Best wishes from

Roger Mayford

and Sam.

Dr MUGFORD'S CASEBOOK

DR MUGFORD'S CASEBOOK

Understanding Dogs and their Owners

ROGER MUGFORD

HUTCHINSON/STANLEY PAUL
LONDON SYDNEY AUCKLAND JOHANNESBURG

To Vivienne, inspired superwoman

HUTCHINSON/STANLEY PAUL

An imprint of the Random Century Group
20 Vauxhall Bridge Road, London SW1V 2SA

Random Century Australia (Pty) Ltd
20 Alfred Street, Milsons Point, Sydney 2061

Random Century New Zealand Limited
PO Box 40–086, Glenfield, Auckland 10

Century Hutchinson South Africa (Pty) Ltd
PO Box 337, Bergvlei 2012, South Africa

First published 1991

Set in Linotron Sabon by Input Typesetting Limited, London

Printed and bound in Great Britain by
Mackays of Chatham PLC, Chatham, Kent

British Library Cataloguing in Publication Data
Mugford, Dr Roger
Dr Mugford's casebook:
understanding dogs and their owners.
I. Title
636.7

ISBN 0 09 174891 7

Contents

Foreword 6
1 In the beginning 7
2 The Mugford way 20
3 Love in profusion 33
4 Close shaves 45
5 Boss dogs 59
6 Fear 73
7 Mucky matters 85
8 On the road 96
9 Dogs at work 111
10 Hobnobbing 124
11 Dogs at law 141
12 The perils of pedigree 159
13 Trainers and training 176
14 Around the world 191
15 Exotica 212
16 Pets – ambassadors to the wild 221
Index 224

Foreword

What we do with our pet animals often reveals the sort of people that we really are more clearly and honestly than what we say or pretend to be with other people. I am a professional voyeur who initially came to work with potty pets out of curiosity about human relationships. I learned my craft with the help of some twenty thousand canine and feline patients, only a few of which have sinned or shone sufficiently to enter the pages of this casebook.

Readers can be sure that the rights to anonymity of my patients and their owners have been protected: fictitious names have been substituted for all except the real life characters that appear in Chapters 10, 11 and 15. In these chapters permission has been obtained from each of the people behind the pets described, including Her Majesty the Queen.

The difficulty with a book of this kind is knowing when to stop, when to publish. My natural tendency is to postpone such decisions, but a remarkably persuasive Faith Evans disciplined me to write this first edition. To her my thanks – and my thanks too to the many hundreds of vets and other colleagues who have stood with and behind our practice over the past twelve years, in Britain, France, the USA and elsewhere.

I
In the beginning

A low sheet of galvanized iron separated four children from the angry whirling dervish that had been someone else's beloved pet. I was one of those children on a South Devon farm; Brandy was a Cocker Spaniel that my elder sister had adopted after finding him lost in our fields. We thought we knew all about dogs, having lived amongst a succession of Sheepdogs, Corgis and mutts that existed more or less in harmony with a changing assortment of other pets such as cats, ferrets, rabbits, tame rooks, field mice and the usual farm animals. My sister confidently announced that we would tame Brandy: we only had to give him a little love and training, she said, and he would stop acting like a monster at sunset.

This unkempt, unwanted red Cocker was my first introduction to pathologically disturbed behaviour in dogs. Brandy was a dog of the 1950s – but in the 1990s there are still far too many dogs around that are just like him: dogs that seemingly go off the rails for no apparent reason, creating misery and danger to those who try to love and care for them. And like some of today's red Cockers, Brandy did not have a bright future. He was dangerous, he did bite my sister over nothing – and one day he was gone, we knew not where. Of course, we cried for our lost pet, but we would have cried even more, in both frustration and rage, if we had known the full story behind Brandy's problems.

I often remember our brush with Brandy when administering to other people's pets. People have a long list of expectations from animal behaviour therapy but knowledge, compassion and results are what they want most of all. We know so much more about why animals do what they do than did scientists in the 1950s. When faced with a dog like Brandy, I can now explain to his owners that he is expressing a genetically determined behavioural trait: it is inherited and something that is quite special to red Cockers. I can tell them that the Brandys of this world are always at their worst in the evening, that they dislike bright lights and often try to cover themselves under chairs or hide in corners. I can explain that most red Cockers hoard bizarre objects like a piece of tissue paper or a sock and defend it as though it were the most treasured bone (they will also defend bones). It also helps to know that novelty, a change of scene, is more likely to snap Brandy out of his deep anger than violent confrontation. Most important of all, we are at last beginning to understand the neurochemical basis of such disturbed behaviour, with a prospect of being able to change it by drug therapy.

Most people will admit to liking animals and at some stage in their lives will have an animal they can call their own: a pet or companion. The role of pets as companions to human beings has fascinated me throughout my academic and professional career, because it reveals the nicer, lighter side of humanity. I am one of those fortunate few whose professional work gives pleasure to others and even more pleasure to myself. The practice I run is concerned with animal behavioural therapy: the application of scientific principles of behaviour modification with a view to making the relationship between a human and an animal work more effectively. The very notion of working as a psychologist for animals evoked a certain ho-ho amongst friends and journalists when I began twelve years ago, but now the field has become more acceptable and certainly my practice much busier.

One of the greatest fascinations of my work is that when discussing their animals, owners are at their most natural and sometimes at their most vulnerable: they reveal their all. We hear and see the truth in their human emotions, with no attempt to deceive or flatter, in a way that rarely happens in all-human psychological counselling. If the practice of animal behaviour therapy is satisfying for a psychological *voyeur* like myself, it also removes an immense burden of anxiety, sometimes of guilt from the owner of the misbehaving pet. There are practical benefits for society too, because so many of our patients, especially dogs, are frankly dangerous.

My good fortune in life began by being born into a farming family. Animals were everywhere, and I was given responsibilities for their care from an early age. I recall an assignment to watch over a herd of sows in a stubble field, where as a four-year-old I was playing with my model farmyard of tin animals mixed up with toy soldiers. It was a warm July afternoon and I fell asleep at my task. Our clever pigs spotted their opportunity to rifle the field next door, but not before first consuming the precious model farmyard, its animals and army. In every respect pigs are remarkable animals, probably as remarkable as the dog in their social behaviour. As a child, I was never struck by the paradox of our unequal treatment of pigs and dogs: our farm Collie, Gyp, lived to a pampered and ripe old age, whereas my pet piglets quickly grew into baconers and went off to market. Such bad luck also visited the cattle and sheep on the farm: my hand-reared lambs, for instance, suddenly disappeared on my return from school, I dared not ask where.

My parents' explanation was always that at least our animals had a good life whilst they were on this earth, even if that life could not be eternal. Of course there had to be exceptions to this general way of the world. They were the chosen ones – our dogs, cats and one Dairy Short Horn house-cow, Cherry, who achieved her natural life-span of twenty-three years.

Non-conformist animals had a poor prospect on our farm: a horse that kicked or a sheep that persistently escaped to raid neighbours' fields would be the first off to market. I was never sure why Cherry evaded this fate. For over twenty years she played a game with the person who hand-milked her. The aim of the game was to unseat the milker and preferably to place a large and mucky hoof into the bucket of milk. Vigilance and a certain authority in my father's bearing meant that more often than not he was the winner. However, as a young lad I also took turns at milking Cherry, and on those days her success rate soared. The trick that I learned from my father was to identify and focus upon a key behaviour which reliably preceded the great hoof plunge. Cherry's tail would twitch and flash in an irregular and sometimes violent fashion in the half-minute leading up to the great onslaught. There were no other behavioural indicators that the milker could rely upon: she did not stiffen, change her position, bellow or snort.

I now appreciate that other such vital but sometimes subtle signs are frequently offered by our domestic pets prior to some massive change in their behaviour. The skill I learned from my father and Cherry was the need to be vigilant in making careful behavioural observations, learning how to correlate events with what came before and what followed. The lesson is as relevant to dealing with an aggressive Rottweiler or a fearful cat as a cantankerous cow. In Cherry's case, the way to foil her kick was to press my shoulder and left arm hard against her thighs, giving a sense of control and restriction to which she responded. Good physical control is still one of the main elements we stress to dog-owners who want to achieve effective behaviour modification of their pets. Life on a farm, working with animals many times larger and stronger than myself, provided a superb training ground for what was to follow.

If my early years with animals schooled me in the arts of understanding, control and kindness towards animals, these skills were severely jeopardized by my formal education at school and university. Science, the biological sciences in particular, showed little concern for animal rights and ethics. Carcasses and organs became a more significant part of the A-level and degree courses which I studied. Still today, students are obliged to go through the same bloody ritual of killing frogs, reptiles and rats whilst learning anatomy and physiology. My school zoology master nevertheless considered me to be an able student, an obvious candidate for an honours degree in zoology. Instead, I chose the unusual path of a joint course in psychology with zoology, wanting to learn more about the behavioural interface between humans and animals.

At that time, in the 1960s, zoologists and psychologists had quite different attitudes towards the scientific study of animal behaviour. Zoologists were beginning to be interested in the holistic approach of the rapidly developing science of ethology, whereas psychologists were still drawing upon the learning theories of Pavlov, Skinner, Watson and others, who studied an individual animal's performance in contrived environments. For example, a pigeon may have to peck a panel in order to obtain corn, or a rat press a bar in order to avoid receiving an electric shock. Complex mathematical models were devised to predict animals' acquisition of complex skills in these contrived situations, revealing something of an imaginary 'black box' which might mediate their behaviour. Unfortunately, the 'subjects' of these experiments lived in highly deprived circumstances, often alone in cages the size of shoe-boxes, with little opportunity to interact with one another or use their natural skills to explore and exploit a varied environment.

The practical difference between a zoologist's and a psychologist's approach shows up in the different working environments in which they operate. The zoologist puts on his welly boots and oilskins to pursue low budget-research on the seashore or a hill – somewhere uncomfortable, or maybe exotic. By contrast the animal psychologist, having spent a big budget on specially-bred laboratory rodents, cages, air-conditioned rooms and the like, stays warm and comfortable indoors. The 1960s witnessed a great debate between psychologists and zoologists as to the best method of developing the study of animal behaviour. The shift of emphasis came with the award of a Nobel Prize jointly to Konrad Lorenz, Nikō Tinbergen and Karl von Fritz. Together these men and their students have shown that it is entirely possible to make worthwhile new discoveries in a scientific way by studying animals in their natural environment.

My own concern was with animal aggression, because I hoped that it would teach us lessons about how mankind might limit its tendencies towards violence and war. My chosen area of study was the diminutive mouse, a species that has attracted a remarkable amount of attention by aggression researchers over the last few decades. We know every detail of its genetics and its social organization and we know that critical early experiences can predispose a mouse to becoming a pacifist or a psychopath. In three years of postgraduate study I became the 'world authority' on a narrow aspect of mouse behaviour: the way in which they utilize chemical signals in their urine and sebaceous glands to communicate emotional states, including aggression. I demonstrated that pheromones or subtle smells do indeed regulate the social life of mice, as we now know that they are also important in dogs, cats and possibly even in man. At the time, the prospects of applying this knowledge about aggression control to other species such as the dog or cat seemed remote, but now I can witness that my earlier research career was not entirely wasted. Rottweilers are not so different from albino mice.

Animal welfare and ethics were not on the menu at my old university, but they were centre stage in my first paid job as an animal psychologist with a large pet-food concern. This international company was interested in all aspects of why dogs and cats do what they do: with one another, with their owners and especially with their food. I was the first behaviourally trained person ever to be recruited into the burgeoning pet-food industry and I worked amongst lovely dogs and cats and stimulating people for nine years. A small team of scientists and veterinarians studied every detail of the nutritional requirements of the dog and cat, which has a practical bearing upon the diets we feed to our pets. The most precisely formulated diet is of no benefit if the animal won't eat it, so it was my job to establish the basic factors which determine how palatable the diet is. Not only must the dog and cat eat their pet food, but for marketing reasons, the pet-food companies try to ensure that the animal appears to enjoy its food, so encouraging the owner to buy more of the same brand. I spent a lot of my time talking to people about their pets' habits, where they slept, the games they played and incidentally what type of pet food their owners bought and why.

I was also interested in the psychological profiling of dog and cat owners. Was there some feature of their behaviour or personality that distinguished them from people who did not own or enjoy the company of animals? Dog owners in particular turned out to be socially adept, with no single personality attribute that could be described as either abnormal or undesirable. In a word these were nice people, a cross-section of all classes and age groups. I will return to the social and psychological characteristics of pet owners in later chapters, but first I want to describe why I became interested in problem pets.

The pet-food company for which I worked wanted to know whether or not dog owners would replace their pet with a new puppy when the present Rover or Bonzo died. A surprising one-third of all dog owners we questioned answered no, the most common reason being that Bonzo was such a tearaway, inconvenience or danger that he had put them off future dog ownership. These problem pets were nevertheless much loved, and their owners stoically put up with the foibles and challenges their dogs threw at them. It seems that about ten per cent of all dog owners experience major problems with their pet's behaviour, but think of the other ninety per cent who enjoy successful relationships with their dogs – it's a better success rate than marriage!

The principal risk to the ten per cent of problem pets is an early death. Indeed, bad behaviour is the single biggest killer of young dogs, the most common reason why owners ask vets to put their otherwise healthy pet to sleep.

Badly behaved dogs also cause difficulties for the wider community and create antipathy towards animals in general and dogs in particular. Indeed, dog-hate campaigns have been born on the back of the presence of faeces in parks, dogs barking through the night, roaming on the streets, causing road traffic accidents, biting children and so on. If someone did not try to remedy these negative aspects of dog ownership, perhaps the right of the majority to own a dog could be threatened. With that, we would also lose the many important psychological benefits arising from the company of animals.

In the late 1970s a remarkable organization was formed in the United States. The Delta Group provided a forum for scientists, veterinarians, sociologists, philosophers and others to explore the several social and psychological issues which determine attitudes to and treatment of animals. The first meeting of like-minded individuals in Europe took place in Dundee in 1978, under the chairmanship of a local vet, Douglas Brodie. There were twelve of us in this pioneering group, including two psychiatrists from the United States, Drs Aaron Katcher and Michael McCullock, who had already conducted valuable research into the psychological benefits that come from our association with animals. The several veterinarians present were drawn to the meeting because they had seen how important it was that the owners' psychological needs and concerns be satisfied while sick animals were undergoing treatment. One of those present, Dr Bruce Fogle, has subsequently gone on to become a well-known and respected spokesman for this shift within the veterinary profession.

I was strangely fêted at the Dundee meeting as the pioneer of quantitative scientific enquiry into this area, because in 1974 I had published the results of the first-ever experiment on the effect of animal companionship upon the mental health and social adjustment of elderly people. At the age of thirty I was suddenly the 'grand old man' of pet-owner psychology and therapy programmes! Thankfully, far superior and broader-based investigations have since confirmed the results of my small study of elderly people in Yorkshire. We had given them each a budgerigar as a pet over a couple of years and compared them with another group who had each been given a house-plant. The scientific data said, and still says, that pets are truly good for people because they help combat loneliness and withdrawal.

It naturally fell to me at the Dundee meeting to focus upon the ten per cent of dog owners who did not enjoy all of the acknowledged benefits of animal companionship. Others present at the meeting threw me a succession of difficult questions which clearly deserved good answers. What is a behavioural problem? What is the frequency of particular types of problems? Do certain types of owners experience particular problems with their pets more than other owners? Do they exhibit a characteristic psychological failing which predisposes them to experiencing problems? Are some breeds more problem-prone than others? Does diet affect behaviour? Can problem behaviour be avoided by better early training methods, changed breeding practices, educational programmes and so on?

To an extent, many of these questions had already been answered by that *femme formidable* of the 1970s, Barbara Woodhouse. In her book *No Bad Dogs* Mrs Woodhouse was in no doubt that problem pets were created by their owners and that common sense, a firm hand and a sharp jerk of the choke-chain could cure most problems.

I found that this approach offended my psychological training and it also contradicted the findings of surveys amongst dog owners who experienced problems. They were not necessarily ineffectual, inexperienced and over-indulgent in the manner suggested by Mrs Woodhouse. I was especially concerned about the violent use of choke-chains in everyday dog training, because we knew from the scientific literature that pain can have a devastatingly disruptive effect upon learning.

The group at Dundee, later to be known as The Society for Companion Animal Studies, made me responsible for answering these big questions, but how could I do that from within a large pet-food company? The only answer was to go into private practice and work with these problematic pets and their owners, to do the best I could in an area where no one else had ventured before. Accordingly, I scanned the literature and found a few interesting and encouraging snippets from the United States, but nobody at that time was doing such work in the United Kingdom and in the whole of Europe there was only one other practising animal psychologist, Anders Hallgren in Sweden.

I began the practice of animal behaviour therapy in June 1979, just at the time when Margaret Thatcher was extolling the virtues of the enterprise culture. If economic growth and technical innovation were to come from the self-employed and small businesses, it seemed an appropriate time to be leaving the big business of Mars Inc. But I was entering uncharted waters, where there were no professional guidelines or proven approaches.

I was already a regular lecturer to veterinary audiences, whom I hoped would encourage me in this new enterprise, perhaps even appreciating the virtue of their receiving formal training in animal behavioural therapy. So my first stop was at the Royal College of Veterinary Surgeons and the then President, Michael Young, whom I knew to be sympathetic to the ideals of the group that had met in Dundee. What about the Veterinary Surgeons Act, which forbids any but a veterinarian to treat animals? This legislation was wisely designed to prevent unqualified or inappropriately qualified people from jeopardizing the welfare of animals. In fact, animals are better protected than people in this respect, as anybody can and does treat sick people with 'alternative' medicine, but only vets can treat animals.

It was important to me that my inquiry into behavioural problems in pets be conducted with the blessing of the veterinary profession; that I shouldn't be regarded as in any sense competitive with it. I wanted to work with and alongside veterinary surgeons, never against them. In this respect I was offered some excellent advice by the then Registrar of the Royal Veterinary College, Alistair Porter. He gave me three recipes for good behavioural practice. First, that I only see cases referred by a veterinary surgeon; secondly, that I conduct no veterinary procedure nor administer any veterinary treatments, and thirdly, that I do not advertise. The wisdom of this advice was confirmed by the experiences of another behaviourist who had offered a therapy service for problem horses. She had advertised for custom directly to the public, not necessarily on referral from veterinary surgeons. Her practice did not thrive.

So it was that in June 1979 I became Britain's first pet animal behaviour therapist. Of course, there was a lot of coverage in the Press, radio and TV about this new institution, the 'pet shrink'. Was I a fraud? Could I possibly be serious? Was this the mad, indulgent face of pet loving? In that first month I was on a high of publicity which generated all of ten cases, every one precious and extraordinary to me in its novelty. I thought it was a promising beginning, but by August only another four cases had appeared and I seemed to be speaking to more journalists than pet owners.

Fortunately, my wife Vivienne had a steady job as a food microbiologist. She cheered me up by reminding me that most new businesses fold in their first year, but she was sure that mine would not be one of them! At least I had time to write scientific papers and articles. The trickle of cases increased and by the end of the year I had treated eighty dogs and cats with behavioural problems. Since then numbers have virtually doubled year by year. I no longer work alone, but have a team of scientists and veterinarians to assist me. Ours is now the largest specialized group of animal behaviour therapists in the world.

At the time I began this practice, our family farm in South Devon became in need of residential care from a Mugford. It was my long-cherished ambition to return to farming and take over where my father had left off. So it was that we moved back to Devon and I immersed myself in matters to do with animals on farms as well as animals in homes. But I found I did not like the face of contemporary farming. Animals had become units of production, with cows grouped in changing herds of a hundred or more individuals having no proper social order, sensitive pigs chained alone as in some medieval torture, and chickens – poor chickens! The days of extensive, humane, mixed farms were over and I had neither the heart nor the stamina to enter the race for maximum output regardless of the cost to animals.

As it had turned out, four-fifths of my cases came from London and the South-East of England or overseas, and I was travelling enormous distances to see them from home on the farm. Our daughters Ruth and Emily seemed to want a father, so we moved again in 1982 to crowded commuter-land in the south-east at Chertsey, Surrey. I practised for three more years in the idyllic surroundings of a small house in a wood, where my tolerant neighbours came to know every permutation of canine violence and eccentricity over the garden fence. Sometimes they had to listen to extraordinary sound effects: growls, howls and whines from pets, or tears, curses and laughter from owners. The nature of my work with animals meant that I could not easily be a desirable neighbour.

Our great good fortune was in knowing the local vet, Carl Boyde, who is a man keen to help any living creature who needs it. He could see my predicament of ever-increasing numbers of patients trampling through our tiny home, whilst he had a nearby farm with under-utilized space but a growing menagerie of horses, llamas, even elephants, to support. So we rented part of Mr Boyde's farm sharing it with all the usual farm species of sheep, cattle, pigs and poultry, all living in a slightly old-fashioned but humane way. Hardwick Court Farm was and is no ordinary farm, rather a gem of architecture and history to the west of London. The much maligned M25 orbital road was planned to go through it, stealing twenty acres in its way. If it stole land from Mr Boyde's farming enterprise, at least it could more easily connect us to my animal patients around Britain.

The extraordinary nature of Hardwick Court Farm is further enhanced by a regular procession of school parties from Inner London, handicapped children from the local hospital, TV crews making use of the olde worlde ambience, a busy veterinary surgery, a practical farm and the Animal Behaviour Centre. Sometimes I cannot believe my luck, being able to help people through helping their animals, whilst having the time of my life in such beautiful surroundings. And it is wonderful to be plotting the latest hi-tech method of phobia management or considering some new advances in neurology on a site that was busy in 1066, with original barns that pre-dated Columbus and in fields manured by centuries of pig wallows.

If I left big business to 'do my own thing' and to do it alone, I could not have anticipated the way in which the Animal Behaviour Centre has grown, and with it the numbers of people involved. We are now a team of eleven and constantly growing in both numbers of people and diversity of skills. The veterinary input is vital, and for the past seven years there has always been at least one vet on the staff. At the time of writing she is Penny Evans, a graduate from the University of Liverpool who is especially interested in the human side of veterinary practice. (She has even married a vet to find out more about the subject!). Supporting us is an efficient team that runs the office and administration, helps with training programmes, organizes puppy play groups, devises new equipment to help animals and so on.

One might imagine that ours would be a restful existence – after all, the company of animals is so good for us, and we can be smart or scruffy according to the day's forecast of weather and cases. There is, however, a strong emotional demand upon any therapist who works through counselling and we are no exception. Our compensation is that we have a farm full of happy animals that remind us that the world is not an entirely eccentric and stress-ridden place. The open-plan office is a constant hubbub of telephone calls, computers printing-out, visitors with dogs, journalists with television cameras and notebooks, and animals of every kind.

The dogs that work with us are a vital part of the practice because they provide models for our visiting patients. The best-known canine in our working team is my Irish Setter Sam, now aged nine. Sam is the specialist at calming down and reforming dogs that are aggressive to other dogs. He goes into what potentially could be a dangerous encounter with tail wagging and a relaxed composure because he absolutely trusts the person handling the canine patient to protect him at the vital moment. Sam is fortunate in still retaining his testicles – most of the other dogs in our practice have lost theirs – but being an entire male does make his situation with other intact males more risky than were he castrated.

Sam's master can take little credit for his wonderful behaviour: he was created by a good breeder and a patient first owner who struggled with his first two difficult years. He was 'hijacked' by me because of his owner's marriage breaking up and when he became increasingly aggressive towards the other four Setters in the household. Sam now meets six or more new problem dogs every day, and neither he nor I can be sure what will happen. Fortunately, his good judgement about matters doggy and his superb timing rarely misleads us: if Sam likes a dog, it's OK. His reward for this good work is to receive perpetual cuddles from every visitor to the office plus the opportunity to go rabbit-hunting whenever the call takes him. Life could be worse!

Sam's best friend is Jasper, another dog with an uncertain past, luckily adopted by my colleague Liz Collier. Jasper has been castrated and knows that for reasons associated with his body and facial markings, perhaps his smell too, all dogs are going to fancy him and that none are a threat. Jasper's speciality is play, with which he can cheer up the most mournful old dog, frightened puppy or belligerent patient. My colleague Andrew has a pretty Collie-cross, Mutley, whom he got from the local RSPCA. Mutley does his job as a stooge dog very professionally, though he is less trusting of unpleasant canine or human characters than Jasper.

Sam, Jasper and Mutley are the key trio for reforming our visiting patients. At the same time there are five or more other dogs who are there just for pleasure, not necessarily having to 'work' for their meal ticket. My daughter's little Corgi, Squirrel Nutkins, is a terrible flirt, inviting all male dogs to investigate her genital regions and then, at the moment of greatest excitement, snapping at the hapless visitor to defend her reputation. Another bitch, Muff, is a Briard. Muff hates men. She may have some good reason to do so, but I am sure it is not to be found in her caring but jokey master Stephen. Stephen's explanation for her snappiness is sensitive ears, but I put it down to her Frenchness and her owner not following our prescribed behavioural therapy. Away from the Animal Behaviour Centre, with less threat and stress than she finds here, Muff becomes an entirely peace-loving dog.

Then there are the farm dogs, a motley collection of Jack Russells, aged Labradors and rangy opportunistic Mongrels such as Sprocket, who belongs to Steve, the farm engineer. Sprocket is by far the most worldly wise of all the dogs at Hardwick Court Farm, an intelligent dog who definitely projects an image of confident independence. Sprocket parades himself before canine patients visiting our Centre, poking fun at their situation and behavioural disabilities. With a disdainful cock of his leg on their master's car, a theft of titbits from their handbag, he is away before you can say scat!

Whilst this lovely farm, its animals and the Animal Behaviour Centre have a certain rural charm, the people who work here have a very serious and professional purpose in life. We are here to save animals, to make their lives better and to make their owners less anxious. Whilst there are very many successes, there are also some failures, where we are unable to achieve those objectives. Not all our patients get better and some owners want more than we can offer. We just have to try harder, to push back the frontiers of knowledge so that mysterious behaviours are at last understood.

Our patients are certainly in better hands when they come to see us today than they were ten years ago, when I had fewer resources of knowledge, methods or equipment. Before delving into my case-book for the main part of this book, I should first describe something of the philosophy, theory and practical methodology which lies behind our work.

2

The Mugford way

There are innumerable 'schools' and approaches to the treatment of behavioural problems in people, so it should not surprise us that there is a fair diversity of opinion when it comes to treating and training animals. The amazing thing to me, a scientist, is how little critical evaluation there has been of these different options. There are, for example, the methods of Kohler and Most, which are based upon the notion of compulsion, if necessary through the use of violence. At the other extreme there is the Pearsall method, which encourages jolly play and reward. There is little or no restriction placed upon animals in Pearsall-run dog training classes, so they have an unfortunate tendency to degenerate into chaos if one dog is exceptionally boisterous or unresponsive. However, at least no dogs or people should get hurt in a Pearsall class.

In the United Kingdom, there was Barbara Woodhouse. Mrs Woodhouse was a true pioneer, who in her time and in her way achieved many good results. At least she decomplicated dog training with her claim that in her hands any dog could be trained in three to five minutes. She emphasized the importance of careful observation of the animal, linked to the delivery of well-timed intervention: this was usually in the form of a jerk to the neck, using a particular style of choke-chain. Harsh intonation of the voice was also a key part of the Woodhouse way. She would berate any owners who were unable to get the necessary nastiness into their hands and voice, and many participants in Woodhouse dog-training classes left feeling an utter failure, unfit to own a dog which they could not get to the standard of perfection achievable by her.

I believe that Mrs Woodhouse's basic intentions were honourable and kind, but that the methods she used were sometimes cruel ones. The Woodhouse way affected a whole generation of dog owners, justifying mass abuse of dogs with choke-chains. As a result, some dogs have suffered severe and irreparable spinal injuries, leading to paralysis and early death. Many other dogs treated in this way just quietly asphyxiate, eventually easing back from their pulling to release blood to their brain and air to their lungs. The basic construction of dogs' necks is much the same as ours, even though they have a padding of fur: they are just as prone to spinal injuries, ruptured discs and trapped nerves as we are. The difference is that they can neither protest nor reveal the pain that they are suffering.

After Mrs Woodhouse, about ten years ago, came the Volhard school in the United States. The basic concept here is strict control and limitation of the animal's freedom to move, using a sliding rope mechanism or a nylon version of the traditional choke-chain. This is worn particularly high on the dog's neck, pressing upon the sensitive *auditory meateus*, the bony protuberance behind a dog's ear. Nerves which connect with this bone are pressed by the rope, thereby creating intense pain, which is why this region of the head was favoured in certain forms of Chinese torture. There is no doubt that a dog will comply with a trainer in order to avoid chronic pain on the scale delivered by this device, and many trainers have taken up the Volhard method on both sides of the Atlantic. Fortunately, the uptake by ordinary dog owners has been low, because their instincts tell them that they should not be delivering such unkind treatment to their four-legged and best friend.

The truth is that dogs are usually easy to train: they have an intelligence and a keenness to conform to their master's wishes which makes complicated and aversive methods unnecessary. We never begin to utilize the full extent of a dog's intelligence in our training. Since consistent repetition of any procedure tends to produce a change in the dog's behaviour, it is not surprising that each of the methods of training described here, and many more, have attracted their disciples. But I and many of the pet owners we see do not really wish our animals to conform to strict universal rules. We want them to retain their personality, their *joie de vivre*, their trust in us based upon a sense of security and affection rather than fear.

The greatest single misunderstanding afflicting the world of dogs is the notion of dominance: the idea that there is a class system with a top dog and an underdog. Dogs are presumed to compete within this rigid framework, scoring points or gaining status at the expense of other dogs in the pack. The owner and his family are supposed to fit within such a pack structure, exerting a regulatory hand over all aspects of the dog's life. I have always been uneasy about this concept because it has been used to justify excessive punishment and force in training, in the way I have already described.

The breakthrough in my thinking about this came after reading reports by two American wildlife biologists with a particular interest in wolves and other wild canids, Randy Lockwood and Mark Beckoff. They observed that the level of violence amongst wolves in a stable setting was low and that most interactions were based upon exchange of chemical, visual and vocal signals. What seemed to lie behind most interactions between members of a wolf pack was a desire for contact and affection: their social attachments.

Wolf packs seem to hang together out of a common sense of purpose: to hunt animals many times larger than themselves and to work as a team. There is some division of labour within this team but the majority of individuals within the pack could not and should not be excessively ambitious in wishing always to take the leading role. Dominance or an executive attitude in all members of a wolf pack would obviously disrupt cooperative harmony, leading to conflict and injury. It is true that some females within a wolf pack are more successful at reproducing pups than others, but raising puppies then becomes a group enterprise for the whole pack, not just the responsibility of the female who gave birth.

These reports on wolf behaviour suggested to me that dogs may develop relationships with people based on self-interest, affection and an altruistic desire to please rather than on a desire to dominate. Reflecting on my childhood days, I recalled many instances in which our working Collie, Gyp, showed that it was loyalty and attachment to my father rather than mere subservience that determined his behaviour. On one occasion I was assigned the role of Number Two Sheepdog, assisting Gyp in close-penning a flock of ewes and lambs queueing to have their feet inspected by my father. Father was called away briefly and I, a nine-year-old, attempted to instruct Gyp in how he should go about his job. He didn't take long to opt out of my attempt at bossy control and ran after my father, a quiet man whom he adored. Before this dog would work with me, I had first to earn his affection.

I realized that if I were going to banish punishment from my own methods of treatment, I would have to find some satisfactory alternative. The answer to this challenge came by reading the literature associated with behaviour modification of educationally impaired children and adults, and discovering a technique that has come to be known by psychologists as 'errorless learning'. The authors of this approach are Thompson and Grapowski, Americans who have revolutionized the teaching of practical skills to handicapped children and adults. The objective is to break down complex sequences of behaviour into clearly defined components so that each link in the chain of behaviour can be acquired and with an emphasis upon reward for success. The aim is to structure a complex task in such a way that the individual elements are so straightforward that there is never any need to punish, because the opportunity to fail does not arise.

I began to test this approach on canine patients who came to me with their problems. Jonathan was a Deerhound who had spent the first two years of his life in a kennel at a breeders'. He was eventually sold to an antique dealer with a smallholding in Hampshire. The problem with Jonathan was that no one had schooled him in the basics of sit-stay-come, so that he regularly ran off from his new master. Once away and on the trail of deer and other tempting wildlife, there was no retrieving him.

When I went to see them I took a long rope, in an endeavour to ensure that Jonathan could never be more then ten metres away from us. If he tried to escape we simply trod on the end of the rope, without saying a word: we did not shout 'Heel' or punish him for going outside the magic ten-metre-circle. At intervals of approximately one minute I called Jonathan by name and if he did not respond, I gently hauled him in on his rope. Close up, he would be given a titbit. We had made sure that he had only received about half his usual food intake for the day so that the remainder of his ration came in the form of these titbit rewards.

Within half an hour Jonathan knew his name and reliably came when called. I had structured the task so that he could never possibly fail to respond to his name, he was never punished for failure and he was consistently rewarded in an appropriate context. I then went on to teach Jonathan to walk to heel by shortening the rope to one metre and walking or jogging at Jonathan's natural pace, each time offering food when he was in the correct physical relationship to me, his head just abreast of my thighs. The key here was to keep moving at the same speed as Jonathan, no matter how fast and regardless of where he wanted to go. (This technique is exhausting for humans but highly recommended.) Having established a good physical relationship between us, I could then start modifying the direction in which he bolted, so that it fitted in with my wishes rather than his. Jonathan was a delight to work with, having been entirely untutored by trainers and therefore displaying no confusing or contradictory responses.

The next and more difficult stage was to teach him to stop, sit and perhaps lie down. I decided that we should use another technique well-known to psychologists, called instrumental conditioning. Jonathan's owner was instructed to wait until his Deerhound spontaneously lay down, at which point he was to say the word 'Down' and offer him a titbit. He was then to excite Jonathan to stand up again and wait for a repetition and again to reward him. 'Down' tends to come more easily than 'Sit' to a large dog like a Deerhound. We decided to teach Jonathan the 'Sit' response by linking it to the 'Down' response, offering food at the moment the hind limbs had touched the floor, but before the forelimbs had folded down to floor level. Just at that midway position, Jonathan's owner said 'Sit' in a quiet, friendly voice, and the instrumental response had been acquired in no time. We now had a dog who had become attached to his owners and whose basic training had been done by kindness. The whole sequence of obedience training had been achieved on the basis of a one-hour training session and a few days' pleasurable effort by his owners.

Unfortunately, many of the dogs that were coming to see me in the early days were already exhibiting long established but extremely unpleasant behaviour: for instance, biting people who came to the door of the house or attacking owners even when they answered the telephone. What could we do to help such people with such dogs? The technique we apply here is referred to in the human behavioural therapy literature as 'response substitution training', which means masking or contradicting behaviour by developing an alternative behaviour whose outcome is more positive. In the instance described above, we could train a dog to lie on a special spot, perhaps a scrap of carpet, in expectation of a food reward, awaiting the arrival of the visitor. Again, there was to be no punishment at all, not even a verbal reprimand.

I put the technique into practice in 1980 and it worked very well. Several thousand dogs later, I can still attest to the power of this simple procedure. It differs from the regular dog trainer's approach of a harsh and dominant 'Down' command, usually given when a dog is about to move into some dangerous or unwanted situation. The emphasis there is too much upon a strong voice, with punishment for failing to comply. In our response substitution method, we pre-train the substitute behaviour to a high level of competence or predictability before using it to challenge the unwanted behaviour. The animal has to *want* to prefer the performance of the new behaviour to that of the old.

So it was that between 1979 and 1980 I would sally forth with bags of baler cord from the farm, every conceivable type of tempting titbit and Barry Skinner's textbook on schedules of reinforcement. Experimental psychologists have determined that it does not always pay to reward every new response that an animal performs, but instead to vary the frequency and timing of the rewards: variable ratio and variable interval reinforcement schedules respectively.

The purpose of the baler cord was to provide that long-distance control over dogs like Jonathan. It was a great relief when a client just back from Germany showed me the first extending lead, where the loose rope was tidily coiled on to a spring held in the owner's hand. I immediately saw the potential of this device for simplifying training, providing long-distance control over run-about pets. I contacted the importers in the UK, Ronnie and Loretta Gee, and we have remained firm friends ever since. The German engineer who first developed this concept, Manfried Bogdhan, is owed a big 'thank you' from all dog owners and certainly from many of my patients, for whom this device was an important part of therapy. The great advantage of the extending lead is that it doubles up as a sound box, which can deliver commands quite as effectively as the human voice. By gently hitting the thumb button whilst swinging the device backwards, you can produce any noise from a light click to a heavy clunk, according to the force and speed used. In teaching heel work, the extending lead is held loosely in the left hand, rather than in the right hand and across the body as in conventional dog training. A light click signals that a heel command is imminent and if it is ignored, it is followed by a heavier clunk sensation down the lead, allied to the verbal command.

Then there was the issue of dog collars *versus* harnesses *versus* choke-chains. Having already looked at the mechanics of the dog's body and found that their necks were as vulnerable to compression forces and whiplash injuries as ours, I had to find a means of attaching leads to dogs which did not cause these injuries. The answer lies very satisfactorily in the traditional dog collar, which has been around for a good many thousand years. The choke-chain is only a relatively recent aberration; it was created in Germany less than a century ago. The chain seemed to me to contradict all that should be good in our relationship with dogs, whereas collars were in more 'user friendly' materials like leather and soft fabric. A conversation with an orthopaedic specialist revealed to me that the width of a collar should span at least two cervical vertebrae to be absolutely safe, which for a Labrador means about one inch across.

In practical usage with an extending lead, a flat collar (as opposed to a rounded collar) delivered just the right touch sensation to a dog, with no pain nor possibility of injury.

I found myself teaching owners and dogs all the basics of control in a few minutes, just as Mrs Woodhouse had claimed for herself using choke-chains and violence. But every now and then I came across a determined dog such as a Jack Russell that would pull and pull, or an exceptionally powerful and large dog like a Great Dane that could literally drag his owner down the street in pursuit of another dog. No amount of kindness, snappy sounds and good timing would work on such dogs and the Roger Mugford method of fast, simple and kind dog training seemed threatened. I looked at every conceivable gadget and device, from German and Japanese spike collars (no thank you!) to ultrasonic devices which we could fit under the dog's throat and activate from a distance, to specially-adapted harnesses and other devices to wrong-foot a boisterous or belligerent dog. The answer did not come to me until 1983.

I was lying in bed at the time in severe pain from my chronic low-back disc problem, pondering my next patient, a Wolfhound that was aggressive to other dogs. I knew he had the power and weight to drag me over unless something clever were devised. I had been brought up amongst Clydesdales and Shires on my parents' farm: the leviathans of the horse world. It had always struck me as extraordinary that we puny people could control over a ton of horse just by a touch of the hand to their halter or bridle. With dogs going increasingly the way of horses in their height and size, it seemed a good idea to try leading the dog from the head rather than tugging it by the neck. Why not base my design upon a horse's halter?

The first canine headcollar we devised was shaped from baler cord, plaited and knotted in a spiders' web of joints and straps. We used my long-suffering Setter Sam as the guinea pig, which he took as a great indignity. Fortunately, we could immediately see that it worked and even my daughter Ruth, then four, was able to lead a dog bigger than herself.

By the time the Irish Wolfhound arrived for treatment we had upscaled the Setter-sized headcollar to one appropriate for his stature. With people, Lupus was a gentle giant, drooling affectionately as we conducted the preliminary question-and-answer session with his owner, me lying flat on the bed, Lupus with his head on my pillow. His aggression, it transpired, was directed at small white Terriers, specifically Jack Russells – he'd been attacked by one as a puppy. If there was a Jack Russell about, Lupus went for it. He was now facing a court order for destruction after having killed one innocent, elderly Jack Russell. Could Lupus be saved?

I drove down with Lupus's owner to the park and we attached an extending lead to this first rough-and-ready headcollar. Just in case anything went wrong, there was also a link to his regular collar. As though on cue, a little white Jack Russell appeared in the park and we gently walked past it. Lupus was apparently a different dog, showing no animosity whatsoever towards the Terrier, calm in the certainty that there was an unbreakable umbilicus between us. Bearing in mind my back worries, it seemed a miracle that I could control such a dog with so little effort.

After this first trial of the headcollar concept, we improved and experimented and my wife Vivienne and I came up with the final design that we now use. We christened it the 'Halti'. It is very like an American headcollar used over a hundred years ago on weaning calves. All this just proved that nothing, but nothing in this world is really new!

No other single piece of equipment in our practice has affected the way we work so profoundly as this canine headcollar. We saw ourselves as having thrown a life line to small people, and especially to women. Machismo and muscles were unnecessary now that all the force of pulling by the dog was dissipated into turning itself around to face the handler. Watching the body of a dog move along the same path as its head was like watching the body of a segmented animal such as a worm, a centipede or a snake, which also exactly follow their heads. The dog seemed happy to follow its head, just like a horse in harness.

Even without complicated theory about why it worked, we quickly understood the benefit of the headcollar in helping elderly and disabled people to handle big dogs. That was the first area of application, but then I saw that the headcollar could contribute to the general philosophy of punishment-free training, errorless learning, response substitution therapy and so on. In particular, it became even easier than before to teach the basic postures of sit-stay-come by instrumental learning with a headcollared dog. The dog could gently be moved into the appropriate posture, the verbal signal given and then the dog rewarded. At a stroke, the headcollar dramatically speeded up the process of instrumental conditioning which I described earlier.

When headcollars arrived on the scene, many traditional trainers shouted 'Foul!', or 'Headcollars are cruel', or 'They *might* damage the neck', or 'The dog appears to be muzzled': I heard every possible justification as to why chains were better than this new approach. But I persevered, patiently pointed out the advantages and kept careful data on each case we treated with a headcollar. None had any untoward effects and positive letters from grateful owners began to pour in. I explained the principle to hundreds of dog clubs, to veterinarians and to anyone who would listen. I quickly became known as 'Dr Halti' and Sam as the 'The Halti Dog', because he was so often pictured wearing one. The idea seems to have caught on in virtually all circles of trainers in the United Kingdom, if not yet overseas.

Another key area of methodological development lay in the use of sounds to distract and interrupt unwanted behaviour. We needed to have a stimulus which could interrupt agitated behaviour in dogs at a distance from the owner, such as when they were involved in a fight. In this situation, dogs cannot be allowed to continue fighting or they will injure themselves, yet the owners must not intervene or they will be bitten. I tested and experimented with numerous devices that might do the job, from explosive fire-crackers to noxious smells, portable water cannon, fine-walled polythene sheeting that would enshroud the combatants and so on. I really wanted to avoid having owners return to the old way of beating their dogs to interrupt disastrous behaviour.

A pressing requirement to develop a practicable long-distance interrupter came with an assignment to treat the Queen's Corgis, who were fighting one another. I began trials on aural alarms in 1984, and finally settled on an aerosol-operated horn with a loud squeal and a high ultrasound content that really grabs the attention of misbehaving dogs. We christened it the 'Dog Stop'. We tried it out on the Royal dogs and when operated close to them it seemed to produce instant peace and attention. It is harmless to the dog and his sense of hearing, if used sensibly and for a brief moment. Aural alarms have been an important step in the movement towards owners becoming dissociated from acts of punishment and, most importantly, neither animal nor human gets hurt.

Early on in our practice I noticed that over seventy per cent of our referred cases were male dogs, many of them aggressive. Testosterone seemed to exert an unpleasant influence over canine behaviour, just as it does over stallions, rams, even man! With the exception of man and the dog, the traditional treatment for aggression in animals had usually been to castrate them, so why should the dog be treated differently? The explanation can perhaps be found in our close and anthropomorphic relationship with the dog, which makes us quick to ask, 'Would we like it done to ourselves?'

The scientific story of testosterone and its effects upon social and sexual behaviour in animals is a complex and intriguing one. There is a priming effect when the young puppy is still an embryo in the womb, there are activating effects at puberty, and a continuing organizing effect throughout adult life. The endocrine picture is further complicated by the matter of sexual experience, when a dog learns to seek and defend his mate from other male dogs. For instance, testosterone levels may be adjusted upwards or downwards by the experience of fighting, where victory or defeat is the outcome. This was my former research area for my doctoral thesis on mice, from which we can draw parallels with hormone action upon canine behaviour. For instance, castrated male dogs are less likely to be attacked by other male dogs as a result of losing the testosterone that controls the smell of maleness. On the other hand, they are sometimes liable to be raped by entire males because their sebaceous and anal glands are changed to produce more feminine odours. Whilst there is not a precise correlation between concentrations of testosterone and aggressive behaviour in dogs, there is usually a worthwhile reduction in competitive behaviour if problematic males are castrated.

Over the last fifty years, numerous synthetic analogues of the natural hormones found in man and animals have been developed: synthetic oestrogens, androgens and progesterone-based compounds or progestagens. Progestagens are extremely useful compounds because they seem to act directly upon brain centres which are involved in the regulation of aggression. They induce a quietening or calming effect in animals as they do naturally in females during the later stages of pregnancy. This more mellow attitude can be exploited in the short term to retrain the animal in more peaceful approaches to the world. The concept of combined progestagen and behavioural therapy was pioneered by veterinary workers at the University of California. Two compounds have risen to particular prominence, one taken as tablets and the other injected. The oral form is of course more convenient, but progestagens are not all good news. The oral preparation in particular can provoke excessive lethargy, increased appetite, water retention and, in elderly overweight dogs, may even precipitate diabetes. My preference is not to recommend progestagens at all, but wherever I sense real danger I first suggest the injectable compound and, as a last resort, the oral preparation.

It is possible to lower artificially the production of the pituitary hormone which stimulates production of testosterone in the testes. The drugs that can do this are known as anti-androgens, and are a useful preliminary or preview of what castration may achieve. Unfortunately, these anti-androgens have only a brief period of effect upon the body, whereas castration is forever and permits long-term, learned readjustments to occur. Many negative behaviour patterns are reliably reduced in intensity or frequency after castration; for instance aggression towards other male dogs, frequent urine marking, hypersexuality, roaming for bitches and some forms of dominance aggression. On the downside, castrates seem to have a lower basic metabolic rate so they require less food; and in breeds such as Setters and Spaniels their coat tends to thin. I believe that these negatives are so insignificant in such competitive breeds as Rottweilers and Weimaraners that I confidently recommend that their males be castrated at an early age.

There is much debate, some well-informed, some emotional, about what is the 'right' age to castrate male dogs. Until recently the data simply did not exist to guide veterinary surgeons as to the optimum time, and current research in practice suggests that there is no one age at which dogs should be castrated. If it is done very young, puppies do not have the chance to acquire macho ways, but it may also be done at puberty (nine to twelve months) or later when testosterone-induced behaviour emerges as a problem.

In later chapters, I shall be mentioning other drugs and veterinary procedures which help in the development of good behaviour in dogs. Crippling, chronic fear is a particular source of misery and I shall describe the application of beta-blockers, and other drug therapies that can be useful for the short-term alleviation of fear. I have also used my physiological training to evaluate critically homoeopathic and other alternative medical therapies, including acupuncture. However, at the Animal Behaviour Centre we generally employ well-established biomedical techniques to support behavioural therapy. These are mostly short-term therapies, designed to improve the long-term probability of behavioural therapy being successful.

Dogs work for many things from their owners: an exchange of looks, a hand on the body, warmth, food, and most of all, play. Play is a crucial activity because it permits them to exercise body signals and strategies with their owners, as well as with other animals. All highly evolved carnivores, from crows to cats to foxes to dogs, tend to be playful in their youth, but our selection of the domestic dog has emphasized their playfulness throughout life. The sad thing is that so few owners know how to make the most of this playfulness. I place a high priority on getting owners to throw away inhibitions and tune in to their dog's desire for play. Body signals form a crucial part of this process, happy facial gestures, bent knees and thigh-slapping all encourage play.

Absence of play brings boredom and deterioration of key sensory and motor reflexes in the dog, as it does in any other species including man. As well as telling people that they should be playful with their pets, I have also introduced special toys to make the process easier. There are two critical requirements for such toys which are often not met by the commercially available products: they should ideally be irresistible and for safety reasons be tough, even indestructible. Most squeaky soft rubber toys meet the specification of being irresistible to dogs, perhaps because they arouse some primal killer instinct to close on small prey such as rats or rabbits. At any rate, most dogs attack squeaky toys but as they do so they often tear them apart and swallow the squeaker, and thereby risk having an intestinal blockage. The way round this is to use thicker rubber and shape it in a special way so that it bounces in an unpredictable fashion, eliciting the same strong chase-grab urge as in the natural predator. Natural as opposed to synthetic rubber also has a flavour which attracts chewing by dogs and is good for their teeth and gums.

The objective of indestructibility is of special importance for tough dogs like Bull Terriers – dogs that go down to the beach and destroy every child's football in sight, with irate parents collecting dues from the embarrassed owner. The solution is usually to be found in tougher and more heavily vulcanized thick rubber toys, or even in solid plastic balls which cannot be picked up or swallowed when the dog plays with them.

Another advantage of play is that it exercises the very considerable intelligence that dogs possess. In particular, challenging search games can be devised which exploit the dog's scenting abilities, with a desire to please and the hope of ecstatic play with the owner as the payoff for discovery. These games are not just working pastimes for professional sniffer dogs.

Animal behavioural therapy can never do more than change the veneer of a dog's personality. Even in humans, instruction, punishment and education have little effect on our basic characters. The child we knew at ten often thinks and reacts in much the same way as the adult at twenty, thirty or more years of age. The debate on the relative importance of environment and breeding has a long history in the biological sciences, ranging from the extreme Marxian view which holds that all our behaviour can be modified by changing early experiences, to the naturist argument that we are what we inherit in our genes. As my experience of working with dogs has increased, I have tended to stand somewhere in the middle, with a bias towards nature. So many of the traits that we see in dogs are unique or common to a particular breed or a few breeds: over-protectiveness in German Shepherds, raging aggression in red and black Cocker Spaniels, tail-chasing in Bull Terriers and so on. But even though the basic behavioural disposition is inherited, the expression of the behaviour can still, in most cases, be modified by experience, training and the environment.

My conclusion about the strong heritable basis of behaviour tallies with contemporary opinions in human psychiatry (controversially stated by Hans Eysenck at the Maudsley Institute of Psychiatry) and with research on laboratory animals. Indeed, harking back to my earlier research career on mouse behaviour, it has been amply demonstrated by Dr Kirsti Lagerspetz in Finland that one can breed for high or low aggression in mice over as few as nine generations. The hundreds of generations over which dogs have been selected have produced dramatic differences in fearfulness, competitiveness, exploratory behaviour, tendency to form attachments, hunger-satiety control and many other traits.

In over fifteen thousand years, the dog has been the subject of the longest-running behaviour genetics experiment that man has ever conducted. Pet owners are very lucky indeed that dog breeders in ancient times seem on the whole to have got things about right. One suspects that behavioural selection then was a good deal harsher than it is today. A dog which bit the hand that fed it in ancient times would surely have been despatched or eaten without further ado. Today, such an owner telephones the vet and makes an appointment to come to the Animal Behaviour Centre! That is acceptable in the short term as long as the affected animals are not used for breeding purposes. Good temperament is vitally important for the future of dogs in society, and we usually suggest to owners that they defer all plans to breed from their problem pet, be it excessively fearful, fearless, aggressive or just plain quirky. It is impossible to prove a heritable basis to some of the strange patterns we encounter but there should be no compromise in the pursuit of breeding perfect behaviour.

Above: Ruling a wolf pack with a heavy hand, but Dutch trainer Martin Hauss dares not turn his back on these subjugates

Left: Jason, a Timber Wolf from Alaska with an eye for chasing Mr Boyde's sheep – patient for Afterthought the Hardwick Court Farm ram, but an inspiration for Mugford

Below: Wolf talk by a Fox, one of the St Louis, Missouri pack with their respectful leader, Dr Michael Fox

Left: Errol James at his desk with brother Flynn below. Not a bad life for a Labrador, so long as there is ample human company or a supply of cars to be destroyed

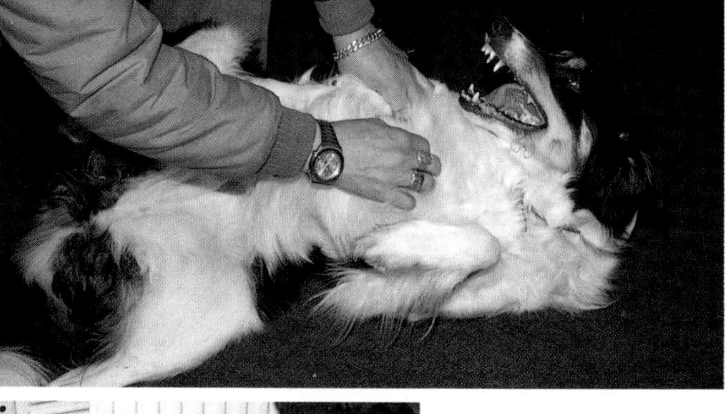

Right: A touch-sensitive Border Collie during the first phase of desensitization therapy

Below: A great-looking Golden Retriever bearing a fatal psychological flaw. Jason showed no hint of his violent potential when visiting our Bayswater Clinic

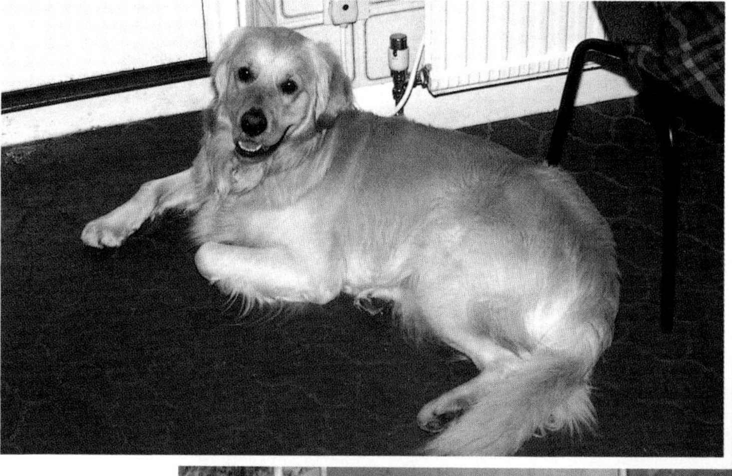

Below: Amita risking her hand with a typically ferocious Smooth-haired Dachshund during Crufts '84. The Long and Wire-haired varieties were all gentle: why the contrast in temperament?

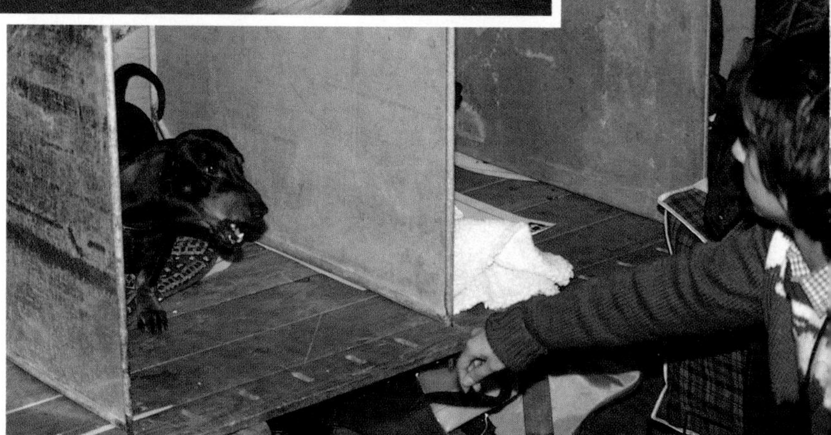

The Mugford consulting technique: let the patient check out his therapist, but be prepared. Richter was a recidivist man-hater when he visited my consulting rooms in Bayswater. *Below:* He had just tried to launch an attack, lucky I had the Dog Stop to hand (*Alistair Morrison*)

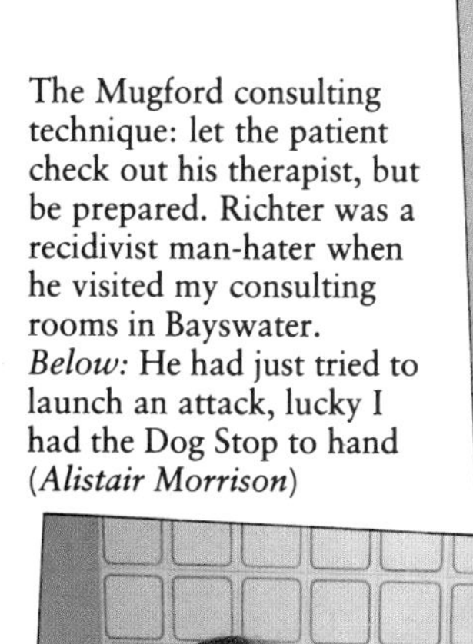

Richter was soon persuaded to like me by food and authoritative handling. Time for play by the Serpentine (*Alistair Morrison*)

Below: Steve Gynn being exploited on the farm as a stooge bike-rider for Smartie, a Westie with a taste for wheels. My vet colleague Penny Evans is seen here teaching Smartie's owners the skills they must apply when they return home

Above & right: Fuji TV from Japan are here filming mad dogs and the English at Hardwick Court Farm. Anything goes for animal film maker, Mr Hatto, and he was a real turn-on for my patient of the day, this over-affectionate English Mastiff

Mr Hatto flattered me with an exchange of presents, in the best Japanese tradition; and exerted a profound effect upon Prince the Percheron, seen here displaying flehmen

3
Love in profusion

The idea that our dogs love us is self-evidently true to most dog owners. However, dog admirers like myself, who are also scientists, have to consider the danger of standing accused of anthropomorphism: assigning to animals emotions and needs which are essentially human. But why else, I ask myself, does a dog roam half across America in search of its lost owners, why did Greyfriars Bobby visit his master's grave each day for years on end at a cemetery in Edinburgh, and why do all dogs appear depressed when we leave them and ecstatic when we return? It is not just that I am a softie about animals; I genuinely believe that there are good scientific reasons why we should look at many of the activities and emotions in dogs as being motivated by an attraction to our company, rather than by fear or a desire to dominate.

The physiology and behaviour of attachment in dogs has attracted a good deal of scientific attention, to the extent that we now understand the basic rules whereby dogs come to depend upon the company of others and why they do or do not panic when left alone. The sad thing is that we see so many patients where love is out of control, where dogs simply cannot bear separation from their loved ones. As Omar Sharif once said, love is all very well so long as you know how to handle it. Benson, an ex-Battersea Dogs' Home mutt, certainly did not know how to handle passion for his mistress.

Sara Jay phoned one Sunday afternoon from a house in Fulham that she said was dripping water from bedroom to basement. I quipped that she was not alone in experiencing frost damage to pipes during that particular summer, which was unusually cold and damp. My joke fell on unreceptive ears, as she burst into tears with the story of Benson. This was serious; it would not wait until Monday, so my understanding wife relieved me of my fatherly duties.

Doneraile Street on a Sunday evening is a very social place. The traditional British pastime of cleaning cars was in full swing, music blasted down from the open windows of bedsits, kids biked and footballed down the centre of the road and dogs were everywhere. This is prime territory for London's dog owners, because Bishops Park, Hurlingham and other good walk spots are close at hand. Most of the houses are terraced, put up at the turn of the century for better-off artisans but now trendy and undergoing mass gentrification.

Benson was a delightful little Collie-cross, brown with dapples of white around his paws and collar. We estimated his age at about two but Sara had only owned him for three months. He came to Battersea without a history, having been picked up on the streets of Clapham. Sara chose him because of his cute eyes and because she felt sorry that he had been persecuted by his cell-mate at Battersea. Benson still bore the scars to prove it.

Sara had bought the house a year before and had spent a small fortune on rewiring, plumbing, new carpets, furniture and all the rest. Originally, it had been a shared project with a prospective partner, but the marriage idea fell through and Sara was left alone with an empty house and a big mortgage. Benson's role was to fill the void of the ex-boyfriend and unreliable lover, as well as guard the house. Because her working day as an estate agent was long, the dog would have to be left alone for most of the day, so an adult rather than a puppy was recommended by the Battersea Dogs' Home staff.

I knew I had found the right address from the piles of furniture, clothing and the like draped over the railings at the front door. A major clean-up was in progress, with wet carpets being lifted as I arrived. The plaster from what had been a masterpiece of Victorian moulded ceiling had just crashed down, sodden from the leaks above. Sara was obviously pleased to have my company at this calamitous moment: I was another pair of hands to heave out the filthy remains. I took myself upstairs to find the source of the flood. It came from a half-inch copper pipe, dented and crushed by the marks of Benson's teeth, and still dripping dirty black water from the central heating system. The wall beside the radiator and pipe bore scratch marks where Benson had pressed and heaved with his forepaws during his battle with the pipe. The scale of damage just did not seem to correlate with the little wag-tailed scruffy dog who escorted me.

I looked at Benson's teeth; they were all present and correct, shining white. However, his gums had been bleeding and his claws were worn from scratching. One could only guess at the demonic state he must have been in to find the strength and persistence to break through the pipe. But why the pipe? Why not some more personal possession of Sara's: the phone-book or stair-carpet, for instance? The short answer to this question was that when he had been alone on previous days, Benson had nibbled each of these and more, and in doing so he had 'trained' Sara to keep all valued possessions high out of his reach. Sara had been to her vet, who had given excellent advice on the need to establish a cooler relationship, prescribed valium for Benson and suggested she contact me for a more structured approach.

Only minor damage had been done the previous week and Sara thought she could cope without me – until Sunday. That was the day she went out to a morning drinks party, and it was also the day of the week that Benson had thought was exclusively for him and him alone. We call this the Monday Morning Effect, as dogs often have a binge of destruction after a weekend of company and indulgence. Another high-risk time is after vacations, again emphasizing the contrast between being together with owners, then 'rejected' and alone. Thwarted ambitions of love often provoke panic and displacement activities such as chewing.

We estimated that 1000–2000 gallons of water had percolated through the ceiling in the three hours that Sara was out, leaving a 4-foot 'pool' in the cellar. Fortunately, the insurance claim was accepted, the final bill being £11,000.

We moved to a dry, upstairs front bedroom where Sara could escape from the holocaust of downstairs and concentrate on what I had to ask and say. It turned out that Benson was her constant shadow, following her everywhere around the house, even to the loo and bathroom. Despite all the damage, she still loved him enough to have him on her knee, where he was continuously stroked whilst being verbally reprimanded for the terrible damage done. It seemed that problems did not begin until she had had Benson for two weeks, when he turned from being a listless, moody dog into Sara's happy and devoted fan. With that change in his mood came increased demands for her company. It was quite flattering to Sara to have such a dog, especially at this time when she was feeling bruised after being jilted by her former partner. Her first response had been to smack Benson on returning home to find things moved, chewed and scratched. She had begun taking him to the local dog-training club, where they advocated strictness and control: Benson was only chewing, they told her, because he lacked respect for her and was 'trying to assert himself'. Quite quickly Sara noticed that whenever she returned home, Benson would look 'guilty', and was reluctant to greet her at the door.

Fortunately, she consulted her vet, who put her right on the harmful effects of punishing a dog at such times. The likelihood was that Benson had performed his damage many hours before Sara's return, so there could be no mental connection between punishment and the act of chewing or scratching. Rather, the association was between punishment and the consequences of the destructive behaviour. The motive behind the 'guilty' expression was to appease the expected aggression or violence from Sara: they were signals of fear, not of guilt.

I ran some simple demonstrations of Benson's great love for Sara. We shut him in the bedroom and quietly listened from the landing outside. He padded up and down the room and we could observe through the keyhole that he had jumped on the bed and pulled her pillow to the floor. He then pressed his nose in the crack beneath the door and sniffed deeply, doubtless picking up our scent. We left the house and took up camp in the front bedroom of the house opposite, belonging to friends. We could now spy Benson's activities without his hearing, seeing or smelling us. It was like a storm developing, first just moving objects, then chewing them, pacing up and down, soft whining and an occasional full-blown howl. Suddenly, after fifteen minutes alone in the bedroom, he attacked the pillow, scattering its feathered interior in all directions. The binge had begun and we rushed back to rescue him. Having watched this sequence, it was obvious to Sara how inappropriate it would be to punish such a distressed dog.

There would have to be some big changes in Sara's general life with Benson if we were to solve his problem. By now I was five years into my practice and we had developed a fairly reliable formula for treating such dogs. I was able to reassure Sara that the prospects of resolving the problem so that she could keep Benson were very good indeed if she followed my strategy for treatment. But the price was high: emotional sacrifices had to be made, including denial of spontaneous affection from Sara to Benson. Confidently, I suggested a ten-point plan for her to follow.

When Sara was at home, Benson was not allowed to follow her from room to room. We agreed on a target of initially ten per cent of her time at home separated from Benson, over subsequent weeks rising to perhaps fifty per cent. The maximum tolerated time alone before Benson showed signs of anxiety was only one minute, so he was to be left behind a closed door for one minute or less. I sketched out a recording sheet or protocol which set out the length of time that Benson was to be left alone each day for the coming four weeks.

During this training phase, Benson really could not be trusted alone in the house and it was decided that he should accompany Sara to work. This was cleared with her understanding employers and Sara's car became Benson's kennel. He loved the car and promised never to violate it!

Before separations, Sara was instructed to be rather cool and offhand, reducing all spoken and physical contact to a minimum. We have plenty of evidence that the routine of departure, using standard expressions such as 'Guard the house', 'Be a good boy' and so on, often precipitate panic.

So far as possible, Sara was to change her routine in the house. I often suggest that owners leave wearing indoor shoes, odd clothes, even no clothes at all, perhaps via an upstairs window rather than from the front door. This reduction of predictability prevents the development of irrational panic.

Silence is the enemy of a dog accustomed to its owner's noises, music and voice. That was certainly the case with Sara, who had a passion for Capital Radio, the London FM pop music station. Like most people she turned the radio off before departing for work each morning. Daylong Capital Radio was prescribed for Benson! Since Sara had a reel-to-reel tape recorder she was also asked to tape everyday conversation and the sounds of Doneraile Street, including a message such as, 'This is your mistress speaking, there's a good boy, I love you, I love you', and so on. It's especially helpful for such messages to be played during the first fifteen to sixty minutes of separation, the period of greatest stress.

Punishment was most definitely forbidden, and the opposite strategy instituted of being particularly loving and sweet-natured at times of reunion. I suggested that a very large brick be positioned in the house which Sara could kick to relieve her frustration about Benson at the moment destroyed possessions were discovered.

Most difficult of all, I prescribed less affection and stroking. This involved considerable self-denial but Sara promised to do her best; at least, not to have Benson on her lap, bed or sofa for continuous petting. She resolved to take up substitute activities such as knitting or boyfriends!

Benson hated to be shut in and had probably only attacked the water pipe because Sara had incarcerated him in the small back bedroom where there were no soft furnishings or personal possessions. She had designated it the 'dog room' but had failed to convince Benson that this was his palace: it had become a zone of rejection, carrying no positive associations. I suggested an alternative approach, where we gave Benson greater freedom, indeed the run of the house. One could imagine the insurance company having nightmares at the thought of the increased opportunities for inflicting damage that this allowed, but my experience indicates otherwise: freedom to roam, and especially to sit on the owner's chair, bed and the like can stop the panic from developing.

When there is a short-term risk of damage, I often recommend that a destructive dog be muzzled or perhaps trained to rest in a destruction-proof crate. I knew that a crate would only worsen Benson's insecurity, but fortunately he readily accepted wearing a Baskerville muzzle. This plastic, lightweight design did not interfere with his ability to drink, pant or even yap. As a short-term measure, the muzzling of destructive dogs helps avoid unnecessary damage whilst a new, more independent relationship is created.

Finally, whilst watching Benson I could well see how great was the state of panic generated by separation from Sara. I could empathize with his situation. When we re-entered the bedroom to which he had been confined, we found his heart rate at about 130, against a normal resting rate of 70–80. He had been panting intensely, and saliva was spread all over the floor and on the pillow he had been ripping up. In a word, Benson had been hyperventilating, degenerating into an hysterical, quivering wreck. I brought up the subject of beta-blockers. Beta-blockers such as Inderal have been widely used in the treatment of hypertension in people, of 'stage nerves' by performers such as violinists with trembling fingers and even as a cure for student 'examinitis'. They are fairly benign compounds though Sara, like most of my owners, needed persuading that the use of such a drug on Benson was 'fair' and safe. Fortunately, beta-blockers do not give a 'drugged' appearance to the dog; they just stop the body from running out of control. After a word with the vet, Inderal was prescribed.

Sara kept admirable records, charting Benson's progress and occasional setbacks over the ensuing two months, and a new *modus operandum* quickly developed. She missed not being able to stroke him as much as before, so she acquired a kitten. A close bond developed between Mr Micawber and Benson that undoubtedly reduced the dog's dependence upon Sara. Eight years later, I still get Christmas cards from Benson and Sara, whose life has moved on into marriage, kids and all that. Benson's was just a passing phase, so common in dogs that have been destabilized by the uncertainties of changing owners.

For some strange reason it is often mongrels and Labradors that are destructive; we rarely see Terriers that panic when left alone. One of the many endearing qualities of Labrador owners is their extraordinary tolerance of deviant behaviour. There are several drawbacks to owning this breed: voracious appetites bordering on gluttony, an excessively loving disposition with a tendency to panic when alone, dog hairs in just about every crevice of the car, home and body. Add to that a powerful tail that has an uncontrollable tendency to thwack children's faces, ornaments and crockery off low tables, and you will see why I am so drawn towards Labrador owners.

Rob and Lucy James were in the garage trade, selling cars from a site off the old A38 near Buckfastleigh, Devon. When I saw them in 1982, they had only been in business for two years. They were still in their twenties, ploughing every penny back into their joint business. They lived in prime territory for a Labrador, close to Dartmoor and the fast flowing waters of the nearby river Dart. They had a smallholding around the garage with geese, sheep, horse and cow droppings: lots of animal artefacts to be consumed, or even better, to be rolled upon.

The local vet called me about the Labradors because he was a friend of Rob and Lucy, having just bought a car from them at a bargain price: perhaps they were influenced by respect for his professional calling. He explained that this was a desperate time as Errol had just destroyed the fifth car interior and their owners could lose no more. And if Errol had to go, Flynn would follow, since they believed the two brothers to be inseparable.

I arranged a visit the next day. It was a Monday in November, the first call of a day planned to take me all over Devon, across Dartmoor to Barnstaple in the north, back to Exeter in the east, to a cat in Newton Abbott and finally home to the farm near Totnes. There were no customers eager to buy cars off Rob and Lucy when I called, which was convenient as it gave them time to talk to me without business distractions.

Errol and Flynn instantly designated me 'friend' on the basis of interesting farm smells on my shoes and trousers. After greetings, Errol took up 'his' chair in the office, which provided a view down the A38 and a spy's eye-view of customers coming and going. This particular spot also had the advantage of blocking easy access to the telephones, so that the dogs engineered extra strokes as their owners squeezed past them to the phone. Rob or Lucy usually ended up part-sitting on Errol as they scribbled notes on the telephone pad. Flynn, by contrast, sat under the office desk where he could be sure of grounding with Rob or Lucy's feet as they worked.

I asked them to leave the office and wait outside. Errol no more than raised his head as though to say goodbye, then settled back on his executive revolving chair. When I made as though to leave the room, the dogs' expression of uncomprehending bliss instantly changed to curiosity and a tense 'ready for action' look. Still they did not budge. I closed the door and sneaked around to the window, where the dogs could be spied through a periscope that I carry for the purpose. Flynn remained beneath the desk but Errol paced about, whining and sniffing the air for signs of Rob or Lucy. At least it was clear that it was Errol who was my patient; it is often uncertain who does what, when two or more dogs live together in the same home.

I was taken to look at the cars. The current runabout was an ancient and battered Rover, taken in part exchange from a local farmer. Farmers are well known for car abuse, but I had the impression that Lucy's taste in cars was for something rather more sophisticated. A quick look at the interior of this Rover revealed why they had been driven to bangers. The whole of the front dashboard had been torn out, most of the wiring disconnected and the driver's seat torn to shreds. Strangely, the passenger seat was left unaffected. The car was worth only the scrap value of the tyres. But this was only the fifth car in a line of breaker jobs. The first had been a Renault 16, almost new, which had cost £1,000 to repair. Then there was the Volkswagen that had caught fire as the electrical wiring was shorted by the dogs. That was a write-off. A Toyota followed, again almost new, the property of a client. That incident was the most annoying of all, since Errol had sneaked into the car through an open window when the dogs had been left locked up in the garage on symbolic guard duty. Errol had done his dastardly work in just half an hour. I was shown the photographs of the Toyota and again he concentrated upon the driver's seat, but also took out the whole of the interior lining, the gear lever, the door winders and the rear seat.

Finally, there had been Rob's pride and joy, his MG. The dogs were not normally permitted in this, but on just one occasion they were taken on a trip to see friends in Bristol. Their owners stopped at a garage to use the loos and in two to three minutes one of the dogs, they believe it was Errol, had pulled away a section of walnut veneer. Rob took Errol out and beat him on the garage forecourt. An immense row had developed with animal-loving customers and staff at the garage, almost to the point of fisticuffs. The cashier phoned the police, Rob and Lucy jumped back in the car and drove home to Buckfastleigh, Lucy in tears. Something had to be done, Rob hissed.

I wanted to re-enact the crime so we chose the old Rover again. It was positioned in a far corner of the smallholding where the two dogs were duly taken. I asked them to do what they would normally do when leaving the dogs. First, all personal knick-knacks and possessions were collected and locked in either the boot or glove compartment. Drapes were placed over the backs of the seats, because experience had shown that this was a favourite area for chewing. Safety-belts, also high-risk targets, were stowed under the seats. Finally, each dog was given a pat and a biscuit, and told to 'be good': 'We won't be long!' One could almost hear the dogs mouthing 'Lies-lies-lies'!

Whilst Rob and Lucy retreated, I took up a spy position from behind a tree. Three minutes elapsed before Flynn settled down on the passenger seat, his favourite position. Errol paced up and down at the back, his whines clearly audible fifty metres away. By the fourth minute he had pulled the rug aside and was sniffing, then began chewing at the fabric of the passenger seat. I sprinted over to release them: I had seen all I needed to see.

We returned to the warm office to review the facts and try to come up with some strategies for treatment. First, I explained that the problem had nothing to do with their failure to 'discipline' or dominate the dogs. Rob was sure that this was the real issue and had even taken advice from a dog trainer on how he could establish a firmer attitude. Like so many others, he had been told that Errol's destructiveness arose from a desire to be boss, a failure to set up strict rules and especially a failure to punish him adequately when he did wrong. It is often tempting to make fun of these misreadings of the canine mentality, but on this occasion I knew that Rob liked the trainer and respected his opinions, so I explained an alternative model.

Puppies, like all young mammals, find comfort in sucking their mothers' nipples. In the absence of nipples they will suck and mouth at their limbs, the limbs of their litter-mates or any convenient item in their environment. As the teeth develop, an intense itching and irritation develops on the jaws which is alleviated by chewing. In part this is an attempt to accelerate the eruption of the teeth through the tender skin covering the gums. The action of chewing also releases pain-deadening endorphins, a chemically-based pleasure system. So, chewing becomes associated with pain reduction and pleasure. In later life, dogs facing stress or conflict often tend to go back to childish or puppy-like habits in a manner Freud termed 'regression'. If stressed people smoke, chew gum, twirl hair, bite fingernails or hit table-tops when aroused, why shouldn't dogs regress to their puppy-chewing stage of development?

Separation from the company of other dogs or people is a profound stress for a dog, more serious than most physical traumas. Dogs usually learn that separation from their owners is a transient privation and that their owners will return in the end. However, some dogs enter a spiral of panic from which the only means of escape is the dramatic oral activity we saw in Errol. Studies we have made of heart and breathing rate show quite clearly that there is depression at the moment an owner leaves a dog, with gradually increasing sympathetic nervous activity during the early phase of isolation. Sudden binges of physical exertion may occur, stimulating an increase in heart and breathing rates to beyond normal levels. For the treatment of such dogs, we can either attend to the symptoms or do something about the underlying causes: over-dependence, over-attachment and insecurity when the owner is away.

In Errol's case, we decided to adopt a plan which encompassed both approaches. We would treat the symptoms by using a beta-blocker to reduce physiological arousal, but we would also change his relationship to humans. After all, he had a most pleasant sibling companion in Flynn, who should have been a near-substitute for Rob and Lucy. It was interesting to notice that the relationship between the dogs was entirely dominated by Errol, that Flynn was almost always deferential. Errol was the more gregarious and open character of the two, more inquisitive about visitors and more likely to pester them for strokes.

If Errol's social life was directed towards people, Flynn remained first and foremost a Labrador. That is the classic arrangement when two dogs live together: the more manipulative and competitive individual tends to form the greater attachment to its master or mistress and is therefore more likely to be destructive. This phenomenon creates the common misunderstanding amongst dog trainers that it is the urge to dominate that actually causes the destructive tendencies. We now know that the priority in treating destructive dogs is not a harsh enforcement policy but rather the relaxed creation of a more confident and independent relationship between the dog and his people.

My first concern when advising Rob and Lucy was for their financial position: how long could they continue to lose the cars, which were their livelihood? Accordingly, I had no hesitation in recommending that they adapt Errol to wearing the lightweight plastic muzzle. He took to it without protest, so we could now begin a desensitization programme in an ancient Morris 1000 saloon car. This was parked at the end of the garage and Errol was taken in and out of it many times for increasing periods. The period was to last minutes, extending to a maximum of one hour at the end of week one, two hours at the end of week two, and so on up to a maximum of four hours, i.e. half a day. Water was provided in the Morris 1000 should Errol need to drink, and the car was always parked in shade or indoors. As with Benson and Sara, I explained the importance of an offhand departure, with no fussy preliminaries or a fond farewell. Release from the car was always a moment for rejoicing, never scolding.

Because Errol was a Labrador he lived for food, and a small proportion of his strictly regulated food allowance was offered at the moment of release from the car. Lucy told me that whereas at the beginning of the therapy programme, Errol had to be dragged into the car, by day three he leapt into it with tail wagging. He had learned that separation from human beings was the price he had to pay for future pleasure.

I took one last photograph of Errol sitting on his executive chair before asking that he never again be allowed this privilege. He was to be distanced from his owners and a bed was to be designated for him which was away from the comfort of their hands and feet. Tough times ahead, the dogs doubtless thought: no more foot massage.

The one-month report indicated that all was going well, but the dogs had not yet been put to the test of an unprotected car. I decided to play it safe and recommended that they substitute some other car for the Morris 1000 and give it another two or three weeks. They then started taking the dogs out and about as normal, always leaving them for a short period muzzled and alone in the car, before being released for exciting walks on Dartmoor. Again, separation from the owner was seen as the price of pleasure. By Christmas, we resolved to give them the treat of a spell in the car without muzzles whilst under careful observation. Errol passed his test; the worst was over.

At a conference some five years later, I bumped into the vet friend who had originally referred the Labradors. Apparently Rob and Lucy had tired of old motor cars and had gone into farming proper, which was more to their liking and better for the dogs. They have a destruction-proof Land Rover pickup, where the dogs can flop muddy and happy with no soft upholstery to chew. There have been no recurrences of car interiors being destroyed, though Errol has suffered a stomach blockage from swallowing rubber piping. It was humbling to learn that I had only helped Rob and Lucy make their dogs more independent – I had not been able to change the compulsive oral habits of a true Labrador.

If dogs did not have a tendency towards excessive attachment, would we love them so much? I think not. Many of my clients give up their jobs and a normal social life in order to hang on to their insecure pets. It is flattering to be ogled at and followed by one's dog, but it is better to have a more balanced, less dependent relationship. This can so easily be achieved by the simple expedient of accustoming young puppies to spending time away from human company. The process of social weaning is made easier using puppy crates: armour-proofed mini-dens which are devoid of electric cables, socks and the shoes so beloved of puppies. If this procedure is followed, there is no need to punish the young puppy for chewing and the negative association of separation in adult life is removed.

I estimate that about one third of all dogs brought to animal charities such as Battersea Dogs' Home present problems of excessive attachment, which lead to destructive chewing, howling or excreting. Estimates from dog pounds in the USA suggest that over half of their dogs present separation problems. For myself, as an animal therapist, these are amongst the most satisfying cases to resolve, because the dogs are always lovable and their owners usually eternally grateful that they can now keep their devoted companions. The ten-point plan that I recommended to Sara invariably brings results – a major advance on the old days, so I never tire of offering advice about the management of love.

4
Close shaves

When I visit Australia, I am drawn to spend time with dingos; in North America with feral dogs, coyotes or wolves. In Africa I am spoilt for choice, so great is the range of wild animals related to our domestic dog. In June 1990, I took a break from a lecture tour in Southern Africa to go dog-watching in the bush in the good company of wildlife expert Joseph Van Heeren, from the veterinary faculty at the University of Medunsa. I wanted to study the behaviour of a pack of seven Wild Dogs, their chemical communication and methods of hunting. These dogs, sometimes referred to as Cape Hunting Dogs, hunt by a devastatingly effective technique of cornering their prey, exhausting it mentally and physically and finally launching a messy group attack. The ones we faced now had been subjects of a long-term study at a cheetah sanctuary near Pretoria. Joseph's previous visits to the dogs had been quite safe but now they were nearing social maturity at fifteen months of age. This was the time to test their natural hunting skills – on us!

Before entering the enclosure that was home to the dog pack, I was taken on a mini-safari to see the other animals in the sanctuary. In the African bush, cheetahs are rarely seen, and then usually alone. Here I saw single cheetahs, pairs, litters of joyful kittens and harmonious groups of teenage cheetahs acting like Olympic cats in training. The Cheetah Sanctuary was established by a remarkable lady, Mrs van Dyke, to rescue orphaned, injured or unwanted animals, and if possible to breed them for release back to the wild. She has devised a management system in which cheetahs thrive better than anywhere else in the world. She also has an open door to any deserving animal, and Joseph took me to see a beautiful Kudu bull whose life he had saved by clever surgery when it was a calf. There were jackals, hyenas, foxes and many more examples of Africa's animals that had been preserved from danger but for some reason could not be relocated back to the wild. But my greatest interest was in the Wild Dogs. I had never seen them before though I had watched them on film and read about them avidly.

I was armed with a camera, sample jars and a puny twig, whilst Joseph carried a small rock, like some Neanderthal hunter facing a sabre-toothed tiger. I had little idea of the danger we were in, being engrossed in photography and recording. Joseph, who was more experienced, had tactfully to edge me away from the objects of our study. Whilst we know that this species is not directly related to the domestic dog, it shows many classic canine behaviour patterns, some in an exaggerated form, that can be observed only rarely or with difficulty in the wolf or dog. I was interested in experimenting with the conditions that precipitate an attack upon prey animals by a pack of Wild Dogs.

We had our backs to a wire fence and the dogs could not come behind us – only face us in a half-circle. They staked us out so that one person alone could not possibly face all the hunters (and would have been attacked had he done so). If we both looked at the dogs on the left, the dogs on the right came closer. When we stared to the right, those on the left came closer and those on the right retreated. We were obliged to scan the dogs continuously along the semi-circle: what had looked like playful spotted Beagles were quickly showing their true carnivorous form. I knew that if I had been alone I would have been dead within minutes.

We could not stay in this position forever; it was time to go. As we stepped forward three paces, the dogs stepped back the same distance. Then from the right, a young dog, perhaps trying to establish a reputation for himself, zipped in behind us. We quickly retreated back to the wire, knowing that if we were encircled we were lost. I raised my hand too quickly to scratch an insect bite and, as one, the dogs moved forward, gazing longingly at my extremity. Joseph hissed that I must remain still, movement being the hallmark of a frightened animal about to run and leave itself open to fatal attack. We both stood entirely still and passive. The dogs reverted to urine-marking, scratching the ground and playing with one another. As we relaxed so they relaxed and eventually moved away. After three minutes, we slowly, but slowly, eased along the perimeter fence towards the exit gate. We were within a couple of metres of it and the dogs twenty metres away. I speeded up; they spotted me and rushed forward. We stopped, then finally made it to safety.

We were not in serious danger because of our knowledge of the basic rules of engagement. The antelope and other prey of Wild

Dogs probably do not understand these rules so well and are often killed when they run away. The rules of engagement governing the relationships between people and domestic dogs are probably adaptations of those governing interactions between Wild Dogs and their prey. About half of our patients are aggressive and many of my owner-clients have been bitten. I am embarrassed to report that I, too, was bitten three times at the outset of my career, though I don't expect it to happen again unless I am really stupid or exceptionally unlucky. I have learned the basic principles: I know that in a tricky situation I must remain still, and above all I must not move my arms and legs. I must maintain eye contact with the potential assailant, I must keep my height advantage by standing and never kneeling and I must be patient and hope to distract the dog with some new pleasant activity, like finding food or play.

The great disadvantage of being the first in a new speciality is that there is no one to turn to for advice about the best way of tackling a difficult assignment: I had to learn by experience. My baptism took place with Marcus, a Boxer in Byfleet, a leafy suburb in Surrey. Marcus turned out to be the ultimate in territorial dogs. It was a quiet Sunday afternoon and I was on the fourth day of a trip about England, seeing dogs of all types from all parts of the country. At that time, 1980, home base was the farm in Devon and after staying with friends for the first couple of days, I had spent the previous night in my car, on Box Hill in Surrey. I was stiff and tired, in no condition for an encounter with an aggressive dog. I had been warned about Marcus in a phone call from his vet, Mike Samuel, who had heard on the neighbourhood grapevine that he was a terror.

Sally and Nick Jensen seemed to be into all sorts of businesses: they were professional photographers, Sally also did a bit of hairdressing and there were catalogues all over the place; these were active entrepreneurs and their lifestyle attracted many visitors to their home. Or at least it should have – as it was, word about Marcus kept folks away, and most customers beeped their horns and stayed in their cars.

Unfortunately I had not yet devised a system whereby I could conduct a consultation on the other side of a wall from my patient but I thought I was protected by my heavy Barbour jacket, my black pilot's flight case and various tasty morsels. That combination had stood me in good stead with previous dogs, so why not try it on Marcus? I have an irritating habit of whistling or humming when nervous and I noticed that that was what I did as I walked down the drive. Nick Jensen was on the phone, so I was kept waiting at the door for a few minutes to ponder what lay ahead.

I was ushered through the hall and into the dining room, from where I could hear Marcus making Boxerish snorts in the lounge next door. We settled down to take the history. It seemed that until just three months earlier, Marcus had been just a slightly tetchy dog who had bitten no one. Then Nick's son returned from leave with the army, and was bitten as he walked through the door. Marcus had known the boy since he was a puppy five years earlier, but seemed to have forgotten his long-standing friend. Since that first bite there had been four other major attacks on people, two of which had led to serious injury requiring medical treatment. The daughter of a neighbour suffered thirteen puncture wounds to her arm, so there was a good possibility of either police action or a civil law suit to follow.

I privately wondered why they had called me in rather than have Marcus kindly put to sleep. Their vet had already broached the subject but Nick had been roused to a libellous temper of McEnroe proportions, so Mr Samuel had kindly deferred the task of persuasion to me.

It seemed that for the last eighteen months Marcus had been given to sudden and intense bouts of sleepiness. Technically referred to as narcolepsy, this could occur at any time without warning, in the house, in the car or even occasionally outdoors. I suggested that at the earliest possible date the dog should receive a neurological examination from a local veterinary specialist. But now it was time for me to meet Marcus, and I opted to do so outdoors.

Marcus was duly saddled up with a thick choker and a short leather thong lead while I waited in the drive for them to emerge. As Boxers go, Marcus wasn't especially large but he was still an impressively lean muscle machine. His russet brown coat gleamed with good health, a clean appearance exaggerated by white 'socks' and head markings. I congratulated Nick on the efforts he must have made to create such a well-laundered dog, contrasting this dazzling specimen with the mucky Mugford dogs back on the farm. I learned that it was no trouble at all to keep him handsome – the poor dog had not been allowed off the lead for the past three years.

Creamy white saliva foamed on Marcus's lips and tongue as he pulled on the choker. I held back as Nick was dragged ahead; Marcus seemed to tolerate me but only because of his enthusiasm to get to the park. I was reassured by Nick that no danger existed – Marcus had accepted me. Suddenly, and for no apparent reason,

Nick veered off to the left into the oncoming traffic. I grabbed him by the coat and Marcus made as if to leap at me to protect his master. Marcus had spotted a child leading a little mongrel on the other side of the road and would certainly have pursued it, if Nick had not somehow held on to the lead. Marcus then calmed down and we just about made it to the park, where he paraded about on a long lead.

Marcus was well known in Byfleet and the park emptied of families and footballers as we approached. He pranced about like a missile looking for its target. Interestingly, he could never concentrate on just one activity, shifting his attention from a stone to a squirrel, to us, to a child; never once was a co-ordinated sequence of behaviour completed.

I asked for a demonstration of obedience, the regular 'Sit', 'Stay', 'Come' and so on. 'Not a chance,' laughed Nick: the Boxer had never been able to learn the simplest of commands. At that stage, early in my career, I still felt it was important that I should handle each of my patients myself, so I cautiously took the lead from Nick and walked ahead with Marcus. He took to me well and could soon be 'bought' by the tasty biscuits I carried in the pocket of my smelly Barbour. Within a minute I could stroke his flank but didn't trust him sufficiently to touch his head, neck or shoulders.

Again and again I tried to get Marcus to sit for a titbit; sometimes he did, most times he did not. I would push him down, give the command and offer the titbit. If he did take it, that in no way increased the probability of his getting it right next time. By comparison, I would expect a mongrel with average intelligence to pick up a new sequence in two or three trials but Marcus, the subnormal Boxer, had not learned it in thirty trials. The only cheering thing was that at least I had physical control of Marcus and he seemed to trust me.

We walked home, with me pretending to do a Barbara Woodhouse 'Heel' act with Marcus on his choke-chain. I got nowhere, which was reassuring to Nick because of his own failure to make progress in six years of trying. I was invited in for tea and we sat down in the lounge, Marcus off lead. When Nick returned from the kitchen I relaxed, taking my eyes off Marcus for an instant as I stretched out to take the tea-cup. Marcus saw his moment and leapt at me.

Hot tea poured all over me and over Marcus, which gave a second for Nick, who was a big guy, to grab hold of his choker. But even Nick wasn't strong enough to stop him, and Marcus succeeded in pulling away to chase me across the room. I had nowhere to hide, nothing to hold that might protect me; even my trusty black case, which might have acted as a shield, was out of reach. There was an enormous gulf of two to three metres between me and the door, but by somersaulting over a fat settee I just made it, the Boxer literally on my heels. The door slammed between myself and Marcus, he in a rage over this lost opportunity. I was thankful to have only a few mild scald marks on my crotch. We resumed our conference on Marcus and his future, this time with a wall separating me from the patient.

My tentative diagnosis was one of profound neurological disturbance producing dangerously abnormal behaviour. In all probability, the primitive hindbrain, including the area which regulates sleep, the reticular formation, was damaged. Lesions or a tumour might affect the hypothalamus, which is known to be one of the key areas regulating aggression in mammals. I counselled euthanasia, based on practical safety considerations as well as on concern for Marcus's ultimate welfare. I was quite unprepared for what followed. This tough, grown man, Nick, began to sob uncontrollably; I found myself comforting him with an arm around his shoulder. Hearing the noise, Nick's teenage daughter came down from her room and proved much stronger than Dad, taking over my role as comforter. I agreed to phone the next day and see if there were any more stones that could be turned to save Marcus. I knew there were none, but I felt that time would make the Jensens see what had to be done.

I did phone the next afternoon, when I was told that Marcus was already dead. On the evening of my visit, he had also attacked the daughter, something that had never happened before. Animal psychologists, VAT inspectors, the general public, even Nick's son could be threatened or attacked by Marcus and that was tolerated, but going for his daughter was the last straw. I struggled for an hour to compose the briefest of condolence letters, trying not to say that the world was a better place without Marcus, but emphasizing that they had done the right thing: they had tried their best, and they were certainly not to blame themselves.

Marcus was by far the most dangerous dog I had seen at this stage of my career. I continued in my positive approach to life and dogs until I found myself back in the same area a few weeks later to see an Afghan Hound. His name was Ali and his problem, a classic one for this breed, was that he ran after sheep. He was said to be a little nervous of people but there had been no serious incidents. As I was chatting with his owners in their kitchen Ali was between us, seemingly inviting contact from me. Without thinking, I was drawn to touch his beautiful long, blond locks but as my hand reached his head he snapped and grasped me by the wrist. 'Aaagh!' I looked at my wrist and saw a red patch spreading over my blue cotton shirt. Then I felt a warm drip, at this stage without any sensation of pain, but within a minute, as the bruising to the underlying bone developed, the pain took hold. Ali had nicked a vein but thankfully not the artery. After the pain, I was overcome by physiological shock just from a single, medically uncomplicated dog bite. It gave me a graphic insight into what an antelope or caribou must feel after a co-ordinated attack by Wild Dogs or wolves.

When I returned home, my wife tackled me on the subject of taking out insurance to cover me if I gave bad advice, became ill or was injured. Vivienne rated me a fairly useful person in a growing family. Until then, I had regarded all such discussions as a source of irritation, preferring to trust to luck. Now however, Vivienne felt justified in taking out a policy regardless of my reckless opinions! In the space of three weeks I had had two close shaves, the latter quite unexpected and with hindsight entirely my fault, because I should not have initiated that movement towards Ali. It was an error of judgement, and I paid the price.

Vivienne's anxiety after the incident with Ali jolted me into realizing that the question of safety needed to be addressed, so I began to talk to veterinary colleagues who had lived with these problems for longer than I had. A traditional technique taught to all vets and nurses is to 'tape' a dog, using a long piece of bandage wound around their muzzle. The problems with this are obvious: the animal is unable to pant, he is frightened and it doesn't take him long to get wise to the sight of a nurse holding a bandage. I was shown some of the muzzles then in use: heavy leather cups with a single strap to tuck behind the ears. This design offered no breathing holes and one size was meant to do for all shapes and sizes of dog. Lacking in finesse, I thought. Pet shops were at that time also selling muzzles made from complicated arrangements of leather straps, each laboriously stitched or riveted to the other. I bought one for the next macho dog I was due to see but it proved unsatisfactory. It took an age to fit, and the German Shepherd to whom it was offered promptly chewed his way through the sides of the muzzle, enjoying the flavour.

For me, the breakthrough on muzzles came in 1985, when I was at a conference in Athens. An Italian gentleman showed me his range of lightweight plastic muzzles, each shaped to the size and proportions of common breeds of dog. Twelve sizes covered more than ninety per cent of dog head-shapes. I promptly bought a hundred for my patients back home.

I felt sure that this muzzle would protect people against dangerous dogs better than other designs, since there was no way a dog could bite through the plastic, either at the front or sides. The next question was how would dogs react to wearing this new type of muzzle? I kept records of the next hundred dogs we saw, carefully observing their reactions before and after fitting a Baskerville Muzzle. As far as behaviour was concerned, there was little change: if they were aggressive to dogs without a muzzle they would still attack dogs when wearing one, and if their dislike was directed towards the postman or an animal psychologist, that too would continue. The difference now was that prospective human victims knew that instead of a toothy bite they got a harmless plastic muzzle thrust into their flesh.

Since this chance discovery in Greece, we have imported many thousands of these muzzles, which have become the norm with veterinary surgeons, trainers and owners confronted with dodgy dogs. We have never argued that muzzles cure bad behaviour, just that they offer time and safety whilst an effective therapeutic strategy is developed. I still have ten fingers but my right wrist carries the scars from that meeting with Ali.

The other breakthrough in handling dangerous dogs was the canine headcollar I had developed with the help of Vivienne and our Setter Sam. Each year that passes in my practice, bigger dogs seem to come our way. Recently, an elderly couple from Doncaster in Yorkshire brought their German Shepherd bitch to see us. Not knowing about headcollars, they had invested in a combination of choke-chain, collar and harness, with three different leads poking out of all this complicated saddlery. Misty hated cats and dogs and was strong enough to drag her owners over in pursuit of her enemies. Her mistress suffered from neck and back problems but she was getting scant sympathy from her doctor and an orthopaedic specialist whilst she insisted on having a dog like Misty. Within two minutes of fitting a headcollar, I could hand Misty back to her mistress who could now enjoy walking a nice, calm dog. The headcollar had converted a pulling strain of more than a hundred kilos to a maximum of two or three by the simplest series of light, fabric straps.

Finally I had to address the crucial question of what is the most effective way to stop a dog that is attacking another animal or person. Do we hit it, throw water at it, rattle a bucket or just pray? In the early years of my practice I had probably done all four and each had, to a degree, been helpful. But I had always wanted something more reliable, something that could be passed on to the owner of a dangerous dog for use with confidence and security. My chance to solve this problem came with my patients at Windsor Castle and the subsequent development of a powerful aural alarm.

In nine cases out of ten the Dog Stop alarm works, and interrupts unwanted behaviour. Unfortunately, however, this method cannot be totally relied on: some dogs don't hear too well because of disease or old age, and some breeds are tone-deaf because of the strange architecture and thickness of their skull-case.

Winston was one such dog. He was a massive, sloppy-jowelled English Bulldog, weighing forty to fifty kilos. (I could not get close enough to weigh him precisely.) I went to his home armed with all the equipment I have mentioned: the headcollar, muzzle, titbits and an aural alarm. Winston was just recovering from a stitch-up job at his vet's: he had injured his face poking it through the front door, from the inside out, when the door was closed. The stitches from a particularly nasty cut to his left ear should have been removed a week earlier but no one could touch Winston's face, certainly not the vet. I was asked to have a go! Winston's latest escapade had begun when he had heard the postman walking up the drive. He couldn't wait for the door to be opened in the conventional way and was attempting to take a short cut. Fortunately, his shoulders became jammed in the splintered hole created by his numbskull. The postman escaped but Winston sustained terrible bruising to his lips and gums, a cut ear, scratches, and he had nearly knocked out one of his projecting canine teeth. I didn't risk a close dental inspection.

I knew already that Winston did not like men in uniform, but would he tolerate me in casual psychologist's dress? The sound of barking on the other side of the now reinforced front door was not encouraging, and I asked his master to tether Winston so that I could at least get indoors to say hello.

Winston, now just eighteen months, had shown a marked tendency to guard his home for the last year. No other living creature apart from his owners could safely enter his fortress: essentially they lived on an urban island. Eric Johnstone, Winston's master, was a big, burly, retired policeman whose children had flown the nest and whose wife went out to work. Winston and he were good mates through the day, taking long but slow walks around the local commons. This had left Winston with muscles like a Japanese wrestler but he could never be a speed-walker. Out and about, beyond his territory, Winston was a charmer to all he encountered. On the border, such as the front door, the visitor was dead, and inside the house, literally anything could happen.

Since we were in this last uncertain category, Eric thoughtfully tethered Winston to a steel post that had been concreted into the living-room floor. A thick, iron chain held the dog to a half-metre radius. I was pleased about that because Eric soon confirmed that Winston did not, after all, like me. It was nothing personal, he added, for fear of offending me, just don't come any closer. I tried bribery with cheese-chunks, but Winston made it quite clear that he would not be bought. Our very largest Rottweiler-sized muzzle was nowhere near the width and shallowness required to accommodate Winston's huge battered face, nor was there sufficient nose to hang a headcollar on. My only hope was that he would respond to the sound alarm, which I pressed as he thrashed towards me on his chain. He may have blinked but there was no other detectable response. I decided to invest some time in Winston and to try and win him over by gentleness and understanding.

Eric had long been a fan of English Bulldogs, and bore more than a passing resemblance to one himself. He knew all about their history, going back to the thirteenth century when they were first employed in bull-baiting. He rationalized that Winston's problem was only a natural expression of this same trait; in the absence of bulls in the neighbourhood, postmen would have to do instead. I made no comment, thinking it would not be productive to contradict Eric's reading of Bulldog history.

I suggested we go for a walk. Encouraging progress was made within minutes of stepping on to the street, heading in the direction of the heath: I was holding the lead and Winston was apparently bonded to me. He was quite gregarious with passers-by; he seemed to have a large circle of fans. Winston was also nice to cats, dogs and squirrels; he was the sort of dog that would have taken pride of place amongst the England team at a World Cup photo session.

As we returned home, Winston visibly stiffened and long-established instincts of alienation were aroused. What I had thought of as progress was really only a temporary respite, accurately predicted by Eric. We have a well-tested regime for modifying the territorial behaviour of dogs, which usually works with guarding breeds like German Shepherds. But with Winston, I could not climb even on to the first rung of the behaviour modification ladder. If the short-term hazards could not be regulated using muzzles and all the rest, how could we possibly begin to encourage pleasant contacts with strangers?

Eric resolved to improve his defences: to fortify the front door, install a second one and put up a suitably worded sign to discourage casual entry. He understood the hazards of owning a dog like Winston, but tended to work around them rather than to try to change the dog's behaviour. Cases like this are always stressful because there is so little in the way of positive feedback during the few hours of a consultation. The primary instrument for testing the therapeutic strategy is one's own frail body, and mistakes are painful! In this case I (just) made it for two hours without sustaining injury. Others had been less fortunate. Sitting in the car after leaving chez Winston, I allowed myself a deep sigh and played loud rock music in celebration of life. Winston did not transform into an angel as a result of my visit, but neither did he succeed again in biting anyone before his death the following year from a respiratory infection.

Back at the farm, I am the biggest guy around, and the one who is deemed to be the most expendable. This makes mine the most popular body on which to test our patients. At least a couple of times a day my female colleagues come up and say, ''Scuse me, Roger, got a moment?' 'Course! Always at your service! Something nice?' 'I wonder if you'd mind just running by this dog, but do be careful: he's involved in a law-suit because he bit a jogger, chased a cyclist and knocked over a milkman!' Sometimes I have to dress up as an old man in floppy clothes, or as a sporty type in jogging gear; perhaps I have to act bold or act chicken, depending upon the circumstances. Role-playing is often very important in the re-enactment of cases involving legal action between victim and dog owner, because we need to be able to state that the description of events given by the defence or prosecution is or is not credible and consistent with the dog's present behaviour as we have encountered it.

I had to play-act recently when treating Xanadu, a Pit Bull Terrier some thirteen months old, who lived with his vet-nurse mistress and boyfriend. Anne was sure that in her caring and experienced hands, a Pit Bull could be a safe pet. She had bred Xanadu herself and on the day of her visit to the Animal Behaviour Centre had left the dog's mother at home to guard her flat in Hornsea.

Xanadu came with a depressing history of attacks on people. His problems had begun when he and his mistress were beaten up by a gang of four teenagers on the London Underground. From that moment on he became suspicious of people, and especially of men. He had bitten her boyfriend, her employer (a vet), several neighbours in the street and most recently had charged and bitten an elderly man who had asked Anne for directions. She now kept him on a tight lead, having no contact with people other than herself and her boyfriend.

My role was to invite an attack from Xanadu so that we could obtain an idea of the initial releasing factors for aggression: movement, eye contact, distance from Anne and so on. With this information, we could perhaps design a desensitization programme that would change Xanadu's perception from one of threat and aggression to one of pleasure and play. Fortunately Xanadu accepted our plastic muzzle and I was instructed to jog by my vet colleague Caroline Barnard. If I stared at Xanadu, he did not go for me as I ran past. The moment of danger came when I stopped to talk to his mistress about his apparent tolerance of me. I asked Anne to shake hands with me and just as she moved towards me he attacked. He had done the same to his previous victims; on me it was a sustained attack which required the co-operative efforts of Caroline and Anne to drag him off. I managed to laugh, but it wouldn't have been so amusing without the muzzle. At least we had defined the risks and could devise a protective strategy alongside formal therapy. Anne submits cheerful reports to us but we remain anxious about the welfare of citizens in the streets of Hornsea.

We are living in dangerous times and my close shaves are of little consequence, because they are part and parcel of the work I do and I am usually equipped to deal with them. My concern is for the safety of ordinary folks who have to share the streets with these dogs. Since World War II, there has been a steady increase in the number of dogs owned, and an even greater increase in the number of large dogs. In the last two decades there has been a dramatic rise in popularity of the obviously 'guarding' breeds: German Shepherds, Rottweilers, and now, from the USA, Pit Bull Terriers. Pit Bulls are a hybrid of several breeds including Rottweiler, Boxer, Bull Terrier and probably other breeds native to the American southern states. Regrettably, they are dogs which have been genetically tuned for the criminal activity of organized fighting. The trend seems inexorable: the number of Rottweilers in the UK probably tops 150,000; Pit Bulls 50,000 and rising fast. Ten years ago I never saw a Pit Bull, and perhaps one Rottweiler per year would come as a patient. Now both are commonplace.

Unfortunately the severity of a bite from either of these breeds is always medically more serious than one from a German Shepherd. German Shepherds tend not to make serious and sustained attacks, but yet are consistently over-represented in dog-bite statistics. They are usually cowardly and, unless encouraged to persist, give only a single bite. Most of us know enough about dogs to anticipate when we might be bitten and to take avoiding action either to diminish the threat or to protect ourselves. The special danger of a Rottweiler is that attacks on their victims are made with little prior warning; they are unexpected. Like the Spanish Inquisition they come like a bolt from the blue, either towards members of the dog's own family or to outsiders.

Most dogs communicate their emotional intentions with their tail: the Rottweiler's tail is amputated at birth to leave only the tiniest stump. Both dogs and people can become confused or mistaken when confronted with a tail-less dog. With luck and assistance from an EEC animal welfare directive, the long-running veterinary campaign against tail-docking now stands a chance of succeeding. There has been selection in favour of calm, cool or arrogant attitudes on the part of Rottweilers which again interrupts the flow of warning information to prospective victims. Of course, there are more nice Rottweilers than nasty ones, and it is certainly the case that most of the latter are entire males.

I am deluged with requests for information about the 1980s epidemic of Rottweiler attacks from all quarters. At first I thought these incidents followed the pattern of incidents involving all dogs, but by 1989 it was apparent that a trend was emerging of greater numbers of increasingly serious incidents. I will even plead guilty to misreading a Rottweiler's body language myself, which had dreadful consequences. I was 'schooling' a male Rottweiler alongside Sam, and both he and I thought that this was a friendly dog, one of those nice Rottweilers. Out of the blue it went for Sam, biting him on his flank and only letting go when I blew a Dog Stop in its ear. Sam was badly shaken and remains afraid of Rottweilers. I feel guilty, but also angry at the carelessness of breeders in allowing such a situation to arise. Time and again, I see or hear about show Rottweilers directing aggressive behaviour at other dogs, even at judges. Yet they are not disqualified – sometimes they win!

With Pit Bulls, warnings of what might happen should the breed become popular, were given by the RSPCA in the early 1980s.

Information from animal welfare and regulatory authorities in the USA all pointed to the disasters that would occur when they moved into urban areas and outside the hands of those who use them for dog fighting. Their high pain threshold makes them quite fearless during attacks on other dogs, people, upon just about anything that moves. Because of the mistaken notion that there are 'no bad dogs, just irresponsible owners', well-meaning, dog-loving folk are tending to replace their traditional mongrels and pure breeds by Pit Bulls. 'With a loving home he will be just fine,' they say, but it is an illusion they deeply regret when their dogs have to be treated for their sudden, extreme violence.

In 1988, I met a delightful Pit Bull in Los Angeles whose owner was only worried about his being a little boisterous. The advice I gave her would have been effective for owners of other dogs: I stressed the importance of not playing tug-of-war, or of over-stimulating the dog, making sure that he was handled by friends, establishing a criterion of stillness before any positive rewards were offered, and so on. A year later I had a letter from her telling me that this seemingly nice dog had been used without her knowledge for illegal dog-fighting by her estranged husband. Subsequently, it attacked and savaged him as he lay in bed, with no provocation except that he had had a drink too many and was snoring in a way which the dog found objectionable. When I see a quote from parents extolling the virtues of their Pit Bull as a family pet, I fume at the risks to which they are exposing their children.

Pit Bulls have been developed for one purpose and one purpose only and that is to give sadistic pleasure to unstable people seeking the entertainment of a dog fight. I have recently been looking into ways of developing protective strategies against these monster dogs, particularly into methods of capturing the semi-wild Pit Bulls and Rottweilers that are used to guard places where illegal drug and money dealing is done. In some of our cities, unoccupied properties are set aside for use by this criminal fraternity, who leave one or more dogs in the establishment to protect their assets. Public and police alike run the risk of mortal injury if they approach them. In the United States and elsewhere, they would simply be shot. That solution is not acceptable in the United Kingdom so we are looking into a combination of sound-emitting devices, lachromoter agents which temporarily blind the dog, confusing robots which rush in all directions and provide substitute targets, and immobilizing drugs. Sadly, man's best friend has been turned into a lethal weapon.

5
Boss dogs

People who love dogs tend to be non-authoritarian types who wouldn't want to suppress or dominate their animals any more than they would their friends. They are naturally indulgent, carefree in their generosity and unthinking in their kindnesses. Most dogs accept these indulgences without exploitation in return, but a few do not. Their owners may either not be very skilful in handling their dog or, more often, they have a pet who is tyrannical in the pursuit of power.

I believe that much of canine society, both in the wild and in domestic situations, is regulated by a calculated pursuit of personal interest based on what produces the best outcome for the individual dog: either co-operation and sharing or competition motivated by greed. Overlaying that pragmatic survivalist strategy are other regulators of canine society: notably social attachment, fear, play, even learned traditions from one generation to the next.

It is obvious to anyone who has watched dogs get along with one another and with people that they do not always have to be bossy or violent to obtain the best payoff. I was vividly reminded of the disadvantages that come from the unilateral pursuit of power whilst studying a pack of wolves belonging to the University of Missouri near St Louis, USA. At the time, I was a Visiting Scientist at the Monell Chemical Senses Center in Philadelphia, looking into the significance of taste and smell in animal behaviour. This particular wolf pack lived in a thirty-acre park and consisted of four males and seven females. They were the pride and interest of Michael Fox, a famous British vet with a humane interest in canine and especially lupine behaviour. Mike and his team of enthusiastic students had been observing these wolves since the pack was formed from abandoned and hand-reared puppies collected from all over the USA. Each wolf had distinctive natural markings and they were given glorious names that hinted at their personalities. Black Tail was the leading male to whom the other males gave up bones, averted eye contact, deferred territory and so on. When the bitch Lola came into season it seemed a foregone conclusion that Black Tail would be her mate. But that was not to be, despite his relentless pursuit of her company and his appealing courtier ways.

Lola had a passion for a smaller male, a three year old named Jackson. She consistently rejected Black Tail, but Jackson had not the temerity (or perhaps stupidity) to mount Lola in front of Black Tail. This dilemma between conflicting passions was resolved in a most unexpected fashion. Another of the males went to the extreme boundary of the park and created a commotion, as though defending the territory against an invader. Black Tail was drawn to the barking and so tricked into deserting his prospective mate. Jackson was upon Lola in a flash and successfully formed a mating tie. When a wolf or dog succeeds in sexual union, other male members of the pack tend to let them get on with it. Black Tail returned from his guard duties and peacefully witnessed the nuptials. Later four pups were born to Lola, maybe fathered by Jackson or maybe by the big, bossy wolf, Black Tail. We shall never know.

There is considerable debate amongst scientists about whether social hierarchies really do exist or whether they are in some way a human invention, perhaps an artefact arising from the method of study and data recording. It may be that there are no simple, linear hierarchies in animals: A dominant over B, B over C, C over D etc. It is certainly rare for such predictable relationships to be found in either wild or captive wolf packs, and in my experience especially rare amongst dogs. What we find is a much more complex and flexible arrangement to do with divisions of labour and coalitions of power, not so different from the organization of human societies. For instance, a person or a dog may be a leader in one situation but not in another. And in some wolf packs, as in some human societies, a despot evolves who assumes absolute power over all others. Such animals can have a damaging effect upon the survival prospects of the rest of the group by continuously disrupting useful, co-operative activities.

I am sure that Jango was born to be a leader. He was a Weimaraner, one of a breed originally created in Germany to hunt big game. Nowadays, the Weimaraners that come to us are tough guys, highly manipulative of their owners and liable to chase and kill small animals like cats or wildlife. I warn prospective Weimaraner owners that they should be prepared for battle and sometimes bites from their dog, especially in males of the breed. The trouble is that they look too beautiful in their so-called 'Silver Ghost' plumage to deserve tough management. Jango was just eighteen months old when he was brought to the farm, in his perfect muscular silver prime. His owners, Jane and Alan Potter, described him as the pushy pup of the litter, who even at six weeks battled with brothers and sisters over a scrap of food or a bone. His breeder noticed that he was always successful in obtaining the best milk supply; consequently he grew heavier and looked fitter than his siblings.

I had been forewarned about what to expect from Jango in a long, tense phone call the day before with Jane, his mistress. I guessed that my training in psychological counselling would definitely not be wasted on this trio, but that my physical brawn might come in handy too. Jane had told me that her husband was contemplating suicide should Jango have to go. I know from experience that a threat of this kind is all too often more than just a cry for help, so I cleared my diary for the morning, letting Alan and Jane leapfrog over other appointments.

The white BMW arrived at exactly 9.30; a colleague on the farm spotted them waiting around the corner until the appointed time. Alan remained in the car while Jane and the dog presented themselves to Cynthia, our receptionist. Jane explained that Alan did not really want to become involved, that the whole idea of coming to me for help was hers and he had no confidence that it would be helpful anyway. I did not deny that her husband could be right, but still persuaded her that we were more likely to obtain results if all three Potters participated in what was to follow. Jane's eyes were ringed from crying and sleep deprivation and privately I wondered how kind I was in fact being to them, offering a 'way out' which might not succeed. Perhaps better to bite the bullet now than later?

Alan came into my small office looking like a crushed old man. In reality he was in his early forties, dressed in informal athletic gear incongruously finished off with long white gloves, which he wore to hide the physical scars of the last confrontation with Jango. His deep depression showed up clearly in his voice and posture. When we began talking about Jango's history, Jane became talkative, almost cheerful in reviewing their good times together. To Jane, Jango was just a dog whose physical company she enjoyed; she was not emotionally wrapped up in his feelings and needs. By contrast, Alan dearly loved Jango, talking like a child of the various 'firsts' that they had enjoyed together: a trip to a hotel, a camping holiday, a night at friends' when Jango killed their cat and so on. This was like a father talking about an errant son who now faced the death penalty.

Alan was a newspaper man, a top dog on his paper used to getting his own way. At that time, Fleet Street was in turmoil with the great move eastwards to the Isle of Dogs. Alan was under great strain at work, hiring, firing and dealing with the unions, leaving little energy left to do battle with a dog at home. Why should he? A dog is for enjoyment! Jango meanwhile was carving out an affectionate niche for himself with Jane, and finding the attentions of Alan in the evenings and weekends objectionable.

As I took the history, Jango's owners admitted that he had always been allowed the best chairs, beds and laps. He had first growled when Alan had ordered him off a sofa at five months old. He began leg-cocking on furniture at six months, and things got steadily worse from then on. There were other warnings in Jango's puppy behaviour of things to come. For instance, he had always been reluctant to give up stolen objects; bones were defended to the last. He had resisted being restrained for grooming or first aid, and particularly hated his paws being dried after muddy walks. There were other 'no go' regions of his body, for instance his jaws, genital area and stumpy tail.

Jango had not been an easy dog to train, prone to running off to play with other dogs. He growled when collected from these canine knockabouts. On advice from the vet, Alan had taken Jango to training classes but these were not to their liking, because tough handling and strict punishment were advocated. In particular, the need to 'show you are boss' was demonstrated by an Irish trainer on his own German Shepherd: he rolled the dog over and shook him by the jowls until 'submission' was obtained, all the while staring and growling into the dog's face. The poor German Shepherd responded by defecating on the feet of his owner. When Alan tried the technique on Jango he got badly bitten.

The last awful battle between Alan and Jango took place three days before they came to see me. Alan was a bit tipsy from his fourth whisky of the evening and decided to 'take Jango on' over his refusal to move from the sofa. When Jane, who was also on the sofa, saw Jango's hackles stiffen, she pushed him from behind towards Alan. I believe that this touch from the adored mistress was interpreted as an invitation or a goad to attack Alan – that certainly was its effect. Jango grabbed Alan's right hand, badly ripping the flesh. Alan mistakenly pulled his hand from the jaws and kicked Jango hard in the belly, whereupon the brute came forward again and held Alan by the arm, making four tidy, deep puncture wounds with his canines.

Blood was everywhere, with Alan in partial shock and Jane crying hysterically. When they stopped shouting and moving, Jango backed away, seemingly contrite. Alan was lucky: other dogs have done worse damage to their masters, and some have killed.

Alan had his wounds stitched up at the local hospital where they advised him to have Jango destroyed; this he resolved to do the next morning. Of course, by the morrow their resolve had weakened and Jango was reprieved. But what were they to do? Friends and relatives were beginning to shun them. Someone suggested a training establishment in North London, which ran 'reform courses' for problem dogs. They visited the kennels and were shocked to find that they were not allowed behind closed doors; what little they could see struck them as brutal and unfriendly. Hence the phone call to our office.

Outdoors, it was fascinating to watch the courage in Jango's body language as he went about the farm. He jumped all four feet off the ground with excitement on seeing his first Bantam and was keen to deal mortal blows to Albert, our paraplegic turkey. He strutted like a Viennese dancing horse in front of the cows, his close-docked tail always erect and wagging, even when confronted by a seventeen-hand Percheron horse. This was a dog afraid of nothing, a dog who had always had his own way. On the other hand, so long as he was not confronted or hassled, Jango was a most likeable dog, especially gregarious with new acquaintances like us.

That happy relationship changed dramatically when I got to work. Since Jango pulled like a shire horse, I knew that a headcollar had to be fitted to achieve safe control. Safe control was not a high priority for Jango: he preferred freedom. My cautious approach to handling him was well justified because at the second try with the headcollar he lunged forward, missing my arm by a whisker. By this stage Alan was shaking, fearful of yet another bite like the one that had demolished his self-esteem a week earlier. For myself there was only a small loss of face, unimportant except for the fact that I had been depicted as something of a miracle-worker in Alan's newspaper just a couple of months earlier. I didn't want to let them down! I joked that St Peter's Hospital was only a mile away, though I still didn't relish the thought of full-scale battle.

Slipping Jango on to a noose, I took him outside, where we began playing with balls and titbits. He enjoyed it and let me pat his body, though not his neck and ears. Sneakily, I slipped the headcollar around his head, leaving the nose-piece dangling. More play, distraction with other dogs and we walked for half an hour. Then over went the nose band without his noticing and I thought I was his master. The explosion of protest in my direction was dramatic. Never had Jango been so insulted in his life!

Alan insisted that we should give up, that he wanted to leave, that he was afraid for me, that it looked cruel, that he would seek another way, that the only answer was for Jango to go. I would have none of this. I could not withdraw from the course of action that we had together agreed. I cheerfully pretended that such behaviour was quite normal in a confident dog like Jango, that it was just a passing phase; I asked them to 'watch me having fun with him'. In the end, Jango did calm down, his docked tail sinking below the horizontal. However, that was not before several more close shaves. He was an awesome opponent, standing almost two metres on his hind legs.

Once Jango had accepted that he was tethered to Mugford via the headcollar, we began simple but effective obedience training designed to emphasize my relative strength and assertiveness over him. The first stage was never to allow him to walk ahead of me but always to have him at my side or behind. The headcollar simplified this process and each time he stepped ahead, an annoying rattle-can would be dropped down a metre ahead of him. He knew the 'Sit' command but had previously refused to obey me; with the headcollar, however, I could make him sit without any expenditure of adrenalin. Then I made him lie down, a process he hated since it meant having his belly touch the ground. Down he went even so, by the simple process of bringing his head to ground level, then gently coaxing his buttocks to follow with a titbit reward when the manoeuvre was completed.

Finally, there was the 'Come' command. By now, he had lost all interest in chasing the livestock on the farm; animals were coming out from behind the bales, nooks and crannies seemingly to mock this great grey brute. When he was about ten metres away from me I called him in, but he seemingly could not hear. Then I reeled him in beside me like a reluctant great sea trout. This old-fashioned compulsive form of training is not to my liking and not one to be recommended for 'ordinary' dogs. Nevertheless, it is useful for dogs like Jango because it establishes simple rules or criteria for obeying commands and accepting authority.

Eventually, I handed Jango over, first to Jane, who repeated the exercises, and later to Alan, who did the same. The changeover worked well, and Jango was for the first time receiving and obeying

Left: During my investigation of the murder of Glenys Coe, I watched her dog Tara come to the spot where her body had lain: she marked it with urine. The Police photographer captured her every move on video for later analysis

Right: My colleague Elizabeth with Sid, a neutered billy goat who hates dogs and trees. We occasionally exploit Sid's temper to subdue the more ferocious livestock-chasing patients before going on to therapy from Afterthought, the sheep

Above: Afterthought as an eager yearling ram, showing early potential for canine therapy

Left: A working pack of four Samoyeds and a Siberian Husky visited the farm. Our challenge: to resolve a long-standing rank order dispute. *Above:* A precarious assignment for Mugford, seen here aboard the sled at speed, around the Hardwick hill. The Husky was chosen to be leader

Below: Visiting dogs usually have a passion for horses' hoof trimmings, of which there are always plenty at the farm. Hoof keratin is indigestible but this Setter puppy would not relinquish its 'trophy' to Elizabeth

Wild times at a puppy play group. All a bit tiring for Sam

Right: Boy meets girl at the play group. Sexual activities can start early in smaller breeds, such as this Westie and Tibetan Spaniel

Below: Afterthought educating puppies during a play group. He is uncharacteristically gentle with puppies, having been raised amongst Hardwick Labradors who made him a good judge of canine body signals (*Alistair Morrison*)

Right: Fritz meeting Sam, his first canine encounter for years. Note Sam's non-threatening body posture, averted eyes, flattened hair and tail tucked under. Next, he goes into 'icebreaker' mode of play-bow, hop and tail wag, so that Fritz the fighter finds a first friend

Below right: Sam is a good judge of canine character, seen here at the end of a therapy session with a Pit Bull rescued by the RSPCA from an illegal dog fight ring. The fighting dogs suffer terrible injuries, mental as well as physical

Below: Sam the protector of my twin son, I think Harry, from a child-abused Jack Russell. So far, all my kids have survived without injury and have total confidence in the company of dangerous dogs

Foot: If Sam is an expert on canine communication, strange cats tend to leave him baffled and anxious; here Sam comes on a home visit to see a cat with a reputation for violence against dogs and men. We both survived the encounter!

Above: Sam faced with a confusing challenge – judging the expression of emotions in this hairy Old English Sheepdog is nigh impossible, so he backs away

Right: Turk, a mentally simple Percheron, trys to steal Sam's show. Turk loves to suck dogs' ears and only on such occasions can he rely on Sam remaining still

Below: Be sure your dog will occasionally let you down: Sam has killed a rabbit in front of visiting owners, a too regular occurrence that loses him fans

Right: At a cemetery in Edinburgh, there is a famous shrine to the loyalty of a dog that mourned for his dead master. On our visit, Sam went straight to it and performed this abominable desecration

Toys lie buried like mushrooms around the farm and dogs come in from far and wide to play

commands from physically in-control people. I noticed that whenever the opportunity presented itself, Jango attempted to urine-mark objects: the slightest relaxation of leash control and he was off to cock a leg. This seemed to be a quite deliberate statement of defiance and I resolved to suppress it. Alan was briefed to drop a rattle-can each time he cocked a leg. Jango's natural curiosity made him turn back and investigate, resulting in a loss of balance. In this way, we blocked his urine-marking and with it the opportunity to define territory and perhaps to signal leadership.

I suggested to Alan and Jane that they should never again allow Jango off the ground since elevation conferred an advantage to him. There would be no more bed-warming with a Weimaraner! I also explained the importance of harnessing Jango's love of company to Alan and Jane's advantage rather than to his own. Specifically, when he came to them with a wagging tail, a direct eye and a demand for a stroke, they were to ignore him. At a later stage, when they felt the time was right, they were to call him over to sit and be stroked. This simple change of the rules of engagement has a dramatic effect upon pushy dogs like Jango. I also asked that they contain their own spontaneous affection towards him, perhaps cuddling one another rather than the dog.

The idea that expressions of spontaneous love could mould and in some cases damage a relationship between a dog and owner came as a surprise to Alan, who was applying his beliefs about tolerant human relationships to the world of dogs. He had not realized that the pursuit of power and privilege is as important to some young dogs as it was to a rising business executive like himself.

Games were to be another key element in modifying Jango's behaviour. His favourite had always been tug-of-war in which a figure of eight pull-toy provided the invitation to mock battle. I suggested they put an end to this kind of rough 'n' tumble, replacing such games with different, people-centred rules. Alan and Jane were always to stand during play, to engage in peaceful games such as 'throw and fetch'. Slow movements and quiet voices were the key elements in this strategy; anything else stimulated Jango and undermined his owners' authority.

Finally there arose the delicate subject of Jango's testicles. It had been made quite clear at the outset of our consultation that Alan regarded castration as a 'no no', an assault upon a dog's dignity. One would not do this to one's friend, so why to a dog?

While sympathizing with his sentimental concern for Jango's welfare, I could not accept the point. I knew that this was a purely practical issue, that it was testosterone that was motivating some of the competitive elements in Jango's attitude to Alan. The problem arose from a play-off between two males, with Jane as the prize. I knew very well from both the extensive research literature and my own experience in practice that castration was warranted. Male Weimaraners are particularly responsive to this operation, so much so that I sometimes feel tempted to recommend routine castration as a preventative measure. Future generations could come from a sperm bank or perhaps from one or two particularly affable dogs.

Twenty minutes later, after an emotional debate covering such intellectual high spots as 'Will he miss them?', Alan gave in to my logic. However, he voiced concern over the safety aspects of handling before, during and after the operation. How could the vet possibly manage Jango? Would he be drowsy after the anaesthetic and likely to snap? How would the vet restrain him? I could not be certain about reassuring him on all these points, so I arranged for him to be 'done' by a vet known for his skill at handling tricky animals: my landlord, Carl Boyde.

Carl slipped Jango on to the backseat of his much-abused Volvo estate where he could lie out surrounded by harnesses, ropes, dirty Barbours, wellies, horse-hoof clippings, a bag with fresh bull testicles, blood samples for the lab and all the paraphernalia of a country vet. On my advice, he treated Jango with the circumspection due to a wild, potentially dangerous animal and trapped his lead outside the rear door of his car. This prevented Jango from reaching forward and simplified handling at journey's end.

I collected Jango that afternoon from the veterinary hospital. He seemed genuinely pleased to be with someone who was familiar to him, in spite of the fact that I had been his opponent earlier on that long day. I took him back to the boarding kennels to which he had been assigned for ten days. I warned the kennel owner to watch him carefully and to be on her guard. Being a sensible woman and one of those 'naturals' with animals who disregards her own safety, she ignored my wisdom! She had evidently got through her life pursuing her carefree strategy without the benefit of Roger Mugford, and she got along very well indeed with Jango.

Casually, she picked up the lead and commanded him to follow, which he did with tail down and a slightly sore gait from his castration cut. The rationale of putting Jango into kennels was to give Jane and Alan time to review future strategy and make the dog feel that home was indeed a sweet place, not to be taken for granted. Whilst Jango was in purdah, his master and mistress were to holiday in the Dordogne, a previously arranged break, but eventually they cut the vacation short due to worry over the dog. They drove directly to the kennels and then home with Jango, without coming by to see me.

A mysterious and unexpected silence ensued in which I failed to receive the weekly reports that I had requested. After a month had passed, I could contain my curiosity no longer. I wanted to know what had happened to this remarkable demon of a dog, so I phoned them and heard, much to my relief, that all was well. There had been only minor growls over small issues like a friend coming to the door, but nothing of significance. Alan was receiving psychotherapy and had taken time off work. He talked of a new career but at least he now had Jango in better perspective. The monthly hormone shots that I had suggested were being given by the referring veterinary surgeon. Both were most grateful for my help but they were still cautious; Jane told me that it would be a year before they could feel confident that Jango was reformed.

I conceded and waited the year. What prompted me to call Jango's owner was that I had seen an identical male Weimaraner who had bitten his master and mistress in similar circumstances. They too were brooding and talking of euthanasia without really wanting to do it. I urgently needed to know whether or not I had been successful with Jango in order to reassure these new owners of a macho Weimaraner. Hooray! hooray! Jango was alive and very well; there had not been a single bite during the year. Their friends were no longer afraid of Jango and he had become a village favourite. Most impressive of all was the psychological recovery of Alan, who had seriously been considering throwing his life away on account of a dog. That is a waste I could not contemplate. When I asked why he had not rung me to tell me the excellent news, he admitted that it was out of embarrassment over the personal breakdowns he had suffered due to Jango. He wanted to put that whole year and all the rough experiences behind him and start again. I well understood his desire to start off anew; failures are a better teacher than successes in life.

As I have said, most of us indulge our dogs and love them in an undemanding way. The cost of a mistake is not usually so high as it was with Jango, though occasionally it might pay to make the point that we can, after all, be in control if we want to be. Every now and again we might usefully insist that our dog sits at the kerb, obeys a 'Come' response and does not literally walk all over us. We must occasionally play at being 'hard to get', switching the balance of the relationship so that affection is exchanged at a time determined by us rather than by the dog.

In matters to do with canine competitiveness, the sex of the dog is an important factor in determining the sex of the victim. Whereas Jango directed most of his attacks towards the man of the house, Susie, a two-year-old English Bull Terrier, was only aggressive towards her mistress, Lara. However, the dog was a slavish flirt towards the husband David.

Susie was a big dog, more like a male Bull Terrier than the usually fine-boned bitch. Her tail was always high, a fearless and proud dog. She was physically reckless and had sustained numerous cuts and bruises by crashing into other dogs, doors, cars and the like. Nevertheless, to outsiders like myself Susie was actively friendly, courting attention by licking my hands, pawing my legs and eventually rolling over in mock submission, inviting a tickle to her tummy. I had already seen the scars on Lara's arms, which were highlighted by black bruises from an attack ten days earlier. Without seeing the bite-marks, one would not have guessed that this dog would bite the hands that fed it.

Susie was Lara and David's second Bull Terrier. The first had been a delight, but had died tragically at four years old of heart failure during competitive agility at her local dog club. Lara had been heartbroken, so David had bought Susie on the spur of the moment as a spirit-reviver. The week before my visit to their home, Susie had been brought to my Bayswater clinic by Lara. The medical and behavioural scenario which unfolded became so complicated that I postponed tests and treatment until I could see them at home, with David present.

We know that in a wolf pack, reproduction is the unique prerogative of one bitch in the group, a canine queen bee. Like bees, she slows down or can entirely inhibit the reproductive activity of other bitches by bullying (social suppression) and possibly by smell (pheromonal suppression). The physiological mechanism by which this is done formed part of my doctoral thesis in the sixties, when I studied the reproductive and social behaviour of mice. It turns out that mice use almost the same mechanism for controlling their numbers as the wolf. The trouble is that man has selected dogs to be exceptionally fertile: their brains and ovaries are not so responsive to social and pheromonal cues as in their wolf ancestors. Susie provided the perfect illustration of how dogs see their owners as fellow members of a pack. I suspected that Susie was trying to capture the biological privilege of sex for herself and objected to signs of sexuality in the competing 'bitch', her mistress Lara.

Susie only began to be a problem with Lara at seven months, days before having her first season. At about that time she suddenly took exception to Lara and Lara alone. Where as a puppy she had just struggled and acted defiantly, now she growled. Four days into her season, she made her first snap at Lara, fortunately not breaking the skin. Being a sensible lady and accustomed to the ways of Bull Terriers, Lara immediately toughened her approach to Susie's general management, ensuring that she was no longer allowed the old privileges of jumping up on chairs and beds. However, it was rather a blow to her, because she took immense pleasure in the spirit, looks and company of her dog. Matters seemed to improve when the first season ended, but not for long. When Lara first contacted me, I asked her to keep a diary of events and going through her diary at the clinic we found an interesting association with Lara's menstrual cycle, particularly on days sixteen-to-eighteen, when she should have been ovulating. We could have been really scientific about this by taking blood samples and vaginal smears from Lara and Susie, but I was pretty confident that there was a correlation from the data I had been given.

The major confrontation occurred as Susie came into her second season. Minutes earlier, there had been a tussle about drying Susie's toes after the morning walk, which had upped the level of violence for subsequent confrontations. Susie had run off with a pair of Lara's pants before launching her attack. Just two bites had done all the damage I could see to Lara's arm; but at the moment she had burst into tears, Susie stopped and tried to comfort Lara, just as would a bitch with her distressed puppy.

The difficulty for me was that most of Lara's management of Susie was correct – a text-book case of how to care for a Bull Terrier. Unlike most Bull Terrier owners, Lara believed that Susie should conform to strict rules; she was a keen member of two obedience clubs and did competitive agility training. All this effort was in sharp contrast to the attitude of David, a City man who was not interested in Susie's care or future: she received only a token greeting from him on his return home. Yet Susie would fawn at David's feet for hours afterwards, positioning herself beside him rather than by the more devoted Lara. Whereas Susie's approaches to David were rebuffed, her approaches to Lara solicited ecstatic affection. This was the only psychological key which I could find to unlock the problem between the dog and her mistress.

The hormonal aspects fascinated me. With Lara's permission, I phoned the breeder to ask about Susie's early days. It turned out that she was one of a litter of eight, of which four male and two female puppies had survived. So far as the breeder could recollect, two further males had died. So the brothers greatly outnumbered sisters in this litter. We know from studies of Freemartin cows that a female calf can be masculinized by sharing its foetal blood supply with her twin brother. If foetal androgens can affect young cows, I wondered, can they also affect the development of young dogs? In Susie's case there was a strong possibility that although she was genetically female, her character was part male. When we took her for a walk we could see this in her general posturing, especially in her contorted leg-cocking when marking territory. Male Bull Terriers are renowned for being much tougher than their sisters: it is a breed that is more sexually dimorphic than most. In that respect, Bull Terriers are like Rottweilers, West Highland White Terriers and Weimaraners in producing macho males but sweet-natured bitches. I knew that simply spaying Susie might not do the trick entirely because that would exaggerate the male side of her brain even more, particularly that which mediates aggression. Yet the presence of both androgens and oestrogens during Susie's season could have been responsible for both an increase in her libido and her increased irritability and competitiveness towards Lara. Careful thought was needed about how to proceed in this complicated physiological scenario. It is well known that androgens increase sexuality in females, in extreme cases precipitating virtual nymphomania. But they also precipitate unpleasant masculine traits like aggression, so it was a tough decision for me to have to make.

In conjunction with Susie's veterinary surgeon, we decided upon the following plan. For the next six weeks, Lara was to be especially offhand with Susie, modelling herself upon David's attitude. She was told not to seek confrontation but if one was inevitable, say in treating an injured paw, she should muzzle the dog to be on the safe side. I recommended that Susie should be spayed after a few weeks had elapsed, whereupon we should review the situation before attempting any more complicated hormonal treatments.

Three months went by and Susie did not dramatically improve; indeed there were several minor bite incidents. David was becoming impatient and wanted Susie to go, if only to stem the floods of tears he was obliged to endure from the distraught Lara. Grasping for straws, I recommended oestrogen replacement therapy to bring out the feminine side of Susie's behaviour. We chose a low dose, 0.2mg, which is near the natural level in bitches. Within a week, Lara could see an improvement and after a few months she was well pleased. We maintained the oestrogen replacement therapy for a year, after which it was stopped. That was four years ago and Susie continues to be a bearable and beloved Bull Terrier.

Sex and aggression are as inextricably linked in dogs as in man. Our bodies exude odours which tell dogs about who we are, our sex, maybe our sexiness and certainly about our emotional states of fear or confidence. A dog like Susie can smell exactly what her mistress has been up to, which can be a sobering thought for those contemplating cheating on their dog. French scientists have recently discovered that dogs may even be able to distinguish between people suffering from distinctive psychiatric disorders on the basis of their body odours. When treating patients like Susie there is always a danger of focusing too much upon the dog and neglecting to explore how the physiological and behavioural state of the owner might play a part. Propriety usually prevents me whipping out a specimen jar for the owner to fill or sniffing their underarm odours, but perhaps I should.

The final irony in Susie's story is that she came from a breeder who routinely hand-rears Bull Terrier puppies because the mothers are so aggressive and often cannibalize their young. We know that in other species poor mothering behaviour can adversely affect emotional development of young. For instance, the Landrace breed of pig is highly strung and they are liable to fight one another under intensive farming conditions. The mothers also tend to eat their young when stressed. I believe that the same principles apply to Bull Terriers as to pigs, and that breeders must select for good behaviour in all respects, including maternal care. Susie's breeder remains unconvinced by my arguments and believes that Lara alone was at fault.

In animals and humans alike, excessive displays of competitive aggression destroy many of the benefits that come from social living. No one member of a pack can be too prickly or obstreperous or the pack will break up. Co-operation is the vital trait which allows dog packs to form working coalitions during defence and hunting and in the rearing of young. There is only ever space for one pushy, executive type, and the trouble is that in some breeds of dog, almost every individual wants to be boss!

The ordered relationships that we tend to find in packs of wolves and related wild dogs are easily destroyed by trouble-makers, a shortage of food or some external change, like a neighbouring pack encroaching onto its territory. With domestic dogs, we humans constantly introduce disorder and it surprises me that most people are routinely accorded such deferential respect by their pets. Yet by making only a few key compromises, indulgent fun can still be had with the majority of my pushy canine patients.

6
Fear

I try not to become emotionally involved with my patients but I frequently do. The type of dog to whom my heart really goes out is one that is afraid, either of something in particular or of the whole world. Life can be a demanding balancing act between courage and fear, between approach and avoidance, between initiative-taking and a retreat to familiar places and pastimes. In the wild, to be excessively courageous is to be dead in double-quick time: the survivors are those who run away to fight another day. Flight is thus a key survival skill, well developed in herbivores such as horses, when they sniff or sight danger. A predator like the wolf also needs to be cautious because there is always a predator or a danger bigger than himself. For instance, wolves had to watch out for sabre-toothed tigers in their recent evolutionary past; now man is the predator to fear.

As a result of research over the last hundred years we know a great deal about the basis of fear in man and animals. We know which part of the brain is sensitive to chemicals that govern the sensation of fear. We know that the adrenal gland pumps up the body with its output of epinephrine and that fearful arousal can be monitored from the metabolites excreted in urine. We know about the heart's response, preparing for fight or flight. We know how animals, even man, can 'poison' themselves by hyperventilating, a sign of over-stimulation by the vagus nerve which regulates the heart and breathing centres.

Then there is consciousness: the knowledge that a particular situation is safe or savage. Most people can make this judgement without suffering crippling fears and phobias. Those who succumb can go to a psychologist or psychiatrist to talk about them and receive treatment. The situation with dogs is vastly more complicated because it is usually believed they are not capable of this rational, weighing-up process. Even with people, the treatment of phobias can be difficult: witness how many middle-aged people suffer from agoraphobia or a fear of harmless spiders, snakes or birds. Since I have been in practice there have been enormous advances in our understanding of how phobias are acquired by people and how they may best be treated; fortunately I have been able to transfer many of these ideas from humans to animals.

Every dog has a threshold beyond which it becomes afraid of worldly happenings. Loud noises are the most common type of stimulus to provoke fear in dogs, and some breeds are more sound-sensitive than others. For reasons that have not been scientifically determined, Collies in their various types are the most sound-sensitive of all. Bearded Collies, Rough Collies and related Shelties often come to us in misery from the bangs, clatters and whines of machinery. Mongrels carrying the same Collie sound-sensitive genes are also over-represented amongst phobic patients, particularly if they had a deprived or traumatized puppyhood.

Lily was just such a part-Collie mutt from Battersea Dogs' Home who had moved north of the Thames to live in West London. There, she was a much-loved member of the Johnson family, along with three noisy boys, husband and wife, guinea pigs, cat, another dog and a vast entourage of relatives and friends. This was a supremely sociable, hard-working and noisy Irish family in which Lily was the only female ally of Mum Johnson, a 'sister' to her sons. We guessed that Lily was now six, the Johnsons having owned her for four years. She was generally good-tempered but had always been nervous around Guy Fawkes Day, and the boys knew that they must never play with cap-guns. This had posed no great problem, particularly as the vet prescribed a gigantic dose of ACP (a widely used sedative) before and during the 5 November celebrations.

Lily became a potential patient of Roger Mugford in March 1989, when she suddenly refused to go out of doors. She dug in her paws and had to be dragged out to the street, tail down. On one occasion she even urinated and defecated in her terror. Of course, she was allowed to forego walks and unfortunately took to doing her business in their tiny back yard – or worse, in the house.

At the Animal Behaviour Centre the family went wild at the chance to be on the farm, just like their Uncle Sean's back home in County Meath. Lily trotted around to see the animals and to play with our dogs in the office, suggesting to us that a pack of lies was being told about her by Mr and Mrs Johnson. She even tolerated a passing tractor which was roaring up and down the lane on dung-spreading duties. This ageless little Collie-cross played with my Setter

Sam like a puppy. It all began to look like a waste of time and effort, even though the outing had been enjoyed by all. We agreed I should visit Lily at home.

The noise in the Hammersmith area of London is horrendous from building works, the rumble of traffic over the flyover, the Underground and the rush of buses and trucks around the Broadway. It is definitely not good dog country. Sam is an excellent judge of suitable territory for canines, and he remained huddled in my car, showing no inclination whatsoever to get out at the Johnsons' house. I was ushered in and Lily appeared from the back of the house, where she had created a den under the kitchen units. She was friendly and seemingly in good health, just as she had been at the farm the previous week. I held her chest to measure her heart rate: it was a normal eighty, though her breathing was shallow. She licked me trustingly. However, when I rustled the lead, Lily's whole demeanour changed: she rushed back to her den and sat with one paw raised in a pose of pathetic supplication. I could now see what I had been told about her earlier at the farm.

Hard man that I am, I decided to try for a walk, but she would have none of it. We carried her to the street but she crouched low and would not budge. Around the corner in a small park she showed a brief interest in doggy smells, and a former canine playmate that belonged to a friendly pensioner. At least we got her walking on the homeward journey but we could not put her into reverse. As we went southwards towards Hammersmith Road, her fear increased. A bus pulled to a halt on Hammersmith Road, the airbrakes hissed; and that was it. Lily tried to bolt and we only just managed to restrain her.

In cases of this sort, we often use a 'jolly hockey sticks' attitude to distract a dog from dwelling on fearful matters, but Lily was much too far gone to respond to this kind of superficial approach. Her heart was racing, she was hyperventilating and salivating, and had she broken free she would probably have rushed off in total panic.

Nothing could be done until we could control her physiological arousal. We managed to get her home, and I called Lily's vet who agreed to prescribe a low dose of valium combined with a beta-blocker. My aim was to slow down Lily's hyperventilation and reduce her blood pressure with the beta-blocker, which should then enable her to form a better mental adjustment to her situation. Until that stage was achieved, Lily would function like a frightened mouse. As it happened, Grandfather Johnson was also on beta-blockers and was able to reassure the rest of the family that since he had come to no harm and was no junkie, why should Lily? They agreed to proceed and I said I would be in touch after the drugs had had their effect.

The next week I called them to find that Lily was no better. I asked them to try it for another week, but next week came and still there was no improvement. I decided to change tack. Were there, by any chance, friends or family outside London where there was a lower density of traffic? Yes, Mrs Johnson had a sister living in rural Sussex. Could she be persuaded to take Lily? I was asked to make the phone call to Big Sister. A lovely Irish voice answered the phone and immediately agreed to my request. After half an hour of stories about how she had rescued her kid sister from amazing childhood escapades back in Ireland, we agreed on a plan for Lily.

The drugs were to continue without interruption, and Lily was to be fed, as a reward, even after the shortest of walks. If there was any reluctance to walk out to the garden or surrounding countryside, she was not to be forced, but carried to the car and given a brief ride to a nearby field or park. Lots of praise, wind-up playful attention and a no-nonsense tone of voice were to be used. It was half-term, so fourteen-year-old Duane was appointed to accompany Lily to her temporary holiday home. This was seen as an immense privilege for him by his younger brothers. Since there was always the possibility of Lily bolting and getting lost in darkest Sussex, I told Duane to make sure that she was held on an extending lead at all times.

As it happens, I was passing through Sussex a few days later *en route* to a radio show, so I decided to drop in. The change was dramatic. I saw exactly the same dog that had visited Hardwick Court Farm: calm, confident, friendly. What would happen when she returned to Hammersmith? We checked that out by going into downtown Crawley, under the flight path of Gatwick Airport. Poor Lily wilted before our eyes. And when an ancient Ford drew up alongside to ask us for directions, polluting us with a squeaky noise from a badly-worn water pump, she bolted.

Back at the farm, I phoned a noise consultant to ask about the frequencies and likely intensities of sound in an area like Hammersmith. He explained that there would be a wide range of noise outputs, with low frequency emissions from underground trains and from heavy trucks physically vibrating the body. At the upper end of the sound spectrum there would be the ultrasonic or high-frequency emissions from electrical and mechanical devices. Both would be well within the extraordinary hearing range of a Border Collie, though they might not be so apparent to human beings. Where did this leave Lily?

We took her back to Hammersmith for a one-week trial, if only 'for the sake of the children', who had to understand the cruelty of imposing the Hammersmith experience upon Lily. The parents wanted me to be involved in this process, a request to which I gladly agreed. I visited them again and Lily was right back at square one, perhaps even worse. Fortunately she had endeared herself to auntie during her holiday in Crawley so back she went. Now Lily is doing fine.

I could say that Lily was our failure but that wouldn't be true, because she demonstrated to us the limitations of animal behaviour therapy when confronted with an unsuitable or hostile environment. Much as I would have liked to bring the traffic around Hammersmith to a halt for the sake of Lily, that was not within my power.

Other fear and phobia cases we deal with tend to have a more positive outcome. For example Bella, a Rough Collie in Camberley, who every Thursday for the month before my visit had inflicted serious damage upon herself and her concerned owners' property. Previously, Tina and her husband Alistair had seen nothing odd in Bella's behaviour, though they had noticed that she had become jumpy when she heard crashing cutlery or the scratch of a knife on glass. Bella's mistress decided to stay at home one Thursday to see what provoked this mysterious change in their pet's behaviour.

At precisely 10.15 a.m. Bella began pacing and whining. Then she rushed upstairs and after attempting to bury herself in the bed, chewed at the door and window-frames. Within minutes, she had become a thoroughly miserable animal. It soon became obvious what was behind Bella's fear when the garbage truck arrived. She flipped at the grinding sound of the compacting steel blades as they ground steel against glass, tin and everything else in the rubbish. Accordingly, I was invited to come the next week at 10 a.m. sharp.

Bella's behaviour was exactly as Tina had described over the phone. Since she began to show fear of the garbage truck when it was at least two kilometres away, I guessed that she anticipated the unpleasant noise of the compacter machinery by linking it to the sound of the diesel engine moving around the housing estate. Collies in general and Rough Collies in particular have spectacularly sensitive hearing, which I presume to be linked to their former working roles; after all, the shepherd must be able to control his dog by whistling commands from maybe half a kilometre away. A by-product of this selection for sensitive hearing is the discomfort these dogs feel at hearing loud noises, especially those of high frequency. The sensation is probably not unlike that experienced by people standing close to hi-tech ultrasonic fire alarms.

As I watched poor, demented Bella run from room to room unconsoled by our presence, it was obvious that instant relief was needed, so we piled in the car and drove to the other side of the housing estate. The surrounding area was deeply wooded, providing a perfect environment in which to conduct a desensitization programme for her fear of garbage trucks. But before we took off for the woods, we worked out the minimum distance from the truck which Bella could tolerate: it was about 500 metres, at which distance she hopped out of the car and walked the streets, conscious of the noise but relatively unconcerned. Much closer than that and she became reluctant to get out of the car, her tail went down and she began to hyperventilate. We could easily hear the garbage truck at this distance from its low frequency thumps, which carry over greater distances than high frequency sounds.

The process of phobic desensitization relies upon the pairing of pleasant sensations with low-level exposure to the fear-evoking stimuli: in Bella's case the complex sound of breaking glass. We decided to utilize the garbage truck as the stimulus, supplemented by home-training sessions using tape recordings. Bella was a wonderful patient because she loved playing with balls. They were a compulsion to her: show her a ball and she became an hysterical, yapping puppy. As soon as she was within 500 metres of the truck, she stopped playing; further away, play could resume. Tina, Bella and I walked around all the estates in the area, playing ball games on open spaces at the tolerated distance from the garbage truck. A hidden audience of housebound residents peered out at us, thinking no doubt that we were raving lunatics.

We spent the whole morning shadowing the garbage truck route until its crew stopped for lunch. I went down to the Council yard to chat to them. A mug of sweet, milky tea was pushed my way and I edged myself between sandwich boxes, tabloid newspapers and one intense young *Telegraph* reader. They were all interested in our morning's work and were delighted to be asked to help. I did not come equipped as a BBC reporter, so had nothing but my scratchy dictation machine to obtain a recording of the truck. I was offered the Rest Room 'beat-box' which had been salvaged from someone's dust-bin, and surprised both myself and them by finding that the recording mechanism still worked. Off I went to get the definitive sound track of grinding garbage. Tape in hand, I returned to Bella's home, but not before the crew had offered to meet up with us again the following Thursday.

I was keen to test the recording we had made on my car tape-deck but it did not sound too impressive. However, through Tina's state-of-the-art hi-fi it had a passable likeness to the sound of a garbage truck. Even if a human ear could spot that it was a poor audio-recording, it seemed to fool Bella. She showed the same fearful symptoms as when she heard the truck itself, which diminished as we decreased the volume. We now had a tool with which Tina and Alistair could continue the desensitization process through the week.

My instructions were never to play the sound recording louder than Bella's tolerance levels and to accompany it with feeding, love and games. A detailed protocol was constructed, specifying the precise volume on the hi-fi, the duration of the exercise and the behaviour to be recorded. We focused on tell-tale negative behaviour such as hyperventilating, low-slung tail, pacing, lack of interest in food and so on. The positive behaviour patterns we were seeking to develop were a playful tail-wag, yapping to solicit play, an interest in food, barking to a knock at the door and an excited reaction to the rattling of her lead for walkies. I arranged to return next week at the same time.

The following Thursday the dustmen were really kind, taking special care not to rev their diesel engine nor run the compaction unit more than was necessary. Three of the four men in the crew had dogs of their own, but their general experience of dog owners was having to complain about bites from ferocious hounds. Bella was obviously different, and for the first time she met and was petted by her 'torturers'. They even asked if next week they could invite Bella into the cab to take a ride. I thought this could be a helpful experience: a change in the context of the phobic stimulus.

I was not present for the first cab-ride but apparently Bella coped, maybe even enjoyed it. The different physical context of exposure to the sound had totally changed her reaction towards it. I have seen such reactions before, where a cycle of fear can only develop in defined circumstances, variation from which eases the fear. Tina and Alistair took it in turns over the ensuing weeks to alternate being at home on Thursday mornings; they had been given compassionate leave to do so by their employers, just as others would obtain compassionate leave to care for a sick child. Bella was as important to them as any child is to a parent, and beautifully typed progress reports were submitted by Tina, a high-powered legal secretary with a tidy mind. By three months the situation was essentially resolved, which in Tina's words was almost a disappointment because they had come to enjoy their Thursday morning breaks, riding around in a garbage truck.

Bella rather nicely illustrates the key elements of my job: a detailed diagnosis from me followed by a conscientious application of a therapeutic programme by the owner, assisted by outsiders willing to help an animal in distress. All I provided was an insight into the cause of the problems – in this case, the genetic predisposition of Collies to sound phobias – and help in creating a reward-based learning system. With hindsight it appears simple, but believe me, it is not always so straightforward.

Just occasionally, I get the opportunity to look like the proverbial miracle worker. I was recently approached by the owners of a couple of Labradors that were said to be agoraphobic. Nervous Labradors are a rarity in our practice because they have been bred to survive the sometimes noisy rough and tumble of life in the country. A tendency to disabling sound phobia would obviously be bad news in a gundog. The essence of their problem was outlined in beautiful handwriting on quality note-paper. The letter read:

> 'We have always had Labradors; we live in the country and we think we know a bit about dogs. However, our present two, Daley and Thompson, seem to have us foxed. They are just over a year old and have never been off our property because we cannot get them to wear a lead. Indeed, getting a collar on to Daley is difficult enough, though strangely Thompson accepts his. We have tried softly-softly approaches and sometimes have been quite firm. Our previous Labrador, who died aged fourteen, showed none of these signs. The dogs came from a reputable breeder and their mother seemed well behaved.
>
> I went to my vet to ask for some tranquillisers for the dog but he suggested I write to you. I can't imagine that a psychologist could be helpful with our dogs unless you are some kind of Dr Doolittle. Forgive my scepticism, but we are at the end of our tether and would really appreciate your help if you think you can.
>
> Yours sincerely, Mrs Jane Hamilton-Moore.'

Mr and Mrs Hamilton-Moore cut an impressive appearance on their arrival at the farm. They drove a white, sporty Ford XR3, and they appeared a confident and successful couple. They owned a large house with grounds and some might have thought it unnecessary ever to walk the dogs outside the land they owned. That was their justification for not trying to walk the dogs until they were six months old. But by then it was too late. The journey to our farm had been uneventful, except that the dogs had quivered in the back seat for three hours. It had obviously been a tough experience and I privately harboured an anxiety that if I did not come up with a solution this couple would feel aggrieved.

First, however, we had to get the hundred or so metres from the car to my office. Both dogs sat quivering in their new collars and leads; they had been lifted out of the car and were determined not to budge from their patch. When I approached to lift the yellow Labrador Daley, he urinated. The black brother Thompson did the same. After ten minutes of cajoling and feeling stupid, we carried them all the way and got wet trousers for our trouble.

Sam, my friendly but insensitive Setter, bundled into the consulting room causing panic amongst my patients. More urine on the floor, more expressions of embarrassment from Mrs Hamilton-Moore. 'Don't worry, don't worry,' said I, weakly. 'It's only cheap carpet!' I resolved to lecture Sam to be more deferential towards my paying guests. A physical examination of the dogs surprised me, because in spite of the appearance of fear from their eyes, ears and tail, they were quite relaxed. They were not shaking as though genuinely afraid, they were not hyperventilating and their pupils were only moderately dilated. Could these dogs possibly be faking? We had seen earlier that they became pathetic heaps if forcibly pulled along and I had every reason to believe what Mr and Mrs Hamilton-Moore said. These were effective people, he the owner and manager of his own company and she a no-nonsense lady used to getting her own way. My vet colleague Caroline ran her professional fingers over the dogs and listened to their hearts. Each gave a healthy thud. These dogs were fit enough to take the flooding approach.

Flooding has a controversial history amongst applied psychologists and psychiatrists because it sometimes makes the patient worse rather than better. In psychological flooding, the patient is exposed to the thing of which he or she is afraid at greater than normal intensity. Imagine someone afraid of snakes being lowered into a snakepit; of butterflies visiting a butterfly-house, or an agoraphobic being dumped into the middle of Runway One at Heathrow. However, for certain human and canine patients, the flooding technique can be dramatically effective and speedier than other techniques. In my professional career with dogs, I had only utilized the flooding technique on six canine patients. I felt that Daley and Thompson were another suitable pair for treatment.

We saddled the dogs up with my own design of headcollar to prevent them from retreating backwards during the walks I planned around the farm. It was a particularly hot June day and I knew it would be thirsty work for us all. Whereas we drank our water, the dogs spurned the bowl I had offered to them. My assistant, Erica, took over Daley, I handled Thompson. To the headcollar we attached a long extending lead, and off we went, with Thompson and myself leading the way. It was an exhausting process; Thompson dragged back at first but the headcollar obliged him to follow, skidding and struggling in protest. I was panting as much as he was – time I took up jogging again, I thought, but I won in just seven minutes. For Erica, a slight nine-stoner, Daley was too heavy. I had to do my bit on him too. Then we walked along together. After a further ten minutes, the dogs were heaving like long-distance runners. The casual visitor might not have liked what he saw – not so much the Surrey Centre of Kindness as a medieval circus 'breaking' frightened animals – but we knew we were making progress, and rapidly.

It was time to hand over to Mr and Mrs Hamilton-Moore, who were sensible enough to trust our judgement. As we passed the leads to them, the dogs' tails bobbed up to near normal; they were relieved to be away from us strangers! There was more pulling as they tested the resolve of their owners, but they could not buck the system any more. I suggested that they stop at hourly intervals on their way home to 'keep up the medicine', and from then on to take them out for regular walks every day.

I asked them to describe the set-up at home. Visitors to their business were usually segregated from the dogs and taken to another wing of their large, rambling farmhouse-cum-mansion. I asked that every visitor meet the dogs and if possible also take them for a brief walk. Every day, twice daily if possible, they were to be taken out for a drive and again a short walk. Every strange dog was to be walked towards, rather than avoided: both Daley and Thompson were afraid of other dogs. Finally, they were never to be soft and sympathetic to the dogs when their tails dropped between their legs: they were asked to use the 'jolly hockey sticks' extrovert approach.

Four weeks later, as requested, came a note with a joyful description of events. The dogs were now quite normal; they couldn't believe how quick and easy had been the transformation. Nor could I, to the extent that I was walking on air for the rest of the day.

The Thompson and Daley situation is by no means an uncommon one. The dogs had been acquired from a quiet farmer-breeder at twelve weeks, later than the optimum age. The litter of puppies had actually been kept in a converted calf-pen, receiving few visitors. The Hamilton-Moores's mistake was in adopting a pair of puppies who became inseparable and uninterested in outsiders. Then there was the division of the house to exclude much contact with strangers. They had thought that this was in the best interests of the puppies: they had not been vaccinated, and their vet had warned them about parvovirus. Similarly, taking them off the estate could expose them to the risk of other infectious diseases, so they were kept at home. Forty acres sounds like an idyllic setting for dogs, but space alone does not satisfy all canine needs.

To use the technical jargon, these dogs were 'undersocialized': they had not had exposure to experiences that were sufficiently demanding, challenging or novel when they were puppies to enable them to tolerate these experiences later on in life. The habit of retreat had been an effective technique for dealing with danger. Why face danger when you can run?

The physiological basis of fear is finely tuned and not easily disrupted by drugs or even positive learning experiences. To a great extent it is genetically determined: an obvious opportunity for breeders to select for confident, extrovert dogs. Too often, there is a tendency amongst some dog exhibitors to breed from nervous bitches in the hope that the experience of a litter will make them more confident. From time to time this may be beneficial, but only as a side-effect of elevated hormone levels during pregnancy and lactation, which act as a kind of natural tranquilliser. For most bitches pregnancy has no benefit, and there is the obvious danger that more nervous puppies may be produced. Even in the absence of genetic influences, nervous bitches can train their offspring to be similarly nervous and mistrustful of new situations: there is a cultural transfer from mother to puppy.

I am always interested in finding a way around these conundrums and one approach has been to focus on the puppy whilst it is young and receptive. That is why I started the Puppy Playgroup at the Animal Behaviour Centre in 1989, where fifteen to twenty puppies come together in a carpeted, specially designed playroom. Wild times are had by youngsters, whose role-models in life are Sam the posey Setter and Jasper, the exhilarating play-freak Border Collie. Puppies like Daley and Thompson come to us at fourteen weeks of age and by twenty weeks they are gambolling about like confident clowns.

Every puppy is handled by every other owner in the group and they meet our no-nonsense dog-devouring pet sheep, 'Afterthought', pushy chickens, contented cats and lots of children. The transformation of subdued and cautious puppies into happy-go-lucky roustabouts is wonderful to watch. I try never to miss Wednesday afternoons; it is the nicest slot in my professional diary. It's the most satisfying too – problems are better prevented than cured.

7
Mucky matters

Too much of my life has been spent tied to the tail end of animals. The process began early on whilst hand-milking Cherry, the house-cow of my childhood. Defecation was one of several weapons which Cherry could employ against humankind and she seemed to know that the splats of warm bovine faeces dispersed more widely and caused greater alarm to those sitting beside her if she hit smooth concrete rather than absorbent straw. I am sure that Cherry knew all about the messages that could be carried in faeces.

Dogs are in a league of their own for chemical communication through faeces and urine. Their reliance on smell poses one of the greatest challenges to us humans, whose lives are so dominated by visual and auditory messages. Imagine the subtlety of dialogue we might achieve if we devoted as much effort as they do to sniffing under strangers' arms and around their anus, licking their vaginal secretions, making oral investigations with our tongues and finally checking out dollops of faeces and sprays of urine.

At a technical level, my involvement with urine and faeces has been continuous from the days when I was working on my doctoral thesis, where I was much concerned with the way mice communicated messages about their emotional state, sexual status and aggressive or peaceful intentions. By analysing their urine and glands on the urinary tract I was able to trace the source of the macho messages from male mice to a tiny gland, the preputial, which we now know exists in other mammals including dogs. Female mice share an odour of peace with their fellows by excreting metabolites of oestrogens in their urine: in madder moments I have contemplated bottling this female essence to spread around the world's trouble spots.

Human attitudes towards this subject are always couched in quaint euphemisms, the direct biological terminology being avoided wherever possible. I have never had this problem myself and have embarrassed many a companion in restaurants by animated talk about the ins and outs of body smells: perhaps the role of an enzyme beta-glucuronidase in the fine tuning of chemical messages in urine. I speculate that perhaps people behave very like dogs when they head for the woods to sprinkle behind trees. When personal space for human beings is in short supply, as in psychiatric wards or prisons, urine is often deposited at the edge of defendable areas in corridors or on beds, in just the same way as it is by crowded mice and dogs.

There is no doubt that dog owners are emotionally affected by their pets' excretory habits and expect them to conform to strict codes of conduct. It is only remarkable that so many pet dogs successfully accommodate these human expectations of propriety. Puppy owners usually embark on their relationship by exhibiting anxiety about whether or not their new pet will get it right by eight, twelve, fifty weeks or never! It is one of the main topics of conversation amongst our Puppy Playgroup members. The truth is that most puppies become house-trained despite rather than because of their owners. (Current thinking amongst paediatricians is that mothers could also benefit from taking a more relaxed attitude about potty training their babies.)

There were no potties big enough for Danube, a Great Dane in North London belonging to a veterinary student. The story I had been told was that Danube had been adopted from the Breed Rescue Society some six months earlier when his mistress, Jennifer, was living at home. He was supposed to have stayed with her parents during term time while she was at the Royal Veterinary College, and be Jennifer's responsibility in vacations. Parental enthusiasm soon dimmed when Danube's absence of bladder control was revealed. Danube peed whenever he became upset and unfortunately many things could upset him: a strange man, another dog passing the house, a sharp reprimand or even a mildly emotional reunion with any member of the family. Jennifer's parents declined to keep Danube so it was away from the countryside and back to the city for him.

Most of Danube's 'kinks' were sorted out by Jennifer using patience, love and kindness. She rarely reprimanded him for his 'mistakes', rationalizing that he had a weak bladder, though clinical tests at the Royal Veterinary College did not reveal any obvious medical abnormality. However, one major problem remained: he always urinated when left alone. A Great Dane consumes more than a gallon of water per day and what goes in must surely come out. Yet there were times when Jennifer simply had to leave him alone: she had to go to lectures, practicals and so on and there were areas of her social life in which Danube could not always participate.

It could be two minutes or two hours – the response was always the same: to empty his bladder. Jennifer's small flat was above a launderette, so it was quite a disaster when urine seeped through the floor to the ceiling below and on to the heads and clothes of customers. Luckily the proprietor of the building was an understanding man who admitted that he had quite a soft spot for Jennifer, an exemplary tenant of two years' standing. Jennifer arranged for me to meet him, just to emphasize the effort she was making to overcome the problem. I went down to the launderette and indeed there was a one-metre diameter circle of yellow on the ceiling. Black tinges edged the stain because the urine had acted like a chromatographic solvent as it moved through the plaster. I made a joke about how the chemical components of the urine had been beautifully fractionated by this process in his ceiling but Mr Kamil was not amused. I had to come up with some results quickly, or Jennifer and Danube would be out on the street.

Danube was a beautifully proportioned blue-grey Dane who had a tendency to adopt statuesque poses in front of human audiences. I fished out my camera from the trusty black bag to catch Danube in a particularly showy pose but I need not have hurried. He held his position without flinching for over a minute. Photo taken for my records, Jennifer rattled his lead, which stimulated instant pandemonium from fifty kilos of demonic Dane. I tut-tutted about the fine chain choker and short lead which Jennifer put on Danube, but decided to keep my opinions about suitable walking equipment quiet until later on in the consultation. Jennifer was dragged down the narrow stairs at top speed and on to the street. Time and our walk went on, but it was noticeable that Danube never once urine-marked by cocking his leg. Great Danes are not usually so keen to mark as smaller, more precocious dogs, but from time to time even they eventually find something worthy of marking. Danube read the chemical newspapers but contributed no editorial of his own.

This part of North London is not good dog country and there was only a towpath on the nearby canal available for exercise. This small strip of green was well populated by other dogs and their faecal remains. I warmed to Jennifer when she whipped out a polythene bag and expertly gripped a steaming pile of faeces just deposited by Danube. I usually carry a pack of paper poop-scoops myself to make the subtle point that faeces are too valuable to be left behind for others to walk on, but Jennifer didn't need telling. Danube was a demanding dog to walk and kept dragging his mistress about on his short lead. I produced an extending lead and fashioned a makeshift dog collar from my trouser belt, not wishing to see the poor dog garotted on his chain. With a more relaxed freedom to walk at his own pace, Danube instantly stopped pulling. I taught Jennifer how to 'click' the extending lead mechanism as a signal for Danube to walk beside her, saving her voice to converse with people or say pleasant sweet nothings to the dog.

We arrived back at the flat refreshed after an interesting walk through this tough, historic part of the city, but Danube's bladder was still full. I palpated it and guessed he had a quart or two ready to void. Time was passing and I had another appointment with a destructive Labrador. I asked Jennifer to feed Danube and spend the next two or three hours walking up and down the canal until I returned later in the evening. Amazingly, I was told that Danube had still not urinated. This was remarkable – as though there were a Freudian block preventing him urinating in front of his mistress, even on an eight-metre long extending lead.

Leaving Jennifer at home, I trotted back to the towpath with Danube yet again. We had just turned the corner of the slipway down to the canal when the urge overtook Danube. A seemingly endless stream of urine trickled down to the waters of the canal. Where did this inhibitory kink come from that blocked Danube's ability to urinate in front of Jennifer, the woman he loved?

Back at the farm, I telephoned the lady responsible for Dane Rescue to obtain more information about Danube's first owner. Perhaps I could speak to him or her? Permission was given and the next day, back at my office, I called Danube's old home. It seemed that he was one of a pair kept by a keen exhibitor and breeder of Danes. She lived alone with four Great Danes and had nothing but their general welfare at heart. Unfortunately, Danube and his brother fought from the time that they were a year old and by fifteen months the situation had become quite impossible. The breeder had no recollection of Danube being anything but clean in the house, but a good part of the dogs' time was spent in kennels, where Danube definitely did urinate. When I asked her whether there had been any unusual occurrences in Danube's life, she recalled an incident when Danube was ten months old and had almost cocked his leg for the first time. Unfortunately he chose to urinate upon electrified sheep fencing and received a painful shock. His mistress was close by at the time and tried to comfort him; all seemed to have been forgotten. However, after my prompting she realized that from that moment onwards she never again saw Danube urinating: he became a cryptic toileter.

I surmised that the unpleasant experience of being shocked had been inadvertently 'blamed' upon the presence of a caring mistress; originally the breeder and now Jennifer. It is unusual to have such a clear and plausible explanation of a behavioural problem, and one which pointed the way towards a practical cure. First I asked Jennifer to rope in casual friends and strangers to walk Danube at least three times a day. They were to carry a chunk of food and give it to him immediately a fair volume of urine was passed. Their only positive interaction with Danube was to be at this moment; they were not to be nice at other times. During and after the act of urination, they were to say a special word of their own choosing. They happened upon the name of the then Prime Minister, 'Thatcher', as the verbal cue. It was an admirable choice, being an unusual sound combination with no conflicting associations, for dogs at least. After one week, Jennifer was to accompany her friends on walks with Danube, when she would say the word and offer food at the appropriate time. On days when friends could not be brought into this enterprise, Jennifer was to take Danube by taxi to a nearby wood where he could be allowed off his lead. We had already noticed that when he could get away from people into dense undergrowth, Danube reliably urinated.

I prepared a detailed report outlining the strategy that Jennifer was to follow and waited for results as impatiently as Mr Kamil. Unfortunately during the first week there were three setbacks, and more warnings from the landlord. Jennifer successfully appealed for time to give the therapy a chance. Luck was on her side, and Danube learnt the new rules: that the presence of people was no threat at all to his right to urinate in peace.

Dogs do not have to urinate and defecate just anywhere: their selection of the right place and the time is just as considered as it would be for people with average-disciplined bowels. Most Guide Dogs are trained to go only on the one-word command 'Busy', and a few pet owners have also taken the trouble to direct their dog's excretions to the bottom of their garden rather than on to other people's gardens, pavements or public parks. It is best to start young, but as we showed with Danube, the tendency to go on command can be trained at any age.

The important thing is always to be close to the dog just as the urge takes him or her. In practical terms that usually means keeping the dog on an extended lead and watching out for the tell-tale signs of the dog about to excrete: sniffing, circling and then release. At the moment of sniffing and circling, I instruct my students to say the chosen one-word command – but not 'Good boy' or 'Good girl', which have other positive associations that can cause difficulties. Then, when all has been completed, offer food. Play is another excellent reinforcement for excreting on command. Dog owners often discourage their dogs from 'going' when out on a walk by immediately turning for home or stopping play when the pet has 'performed'. I recommend that a decent interval of perhaps five minutes of intense fun and play should follow the witnessed act of urination or defecation.

If excretion is a conscious and controlled affair for dogs, the desire to deposit chemical signs is a compelling matter of instinct for them, not easily discouraged by owners. To train an entire male dog not to lift a leg is perhaps as challenging as to train a hot-blooded male not to gaze at women.

Recently, I made a house-call to a family who were beset by a classic case of chemical overload. Litmus was a Yorkie, the grand old man of the house and eight years old. Despite failing teeth, he had a lion's heart and dominated his pack. The pack consisted of two other dogs, Cavaliers called Bill and Ben, aged one and three years respectively. Bill was always a smelly dog due to an anatomical defect which made him fire urine up his abdomen and down his right forepaw when leg-cocking. It is a problem we sometimes encounter in Cavaliers for which the only solution is surgical alteration of the angle of the penis. John and Clare Lockwood had come to terms with Bill's little problem but not when all three began urine-marking here, there and everywhere in the house. It had only been going on for six months but during that period the effect had been devastating.

The Lockwoods were keen travellers and collectors. Everywhere I looked there was a Greek icon, a Roman vase, an ammonite, oil paintings, 1930s Bakelite radios, yet all in an ordered and tasteful fashion in a large, rambling house. Two well-scrubbed, house-trained children appeared but were commanded to disappear, probably because the parents felt the topic of our impending conversation might seem rude to young ears.

It seemed that the problem was only to do with urinating; the faeces were deposited out of doors, on walks or in the garden. I was taken on a house tour to inspect the scenes of the crimes. I started a list, and after the thirtieth location acknowledged that we could summarize the problem as 'everywhere'. Almost every piece of furniture, the lower stairs, satchels, bikes, clothes of the family, even the ankles of visitors – just anything more than two to three inches off the ground was urinated upon. We went for a walk so that I could collect data on the order in which the chemical messages were being deposited. It was absolutely characteristic: first Litmus, seemingly the leader of the trio, then repeatedly and in no particular order, Bill, Ben, Ben, Bill etc. The two Cavaliers were in continuous olfactory conflict and their challenges to one another were initiated by the chemical message of the master dog Litmus.

I got down on my knees to take a detailed sniff. It had the stale pungency of an unventilated urinal: not just a matter of bacterial decay but also the sweet smell of steroids. The oily quality of the urine could be seen on white fabric such as Clare's bedroom slippers which had received a dose that very morning. The nylon tufted front of her slippers had a greasy feel to my fingers, attributable to the preputial and other sebacous additions to the urine. We know that these glands are partly under the control of male hormones: testosterone precipitates so many problems in this world.

To date, the Lockwoods had been using expensive and proprietory household products to clean the mess up, including gallons of disinfectant. I recommended a well-known brand of cold-wash biological detergent as a more economical and effective approach to the problem of tearing the urinary chemicals from their fabric hosts, digesting the protein residues with the enzymes that make 'white washing whiter still' in TV commercials. I could find no fault in the general husbandry and management of the dogs except the fundamental relationship between Bill and Ben, which was to be the focus of my advice.

The problem seemed to emanate from the rank order dispute between Bill and Ben, which good and well-established principles of pack management should easily have resolved. Like many dog owners, Clare and John tended to treat the Cavaliers as slightly brain-damaged equals, with Litmus the diminutive Yorkie their top dog. Thus, Litmus was fed first and given rights and privileges which were denied to Bill and Ben. I say 'brain-damaged' because many veterinary neurologists argue that the architecture of Cavalier brains has been dramatically changed by the contorted skull-shape selected for this breed. Indeed, in some Cavaliers varying degrees of hydrocephalus can be seen, which may have a damaging effect upon their cognitive function.

I was not in a position to administer an *ad hoc* canine intelligence test to Bill and Ben, but they both struck me as chaotic though lovely dogs whose chief mental achievement was repeated urine-marking. I advised the Lockwoods to have both dogs castrated so as not to change the relatively harmonious relationship between them: at least they did not fight one another. I proposed a cleaning regime which started with the biological detergent solution, following by a scrub with surgical spirit and finally soaking the affected corners of material in a mild oxidizing solution of hydrogen peroxide.

At the time of my visit, the dogs could not rely on walks through the week when the family was at school or work. I proposed that they draw up a rota involving parents and children alike, which ensured that the dogs had at least two walks every day. This provided them with an opportunity for chemical investigation and urine-marking outside the home and would, with luck, diminish the communicatory significance of marks within it. The Lockwoods were softies towards the dogs, unwilling to place much restriction upon their general lifestyles and interactions together. I suggested that as a compromise the dogs should sleep in daughter Andrea's bedroom during the night. Through the daytime, the dogs were to be confined to one room only (the kitchen) with supervised access to the garden at hourly intervals. After the dogs had been castrated and recovered from the operation they were to be permitted steadily increasing use of different rooms of the house, still under supervision.

It is too early to say whether I have been successful with the Lockwood dogs but the signs are good. The composition of urine and the frequency with which it is deposited is always changed rapidly by castration. Cavaliers are especially high on the list of breeds that are particularly susceptible to this problem. I have no scientific explanation as to why this should be so, but surmise that there has been genetic selection for precocious sexual development; Cavaliers are often physically and sexually mature by five to six months of age, compared with twelve months or more for larger breeds of dogs. Perhaps they generate higher titres of testosterone than in other dogs, driving brains and bladders towards more masculine modes of behaviour.

Smooth-haired Dachshunds are also memorable characters within our practice, both for their determination and for their tendency to defecate at the least convenient time and on the least appropriate spot. Of course, they also have many endearing qualities, such as a strong desire for close body contact with their owner (their thin coat leaves them feeling the cold). Dachshunds are remarkably intelligent and can make formidable house-dogs, having keen hearing and a vice-like bite awaiting the ankles of unwanted visitors.

Lord X was in his eighties and had had a succession of Dachshunds throughout his life, first whilst in the Indian Civil Service and later in other corners of the Empire. He was a grand old man whose family had lost its estate and money in the Irish troubles of the 1920s. He now lived in somewhat reduced circumstances in a three-roomed flat which was packed with photographs and memories from better times. Danny was the Dachshund of today, watched over by a gallery of six other Dachshunds from the past. Lord X's sweet recollections of dogs were being soured by Danny's habit of placing a well-formed bolus upon his writing chair at least once a day.

Danny was referred to me by one of London's best-known vets who had himself been well bitten by the Dachshund bug. This vet and his family had been keepers or victims of a succession of pet and rescue Dachshunds and he introduced me to the finer points of the Dachshunds' psyche: in a word, he told me, they are wooden-headed. Everyone at the vet's was fond of Lord X and I was told to proceed at my most delicate and most patient.

I did not need this advice because I took to him straight away. There was no air of bombast or upper-class superiority about him: he knew he'd had a good life and done good work and he was trying to continue in the same tradition. Driven by a sense of duty, he was still a regular attendee at the House of Lords, where education, inner-city deprivation and the Third World were his special interests. Danny had been a popular companion to Lord X in his social life, even accompanying him to his club. However, they had recently been asked to leave after Danny had hopped onto his master's customary chair and performed as he had done on Lord X's chair at home. This was behaviour that was definitely unacceptable to the club management.

On the day of my visit, Lord X's maid was in attendance, an affable Irish lady who complained that Danny was 'a sod, who needed a good sort-out with a cane', something she 'had never seen Lord X do, and the consequences were there to be seen'. Well, smelled. I thanked Mrs O'Connor for her interest and asked her to show me the precise places where Danny had sinned. There were only two spots: the chair I have already mentioned and Lord X's bed. At this point Lord X had to leave for a luncheon appointment and begged my forgiveness. He was back in ten minutes, having forgotten his tobacco pouch.

I always feel that it is good for my ego to have the occasional client walk out on me, although I know that at the time, Lord X did not intend to be rude. He had just absent-mindedly forgotten about his previous engagement and was 'sure that Mrs O'Connor would put me right'. How right he was! After half an hour, I made my apologies and retreated, not much the wiser nor certain as to what I should recommend. In the short term, I asked Lord X to cover his bed with a polythene sheet so as to discourage the dog from coming on to it. This, he explained on the phone, would be quite impossible, as the dog needed his body warmth to get through the night. The same applied to the chair beside his writing desk, which was as much Danny's as his own when they were writing together. Perhaps there is, after all, a correlation between the personality of owners and dogs.

One of the vet nurses who cared for Danny lived nearby and she had invited me to call in and report on my patient, if necessary to bang my head against the wall and generally vent my frustration. Her own Long-haired Dachshunds, which showed no desire whatever to defecate on their mistress's possessions, provided inspiration and therapy for me. The nurse offered to have Danny for a week, just to see how he got on in a new environment and with her dogs. I phoned Lord X and he happily agreed to our suggestion. I drove off to collect Danny, who departed like an evacuee with his favourite toys, brush, comb and fancy bed. The bed was remarkable for never having been used, Lord X's being softer and warmer.

Back at the vet nurse's place Danny freaked at the sight of the other dogs, woofing with alarm from beneath the sofa. I reached down to tempt him out and touched something warm and sticky. He had defecated, despite having just come in from a walk. Polite words failed me, but the patient nurse was happy to continue the experiment. She reported back that Danny was a tough and thoroughly mean blockhead who stole toys from her dogs and never obeyed a command. All he wanted to do was sit on laps or warm human bodies. But he never once defecated indoors again.

The week was up and it was time for Danny to go back to his master. I recommended a low-residue prescription diet from the vet and asked Lord X to walk the dog with a titbit in his pocket as a reward for every observed defecation out of doors. Mrs O'Connor was asked to give the chair and bedding upon which Danny had defecated a thorough clean and wherever possible to feed him at these locations. I tactfully suggested that access to the bed and the chair be denied by closing the bedroom door or by covering the bed when Danny could not be watched. All this advice was sensible and could do no harm, but I was still uncertain as to whether it would do the trick. Somehow, I was still not sure that we had grasped the underlying cause of Danny's behaviour.

My worst fears were realized when, a month later, the vet nurse phoned to say that Lord X wanted Danny put to sleep. I phoned him immediately and found that indeed nothing had changed, but neither had Lord X's great affection for this wily companion: he was simply in despair. As a desperate measure, with no real expectation of success, I suggested we have Danny castrated. The grounds for recommending this were weak; Danny was no more than an averagely dominant Dachshund in indulgent hands. Thankfully, Lord X agreed to my proposal and the deed was duly done.

After another month had elapsed I phoned to find out how things were going. No one was more surprised than I to hear that the situation had vastly improved; my gloomy prognosis had been unfounded. I did not speak to Lord X, but to Mrs O'Connor, who took some pleasure in telling me where I had gone wrong earlier. Didn't I realize that Lord X was incontinent? His laundry bill ran into hundreds of pounds and she was forever changing sheets: the dog was merely copying his master, she insisted.

I tactfully extracted myself from the telephone conversation while privately considering the possibility that I had missed a crucial aspect of this man/animal relationship. We shall never know, because Lord X only lived for another few months. The caring vet nurse found Danny a new home and the problem never recurred.

8
On the road

For a couple of months each year Sam and I travel around the country to see our patients, meeting either at their house, at a vet's premises or in my specially converted van-cum-mobile clinic – a Murvi. We were coming to the end of one such trip when we met an intriguing case in Cheadle Hulme, a farm Collie called Gill who had declared war on moving vehicles.

Her mistress, Mrs Slater, had driven over the Pennines with Gill in a battered old car and looked distinctly out of place in the white-tiled, hi-tech consulting room where I was waiting to greet them. Mrs Slater was a farmer's wife, sheep were their business and Gill was an important member of the team. I got the distinct impression that Mrs Slater still believed in those dark stories about Lancashire and Cheshire folk being agin Yorkshire. She did not like and did not want to be liked in the bustling and prosperous town of Cheadle.

Gill's medical notes made fantastic reading: she'd more than spent her allocation of Collie lives. Her days revolved around chasing things on four legs, but in the absence of sheep she would turn to four wheels. Since ten vehicles a day passed her farm gate, she had ample opportunity to indulge her chasing tendencies and to give each a spectacular welcome. Cars could be seen winding round the narrow moorland lanes a good mile from the farm, and there were no other noises to drown out the approaching engine. The Slaters were too preoccupied with agricultural survival to be keeping an eye on all of Gill's foibles, so collisions between Collie and car were inevitable.

I examined her latest road traffic accident wound, which had healed well. Her owners could ill afford the vet's bill, though their vet ran them a 'slate' which did not have to be paid until the lamb sales in November. Writing was not Mrs Slater's strong point, so I took Gill's history from scratch, without the benefit of preliminary notes from her owner.

It appeared that Gill had been 'trained' both to work sheep on the farm and chase cars on the road by her mother, Bonnie, who had died a year earlier after being run over by the post van. Bonnie had been a valuable bitch, enabling the Slaters to manage a thousand sheep on two thousand or more acres of national park moorland in a way that would otherwise have been impossible. A good dog can go places and do things that no man on foot, horse or even motorbike could do. To lose one Collie to traffic was bad enough; two would be a disaster.

We walked around Cheadle Hulme with Gill on a long lead. She showed no interest in chasing traffic, though Arthur, the fat cat who graced a wall *en route* to the nearby park, elicited a fair amount of excitement from her. I learned from Mrs Slater that no cats remained in her part of Yorkshire: they had all been moved on by Gill, and before by Bonnie. Gill's chase after Arthur was so sudden that I was taken by surprise, and Arthur nearly came to grief. The opportunity gone, Gill seemingly resolved not to put a foot wrong again.

In the park, Gill sat and stayed while we hid behind trees. She played merrily with passing children and dogs. It was exasperating for both myself and Gill's mistress, but we were up against a dog who was clever at choosing her moment and her target for attack. Rather than waste Mrs Slater's time, I sent them home and said I would visit them on the way to my next case in Nottingham.

The following night, a Friday, found Sam and myself motoring through dark and hostile lanes over the Pennines. It had been raining non-stop for an hour and gigantic puddles stretched forward in the headlights. We were descending by the Dower Reservoir on the Sheffield side of the Pennines when a terrible urge to sleep began to overtake me. My preference would have been to 'camp' in my van in some deserted spot, with a plunging stream and sheep for company. On national park land that is almost impossible; they don't cater for nomadic animal psychologists. Fortunately, I spied a rough road leading high into the wet gloom, one could not tell where. The weather was much too awful to get out and investigate, and my ever-unreliable torch had just died.

The road was steep and rocky but I drove fast and amazingly we 'landed' on the floor of a gigantic quarry, overlooking the Dower Reservoir. Even in my headlights I could see rabbits, so I let Sam out for his favourite recreation. After fifteen minutes or so, I began to be anxious that he might have met the same fate as Gill's mother.

But remarkably and as always, Sam did come back, filling the van with all the steam and smells of a happy wet dog. The deluge of rain continued outside, but I was well into my cookery and 'Week Ending' on wonderful Radio Four.

This was my ideal: interesting cases behind me, solitude with my good mate Sam for the night and, if I was lucky, fabulous new country to explore before moving on to the next appointment. My hopes on the wildlife and scenery fronts were fulfilled next morning, as we scrambled down the hillside to the shores of the reservoir. Sam's never-ending passion for water fulfilled, we broke camp and headed for the Slater Farm.

We had agreed in Cheadle Hulme that Gill would be given just one more day of freedom to terrorize road users. It was eight in the morning as we negotiated the soggy road through Forestry Commission plantations, round hairpin bends and through swollen streams. As the farm came into sight, there was no indication of the danger about to leap out. Mrs Slater reckoned that Gill had tuned into the Murvi's growling diesel engine more than five minutes before I arrived: she was crouched on a breeze-block platform that had been used for milk churns in a previous era of dairy farming, and which gave her a metre-high springboard from which to hurtle after her victim. I noted that she did not come ahead of my wheels, but cleverly attacked from behind. I continued to travel at twenty miles an hour, a comfortable hunting speed for Gill. However, as I slowed down she made for the rear wheels, making useless but dangerous pecking actions at the tyres. Apparently with slow-moving motorcycles she had actually succeeded in biting wheels, risking death from being dragged under the mudguard. The Murvi wheels were too broad and tough for Gill; she gave up on me and sidled back home.

This half-minute of real-life drama with Gill had been more useful than the whole hour we had spent at the Cheadle clinic talking about her ways. Clearly her behaviour was precisely refined, adapted through hundreds of chases after vehicles of varying speed and type. So long as they went at a constant speed she was moderately safe, but if they slowed down she ran the risk of running under the wheels. Any number of punishments had been administered in the presence of vehicles and their frightened drivers, but all they had achieved was to make Gill's hatred of traffic the greater.

Over the kitchen table and welcome coffee and toast, we compiled a list of the vehicles she hated and those she just tolerated. Most disliked of all was the post van, which reliably came at ten past nine

– just a few moments away. If there was post to be delivered to the farm, Gill did not chase but allowed the postman to enter the yard; indeed she would roll over for a tummy rub before letting him deliver the mail and drive on in peace. It was only when he drove straight past, leaving her empty-handed, so to speak, that she declared war.

The next farm along generated at least four passing car trips a day, taking the children to and from the end of the lane for the school bus. They tended to plunge on, hoping for the best. By contrast, some incoming folk with a cottage holiday retreat were less bold: they usually slowed down and sometimes stopped. They had even tried to make friends with Gill, offering titbits and leftover sandwiches. This tempered her aggressive reaction but she still risked death by standing in the road looking cute whilst begging for food. I ran a few more trips myself in various farm vehicles, including an open top Landrover. Gill was not to be fooled: these were friendly vehicles, not the enemy that warranted an attack.

Analysis of all the incidents which had been observed by the Slaters suggested that Gill was remarkably clever at distinguishing one vehicle from another. Even a minute change in the driving habits of her 'victims' could dramatically change her response. I was working on the assumption that her behaviour stemmed from the combination of a normal hunting chase with a keen defence of territory. Those vehicles which might be expected to carry friendly people, especially people with food handouts, were stopped but not chased. Those liable to pass by leaving nothing behind but dust and fumes would be attacked. I needed more information to confirm this analysis, so I pretended to go through fond farewells and drove off. I then returned, roaring past the farm at a constant speed and offering Gill another wonderful opportunity to show off her skills. She was tempted and ambushed the Murvi, just missing the wheels and pursuing us for a hundred-metre canter up our slipstream.

I repeated the manoeuvre, this time coming to a sudden halt outside the gate. Gill instantly became friendly, begging for a food handout. Of course she recognized my voice and made a hopeful bid for chunks of Sam's breakfast leftovers. I commanded her to sit, threw her a morsel then drove off. She did not follow.

I had met Gill's sort before in Devon, Wales and, particularly, in Ireland, where every other farm dog is bored to tears with its lot in life and creates its own fun by pursuing the wheels of passing traffic. When I first launched into animal behaviour therapy I thought that a well-timed ambush was the way to stop this behaviour. For instance, I would set off on a bicycle with polythene bags filled with water to hurl at such dogs, or be hidden on the back of Landrovers to throw out rattling tin cans and whole buckets of water. Such dogs would reliably stop chasing the particular vehicle or bicycle which had been used as a launch pad for punishment, but they carried on chasing other vehicles. It took a few manic Collies to teach me that this traditional dog trainer's approach was not producing long-term benefits. I had to devise more scientific alternatives of response substitution training, which is now my ideal strategy for treating car-chasing dogs.

The one reliable feature of all Border Collies is that they are fast learners and remarkably attentive – which in our terms means intelligent. If the task is made simple and straightforward, they can quickly acquire new behaviour and new attitudes. But how could we make cars good news, a source of positive rather than negative feedback? The technique is simple, and it proved to be effective with Gill.

I advised the Slaters to equip the churn stand with some modest home comforts for Gill's benefit. Dry, straw-filled hessian sacks were laid out under a simple awning, turning the spot into a comfortable perch where Gill would be likely to lie in preference to stalking about on the road. My second piece of advice for the Slaters was to ask regular visitors or passers-by to stop and to take Gill a small titbit on her churn stand. She had to lie down on her sack and could then be given the reward. A small pot was fixed to a ledge on the wall for storing a supply of tasty, dry, chunks of meat, so that those passing empty-handed could still participate in the 'Be nice to Gill' campaign.

Any encounters with vehicles that found Gill off her perch were not to be rewarded: she was to be ordered with a simple 'Up' command to get back on the churn stand, and if she disobeyed they were to drive on. After two to three weeks of this regime, I suggested that vehicles just stop outside the gate, and if Gill was not on the ledge they were to drive on without commanding her to go back on the stand. I hoped that Gill would quickly see that the prospect of a food reward and, importantly, contact with the people she liked, depended upon her being safely positioned high off the ground, away from the dangerous road.

The beauty of this technique was that it provided amusement for neighbours, confirming that the Slaters were really trying to do something about reforming their daft dog. Being agreeable country folks, they were happy to give up a little time for the sake of an animal who was already a local talking point and butt for jokes. It also did away with the need for punishment, which was against the best instincts of the Slaters and certainly against my own practical experience and scientific training. The technique that we had chosen for Gill had actually improved her lifestyle, by providing increased contact with people. She was still available for work, but she no longer needed to be chained up in a cowshed, which had become the Slaters' way around the problem.

By eleven o'clock Sam and I had finished with Gill and were ready to depart. I would have loved to have stayed to work in Gill's environment, in this beautiful country so far from urban bustle and pollution. But I also knew that I would probably have become a bit like Gill, bored and understimulated without the stress and challenge of my troubleshooting life.

Our relationship with cars is a classic one of love and hate. Cars offer freedom and increased opportunity, but we often feel guilt at the expense and pollution that they bring with them. Many dogs also have an ambivalent attitude to motor vehicles. For most dogs the car, the truck, even the bicycle, bring new vistas and pleasures that are more exciting than a walk from home. Within a few weeks of adoption, puppies happily climb into cars contemplating only the pleasures of arrival. That pleasure can be expressed in many ways, at best a happy wagging of the tail, at worst hysterical whining, pacing and salivation – in a word, crazed behaviour.

Having dogs that are hysterical car travellers can seriously jeopardize the driving skills of owners and certainly undermines their mental health. So it was with Dr and Mrs Evenson, who were the 'victims' of a wonderful trio of three Rough Collies: Simba and Jason, both males, and their young sister, Gemma. The Evensons were very conscientious dog owners, anxious not to displease their neighbours by letting the trio roam about their quiet, neatly maintained suburban crescent. It had always been their habit instead to pile the dogs into a tiny Metro, a mobile kennel which transported the excited dogs to a nearby common. This had been the Evenson routine for fifteen years, making at least two generations of Rough Collies infamous in the area where they lived. One could always tell when the Evensons were on the move by the shaky progress of their Metro weaving from side to side, as the persecuted driver attempted to compensate for movements of the dogs on board. The cacophony of barking was moderately well-muffled in winter when the windows were closed, but then poor Mrs Evenson was reduced to peering through a tiny spot of windscreen not fogged up by the dogs' hot, moist breath. In summer, with the windows open, they could be heard a mile away.

I originally attended the Evenson household because Simba, one of the two male dogs, had taken a violent dislike to a television repair man and they wished to avoid a repeat with other visitors. It was a straightforward assignment in which I could determine precisely the circumstances that produced this out-of-character behaviour in Simba: a stranger kneeling to repair the TV at Simba's head height, using electronic equipment to test and repair a machine which may have emitted noises that the dog found painful. The TV repair man had been bitten on his shoulder at the moment he looked away from Simba and when I re-enacted the procedure I almost received the same treatment. Standing and moving about normally posed no risk. Mrs Evenson barely mentioned to me the dog's performance in the car, assuming that was their normal and natural way. As part of a home consultation, I investigate every facet of a dog's routine behaviour, including the car. So it was that I suggested we take the dogs out for a ride.

Regrettably, on this day I had no industrial ear-protectors in my black bag, something I normally carry for such occasions. The exterior of the Evenson's car was neat and tidy, giving no hint as to its true function. Inside all was apparent: chunks of foam had been snapped from the back of the front seats and when the dogs entered and began to whirl about, a fog of dust and hair from previous trips was stirred up.

No asthmatic would have survived the journey that awaited me. All the noise came from Simba and Jason, with Gemma mostly cowering, seeking refuge from her big brothers. She was a sweet bitch, and their barking clearly distressed her. It was a difficult situation: my instincts were to use the Dog Stop alarm to quieten the situation, but that would have been unfair on Gemma, the innocent party. Rough Collies are notably sound-sensitive and Gemma might react badly to this loud aural alarm.

The trip was only two miles so I thought it best to keep my head down, plug my ears with fingers and tough it out. Mrs Evenson bellowed a conversation about sweet nothings, not really focusing upon the painful situation that had developed. The worst crescendo was reached as we turned off the main road and down a bumpy, unmetalled road on to the common. At this moment, Gemma came out from hiding and was promptly attacked by bully-boy Simba. As we stopped, they tried to jump into the front seat over me, to escape via the passenger doors rather than the tailgate. More cursing and whacking of dogs from Mrs Evenson, who then quietly asked, 'Dr Mugford, is this normal for Rough Collies?' I laughed pityingly and replied that whether or not it was 'normal', the quality of her life would definitely be improved if I could find a way of quietening her dogs.

The five of us had an enjoyable twenty-minute walk on the common, during which we saw a little bullying of other male dogs by Simba, a little rabbitting by Gemma and a keen interest in joggers by all three. Most worryingly, there came a charge of riding-school ponies down a sandy gully, offering no escape into the bushes on either side. All three dogs looked poised for a daring attack upon superior forces, but fortunately the instructress chose to turn her cavalry around and take another path. We returned to the Metro kennel-on-wheels.

The homeward journey was an improvement on the outward, with only a whimper as we turned into the Evensons' drive. This contrast in behaviour between outward and return journeys is quite classic in car-crazy cases. The barking is an expression of vocal excitement at the prospect of release for an enjoyable pursuit, like walking and being amongst other dogs. But by now I was pressed for time and I knew that after all this excitement, the dogs would not be in the right mood for testing various routines of behaviour modification in the car, so I promised to return the next week. I did so armed with any number of sound-making devices: an ultrasonic alarm, the Dog Stop, a rattle can, a klaxon horn as well as a water pistol, a range of titbits, headcollars, leads, even a black shroud-sheet and internal dog kennel. Making the Evenson pack safe on the road would be a major undertaking.

I began by trying to tether Simba and Jason on the headcollars, with their heads close to the floor of the Metro. Simba accepted this well, but Jason panicked and struggled, so we decided that this was unacceptable. Besides, Mrs Evenson alone could barely cope with getting the dogs into the car, let alone attach complicated tethers to Simba and Jason. We set out for a repeat run to the common, focusing on the events which precipitated the greatest vocal response. This began with the approach towards the car, increased when Mrs Evenson opened the door and sat in the driver's seat, and got even worse when she rattled the keys, started the motor, touched the gear lever and, loudest of all, released the handbrake. There was a progressive increase at each stage of what should have been the simple business of making a short car journey.

I asked Mrs Evenson to stop the car and with it the dogs froze, though they continued barking for a minute. Blessed silence pervaded the little car but masochist that I am, I asked Mrs Evenson to restart the engine. The row immediately began and worsened as the car moved, so again I asked Mrs Evenson to stop, this time suddenly. The dogs quietened but looked confused. I was trying to establish whether or not we might use 'Stop' as a means of punishing excited behaviour in the car, then 'Go' to reward silence. In other cases, where only one dog was misbehaving in the car, the stop-go technique had proved highly effective. With two or three dogs, social facilitation or mutual winding-up tends to undermine the method because the timing of reward and punishment cannot precisely match the behaviour of each dog. I had at least to try it out on the Evenson pack. We stopped and started for twenty minutes, without making much progress. The excitement of one dog fed that of the other; there was a crazed social synergy at work against us. All we had achieved was the acrid smell of burning brake and clutch linings, plus confirmation amongst residents that Mrs Evenson and possibly her co-driver were completely nuts.

What about attempting a reduction of sensory stimulation? We pinned and taped the black sheet round the outside of the car, reducing the dogs' vision only to the way ahead, over the driver's shoulders. This produced some small improvement, but it was only due to the novelty of the situation, not to the fact that they could no longer see what was happening outside of the car. In many other cases that I have treated, visual restriction has been very effective, which is why I sometimes recommend keeping a dog's head below sill level in the car, using a headcollar tethered to the base of the floor.

We returned to Mrs Evenson's home and took out the dogs while I assembled a wire-mesh crate in the car that was just big enough to get Simba into. Those familiar with the dimensions of a Metro will realize that even a small crate wouldn't have allowed us to close the rear tailgate, and besides, poor Jason and Gemma would be squeezed into the tiny gap between the crate and the car. Clearly that was not to be the solution. Neither did I succeed with the water pistol: all three dogs seemed to find enormous pleasure in snapping at the water spray, a trait commonly found in other Rough Collies of my acquaintance.

The next stage was to experiment with separating Simba from

Jason in the car. When we did this, Simba became noticeably less enthusiastic and hysterical and much more responsive to the simple commands of 'Sit' and 'Quiet' from the now hoarse Mrs Evenson. I resolved to try the Dog Stop alarm but first Gemma was removed and led to the front porch, looking miserable at having had to endure such a long preamble to her customary morning walk.

We started the car and began driving down the road. After a slow start Simba got back into his usual voice, but at one squirt of the Dog Stop he became a quivering though attentive Rough Collie. He lay down and looked appealingly at his mistress. She patted him, from which he took instant comfort and began howling again. On the second occasion I just raised the Dog Stop without squirting it; he gazed at it and went silent again. On the basis of a single trial, we had Simba in our power. But this might not be a practical or humane solution when all three dogs were in the car because I did not want to expose Gemma to it for activities she was not herself performing. We drove around the block, returned Simba home and replaced him with Jason. Jason on his own was not nearly so noisy as Simba had been and it was not until he saw the woods that he began to howl. Again, one blast of the Dog Stop and he fell into a sullen silence. He remained quiet until we returned home.

Now for the big one, Jason and Simba together in the car. The progress we had just made with each of these males separately was lost when they were together, and loud ructions began. The mere sight of the Dog Stop didn't succeed in silencing them and so after half a minute of their demented screechings I sounded it. An acrid and unpleasant smell of voided anal glands came from Simba, a moment of great concern as the dogs were now long overdue for their regular appointment on the common. We drove on to the common to release them for their constitutional, the dogs in stunned silence throughout. Mrs Evenson was pleased about this, though I was anxious that I might have produced some permanent, more nervous rearrangement of Simba's approach to living. I need not have been concerned: he was made of sterner stuff. Finally, we returned home and collected Gemma, who had no knowledge of the horror of a whistle from this alarm. We seemed to have found the key to quieter journeys for Mrs Evenson.

I have kept in contact with Mrs Evenson over the last three years because she regularly returns to buy a refill aerosol for her Dog Stop and gives me a detailed update on events. Her husband has now given up his university lectureship so they have more time to devote to the dogs, to observe and record the minutiae of their behaviour and to devise lists of penetrating questions on why they do what they do. Dr Evenson is clearly an intelligent man for whom the company of three dogs is both an inspiration and a welcome distraction from other facets of life.

As I drive about the highways of Britain I very often see a car with a Jack Russell, a Border Collie, a German Shepherd or some other intelligent working breed of dog behaving in the same over-excited manner as the Evensons' Collies. I have noticed that in such cases the owners often wear earphones, or have the radio turned up loud: in other words they have retreated into some pained, private world so as to insulate themselves from the yapping dog behind. Because these people run the risk of a perpetual migraine, let alone being involved in a road accident, I usually try to drive up alongside and pass a standard therapy leaflet to them. On the ten or more occasions I have done this, four of the beneficiaries have telephoned me afterwards thanking me for my sympathy with their predicament.

Fully seven per cent of my canine patients in the United Kingdom are car crazy, just like the Evensons' Collies. Yet overseas, I rarely encounter this problem. When discussing this with a friend and colleague in Los Angeles, Dr Dick Polski, Dick told me he rarely encounters such problems on American freeways. We compared the habits of dogs and their owner drivers in Britain and America, wondering why they should be so different. The answer seems to lie in British dog owners' commitment to regular exercise or walkies, not found to the same extent amongst American dog owners. In Southern California, a trip in the car is an occasional experience, often of quite long duration when, say, the family decide to up and away to a weekend retreat in the Sierras, one or two hundred miles away. There is no regular daily or twice-daily trip to a park around the corner, a habit that is so much a part of the British dog-owning scene. On the other hand, some American dogs virtually live in their cars, as befits a continental and largely mobile society. For example, those aged Winnebago-living communities that migrate north in summer and south in winter simply carry their pets along with them, growing through a seasonal cycle like the proverbial swallow.

Many an American dog I have met has visited virtually every State of the Union. One such well-travelled dog was Rocky, a Jack Russell belonging to Fritz Jannson, a trucker working out of Detroit. I was in Detroit to give a lecture to a local veterinary group, and the case of Fritz was referred to me by one of the audience. Jack Russells are an extremely fashionable but still unusual breed in the United States, though word of their remarkable protective courage is out amongst the trucker community. Fritz was an owner-operator whose regular contract was to move car parts to Florida, with a return journey of fruit and veg. Rocky was his constant companion on this 4000-mile round trip, and he was known at all the roadstops as a mean dog, revered but also feared.

I went to visit Fritz and Rocky at their trailer-home in south Detroit. The Jannson truck was a Mack, with glorious gold and blue scrolls on a red background extolling the virtues of his wife, his truck and his interest in music. The triple air-horn was mounted above the cab like a destructive raygun, should another road-user step out of line. The chrome was beautifully polished in a way one rarely sees on European trucks. Fritz explained that he had $100,000 tied up in his rig, it was all his and the bank could go to hell. Rocky did a great job of protecting his asset when he slept in the bunk out back, because there were always bandits on the road ready to steal a truck and contents and recycle it out of the State or even over the Mexican border. Rocky was as good as a loaded gun by his pillow.

The trouble was that Rocky did not differentiate between friends, neutrals and the enemy. Police cars were a particular target and he ran forward and back across the dashboard whenever a patrol car overtook, or worse, paused in front of Fritz's truck. This aroused mild curiosity amongst the traffic cops, who would then pull Jannson's truck over for questioning. One day, the inevitable happened when Rocky climbed out of a crack in the window to bite the patrolman. Fritz's concern was that his licence as an inter-State shipper would be in jeopardy, but he did not wish to leave Rocky at home in Detroit in the care of his less-than-reliable wife. Could I help?

My first request was that Rocky be muzzled before I came anywhere near the truck. This done, I ventured towards the Mack. I could now sympathize with the attitude of the policeman who had been mauled by Rocky. There was no stopping this dog, whose ancestors had fearlessly tackled rats, foxes and badgers back in England.

Fritz reckoned that they covered 100,000 miles a year together on the freeways, and on all those journeys Rocky had just three friends: operators of truckers' stops who had befriended him with food and shelter. Everyone else might as well be dead. My job was to rehabilitate and resocialize Rocky towards humankind and wean him away from his selfless devotion to Fritz and the truck. It was quite a challenge, but I believe I was moderately successful in adapting standard therapy to the unique situations encountered in the life of a trucker's dog.

I began by creating a safe resting place from which Rocky would not wish and would not be able to launch a dangerous attack. We bodged a small platform from string, wood and canvas just below the heater-air conditioning controls in the centre of the dashboard, a customized canine hammock that protruded into the leg space of the centre seat. It was just Jack-Russell-sized. Rocky could curl up there and sleep in comfort but at the same time could see outside the truck and direct his destructive hatred at passing traffic, especially motor cycles and police cars. I had to show Fritz how to be strict in repositioning Rocky on his hammock and not let the dog onto his lap or dart up and down the bunk seats. Next, Fritz's trucker and road-community friends were to be asked to meet Rocky, take him for walks and generally be human towards him. In England this would have been remarkable enough, but in the even more stand-offish and self-conscious world of American truck-drivers it must have seemed bizarre in the extreme.

I accompanied Fritz to the loading bay of the Ford factory in Detroit, where the black warehouseman knew and feared Rocky as a worse adversary than any police Rottweiler. 'Man, you must be jokin', you wants me to be nice to that critter: one of these days he's bound to bust through the glass!' As we were speaking, Rocky was hurling himself against the driver's window, pressing his snout and tongue through the one-inch opening of the side window. I sympathized with the warehouseman's point of view. We dressed Rocky in a muzzle and repeated the procedure with more confidence that perhaps I was not such a lunatic after all. If he failed to inspire fear in his victims, Rocky's main weapon was destroyed. I showed that I could enter and leave the cab in safety with Rocky wearing the muzzle, and that the second or third time around he even seemed to greet me as a friend.

I brought a shrivelled burger as a source of tasty dog food, and shoved it between the cracks of his muzzle. We were making progress. At the same time, Fritz alienated himself from Rocky by absenting himself in a direct and theatrical manner at each bark or threat. By fine-tuning the apparent rejection from his owner to the moment of a territorial attack, we slowly succeeded in diminishing Rocky's 'nastiness', at least on that one location of the Ford Motor Company's factory. I ran through another eight key points of care, training and husbandry which I wanted Fritz to attend to in Rocky, and left them on a warm note of friendship. This was a case and a situation that I could never have dreamed of seeing in England: it was another world.

All was quiet for two months, and then I heard through my veterinarian friend in Detroit that the hammock technique had worked well and that Rocky was now seemingly bolted by invisible fixtures to it, such was its association with warmth, pleasing attention from Fritz and food handouts from visitors to the cab. And yet, when Fritz was asleep in the back of the cab, Rocky remained a terrifying guard dog, loyal defender of the rig.

Whereas most dogs find car travelling a pleasure, just a few are afraid of road vehicles and hate journeys. I am reminded of a Great Dane in Hampshire who was terrified by the prospect of a journey, usually because it involved a visit to the vet's, to dog kennels at holiday times or to some other place with negative associations. His owners normally used a small Japanese saloon car for their runarounds, and there was no possibility of Nixon, the lolloping Dane, ever being comfortable on the cramped rear seat. Using my capacious Murvi van as a training-ground, we succeeded in tempting Nixon aboard as though he were walking into a large kennel. Any rocking of the vehicle, however, instantly turned him back into a quivering coward. In Nixon's case, the solution was to jack up the Murvi on bricks so that there was no movement. Having demonstrated that the therapeutic technique could work, Nixon's owners bought a cheap ex-builder's Ford Transit van for him, which they kitted out as a comfortable if basic stationary kennel. Once Nixon had begun to tolerate the vehicle, it was moved a little at a time. The same concept is used by psychologists to treat phobic human patients by systematic desensitization.

The time to tackle 'matters motor' with dogs is when they are puppies. Unfortunately, their first association with cars is often negative: puppies vomiting from travel sickness on the journey from the breeder to a new home. I always question in detail owners of dogs that are hysterical or afraid of cars and we often find that some drama occurred during that first journey which set the emotional tone for subsequent contact with cars. A good problem-preventative tip is to ensure that the car is often used as a non-exciting and unremarkable vehicle that goes nowhere in particular, such as round the block, to the supermarket or perhaps a multi-storey car park and back. The car is not then always used as an intermediary between home and walks. Finally, it pays well to train a dog to lie down in the back of a car, on a surface designated for the purpose. I am less keen on dog guards, which tend to induce undesirable behaviour because the dog is isolated from the owner and can more or less do as he pleases; better to maintain verbal and physical contact between owner and dog. The recent introduction of harnesses which may be attached to seat belts is an interesting innovation and one that has worthwhile road-safety benefits. With a dog wearing a safety harness on the back seat, you can still fuss, touch and talk to the animal as a reward for calm behaviour.

It is a tremendous convenience to have a dog that tolerates car travel, and it helps the dog too. The chief benefit is that instead of being left at home bored, the dog is able to participate fully in the life of his owner. And dogs bring valuable company to people like me who have to make long and sometimes boring trips from one end of the country to another. I know the very real pleasure that Sam brings me at such times, though I suspect that Sam himself is more turned on by the faint smells of rabbits and pheasants which occasionally waft through the car's ventilation system. I miss him when driving abroad but I have to leave him at home because of UK quarantine regulations.

9
Dogs at work

My parents' farm Collie Gyp fulfilled two important roles. First he was my fantasy Lassie, he of Hollywood fame. Gyp and I played hide-and-seek up trees and amongst hay bales; we dug up treasure together in an old pond, and in the evenings we stalked rabbits, an unbeatable team with my superior eyesight and his superior sense of smell. But my father also relied on Gyp to bring in the cows, move sheep and stop runaway pigs. He was a true working dog.

The people who train and employ working dogs have some of the same emotional detachment about welfare and animal rights as farmers. A job has to be done and the dog has to work. Working dogs are sometimes depicted as the pin-ups of the canine world, the stars that outshine their less talented pet cousins. The truth is that all dogs have it in them to guide, herd, guard, sniff, retrieve, race or pull; but only about five per cent are worked by professionals. The trainers in each of the above specialties have their own tricks of the trade but they do not usually have a scientific training or know much about animal behavioural therapy. Thus it is that I am often called in to treat working dogs.

Everybody loves a Guide Dog but they, too, can have their problems. One of the several that I have treated was Tina, a pure-bred Labrador from Loughborough who was one of the more resourceful Guide Dogs I have met. Fortunately, she was owned by Pam, an experienced doggy mistress who, together with her husband John, edited the local talking-tapes magazine for blind people. Pam had had two Guide Dogs before and thought she knew all the canine ropes until Tina with her attendant naughtiness came into their lives.

Pam – or was it John? – was very houseproud. Everything was of smart Swedish design indoors but the garden was given over to Tina. Her principal leisure activity seemed to be chewing shrubs, digging holes, burying toys and generally trying to mimic the life of a wolf.

I could see that food and play were the most important factors in Tina's life, followed by an overwhelming desire to lie in or on the cool, moist earth. She was seemingly in a state of constant hunger, and burrowing provided both distraction and edible morsels like roots and grubs. Unfortunately, *ad hoc* wolf dens were not easily accommodated in the small suburban garden which she shared with Pam and John. The compensation for her behaviour was that she was a good Guide Dog, coping well with heavy Midlands traffic and allowing Pam to hold down a well-paid job. Tina seemed to cope with anything on new territories or old, climbing in and out of trains, buses and offices with ease. Nor did she mind loud city noises like lorry airbrakes at pedestrian crossings – so long as she was in her working harness. Take off the white leather straps and handle, and she reverted to Tina the tearaway.

Pam and I walked Tina to the nearby park so that I could watch her behaviour. The Guide Dogs for the Blind Association's ruling is that dogs should be taken to an area of long grass, where they should be released and commanded to do their business. After a few minutes of free play, a well-tutored dog should return to its owner and immediately accept his or her authority. Tina enjoyed her freedom too much, staying an irritating metre away, just out of range for Pam, who might have to spend five minutes or five hours in the park attempting to retrieve her. I saw Tina take a titbit from Pam's right hand whilst dodging her left hand if she moved to grab her collar.

Clearly the first thing we had to do was to find a way of improving Tina's recall. Between us we devised a game in which Tina was obliged to place her jaws into Pam's cupped hands, the payoff being play with a short length of rope. During the early stage of training, she was to be restrained on an extending lead and Pam was gradually to reduce the proportion of 'rewarded trials' to about a quarter. In other words, I introduced a note of uncertainty and risk to the game, a quality which Tina found addictive. She was still to be encouraged and permitted to play with other dogs, an activity she greatly enjoyed, but play with Pam was to become relatively more attractive than it had been before my visit.

As she was a pushy dog, Tina loved nothing better than pulling contests with her mistress. Normally this behaviour is one I would discourage, but because Pam was such an effective lady there was little prospect of her relationship with Tina turning sour. Most important of all, I counselled Pam to be less assertive when training Tina to come to her name, contrary to the 'You must be the boss' advice of traditional dog trainers. She was told to build upon her dog's sense of fun rather than upon a sense of duty. Such a simple change in attitudes can bring about dramatic improvements in recall training and Pam was a receptive student as we applied the technique to Tina there and then in the park. We returned home at a brisk pace: either Pam knew every bump, hollow and danger on the route or Tina was an amazing guide dog.

We had solved the easy problem – now to tackle the big one. Tina's second consuming passion, after the company of other dogs, was scavenging for their faeces. In a word, she was coprophagic, clearing up the poops behind the rest of dogdom. My general advice to owners of coprophagic dogs is straightforward: increase the fibre content of the diet whilst also increasing the frequency of meals. Though this was hardly possible for Pam, I also usually recommend that the dog be watched at all times and distracted from making contact with faeces. I ask owners to relax and accept that coprophagia is a normal biological response for a hungry dog, behaviour that increases their energy intake but usually does the dog no particular harm. For Pam this advice was of no consequence because she could not see whether bits and pieces of faeces were lodged upon Tina's teeth and gums or smeared on her fur. Tina's whole future as a Guide Dog was in question since the Management at the Guide Dogs for the Blind training centre at Leamington Spa, Warwickshire was then of the opinion that coprophagia was a vice serious enough to have her withdrawn from service, even put to sleep. More enlightened policies about this common problem now prevail. But Pam and John loved Tina far too much to contemplate losing her; they would rather have a smelly dog than a dead dog.

I decided to start with a technique that I had previously employed only in an experimental setting at the research kennels of the pet food company where I had worked. There had been many coprophagic Beagles and Labradors in their kennels; presumably eating faeces provided a pleasant variation from the boredom of kennel life and a predictable diet of commercial petfoods. I had studied the nutritional aspects of coprophagia in these dogs and discovered that useful fats and other nutrients are contained in dog faeces. When 'recycled', the fat content dropped from about eight per cent to three. In other words, dogs eat faeces in pursuit of energy when they are hungry.

Labradors are popular as Guide Dogs but they are naturally prone to gluttony and thus to coprophagia. I had already demonstrated the benefit of a double-ended muzzle on such dogs but Tina, it turned out, was too clever for this solution: she simply pressed the muzzle on to soft faeces and licked them from the plastic lattice. Removing such a mucky muzzle would be no pleasant task for a blind person nor for anyone else.

I realized that I would have to adopt a more scientific approach, and again my thoughts turned to our earlier studies. I have always been interested in feeding behaviour and a body of research work known as conditioned-aversion learning, which some psychologists have also called one-trial learning. Rats that receive a sub-lethal dose of traditional poisons learn to avoid the foodstuff which they ate just before they began to feel ill. Clever rats are especially careful to sample novel and potentially dangerous foods before tucking into a large meal. Could a carnivore like the dog utilize similar detective skills to test unknown foods? The scientific literature hinted that they could. When I visited the National Parks and Wildlife Center in Denver, Colorado, in 1974, Dr Stephen Shumake had demonstrated to me that coyotes will also learn to avoid bait that makes them ill. The objective of his work was to stop coyotes predating upon sheep flocks by putting them off eating mutton. Nowadays, I sometimes use the same technique to teach pet dogs not to chase sheep.

In my former job with the petfood company, I adapted the technique used by Shumake on his coyotes and dosed coprophagic Beagles with harmless salt, lithium chloride, after they had been observed eating faeces. They stopped eating faeces after two or three such treatments, apparently because they 'blamed' their illness upon the smell and taste of faeces. This technique was all very well for treating laboratory dogs who could be dosed by intubation directly into the stomach, but it was not suitable for unskilled pet owners. The answer came from my resourceful wife Vivienne, who 'buried' the small quantity of lithium chloride crystals in home-made 'crack' caramel she prepared for the purpose. Dogs like toffee, and as it melts in their stomach there is a slow release of salty lithium.

Vivienne cooked three toffee pills for Tina, each one containing three grammes of lithium chloride. Tina's vet was present for the first treatment, and sure enough, Tina was as sick as the proverbial dog after eating a dollop of faeces in the park. She recovered her customary perkiness within half an hour and was outwardly physically unaffected by our treatment. She ate no more faeces for two whole days – remarkable progress – but then the bad old habits came back. With the vet's and my approval, Tina was dosed with the second toffee pill after she had been witnessed chewing on a tasty stool. Ever since, I am pleased to report, Tina has let other dogs' faeces lie.

Pam and John have since become firm friends of our practice and have featured me twice on their talking-tape magazine. Part of me occasionally feels sorry for Pam's misfortune at being blind, but then I envy the order in her life and the pride she takes in overcoming her disability. She is young and active, and the companionship offered by Tina was perhaps less important than it might have been to an elderly or sedentary blind person. Tina was first and foremost a working dog, with just a few behavioural blemishes which stopped her achieving her full potential. A kiss from Tina need no longer elicit in Pam a shudder at the thought of what she may have been eating earlier in the day.

I have also been called in to treat a Guide Dog afraid of thunder and another that was aggressive towards other dogs. But even more interesting are the long-term efforts of the Guide Dogs for the Blind Association (GDBA) to improve on the way they do things. They were the first professional dog organization to exploit fully our scientific understanding of early learning in puppies. They have consulted me about stress in working guide dogs, selection of breeds and cross-breeds, environmental enrichment for dogs in their palatial kennels and the provision of special toys to keep young dogs happy. Even Guide Dogs can pull too hard, because they are meant to walk ahead of their owners and not alongside in the conventional 'Heel' position. The GDBA now use the headcollar I designed to teach excessively headstrong, pulling dogs to walk in the desired position without needing to resort to punishment by cruel choke-chains. When headcollars were first used on some Guide Dogs, letters of complaint were received about them being 'muzzled', but Haltis are now accepted as normal equipment.

As time goes by and the value of the companionship of animals becomes more widely recognized, new applications and jobs for dogs in society appear. In the United States and now in the United Kingdom and elsewhere, the Hearing Dogs for the Deaf Organization uses specially trained dogs to alert their owners to a knock at the door, the telephone ringing, pans boiling and so on. Theirs is a most demanding occupation, stretching knowledge of dogs' senses, learning and behaviour to the limits.

Another newcomer to the world of working dogs is the so-called 'Assistance Dog', who is trained to help the physically handicapped.

The boundary between companionship and bondage in the relationship between people and dogs is a delicate one and I sometimes have my doubts about the ethics of using dogs in this role: pulling paraplegics in wheelchairs, picking up dropped objects, opening doors and the like. On the other hand, I have no doubt that for the recipients of these trained dogs, there is much more than convenience involved.

My favourite animal charity of all is the Pro Dogs Organization, which pioneered a PAT dog visiting scheme. This is a voluntary effort in which owners of selected dogs take their pets along to institutions housing lonely people in need of cheering up. They may be young, middle-aged or elderly, mentally normal, subnormal or advanced, emotionally well or traumatized but all are in need of the unconditional love and stimulation which a cold, wet dog's nose brings. PAT dogs' work is particularly important in the hospices, which are becoming such an important part of the new way for the dying in Western countries. Hospices should be, and generally are, happy places and it is entirely right that dogs should be a part of that informal scene. Sometimes, however, the dogs go wrong, becoming excessively nervous, too selective of which resident to like and which to avoid. There are strict rules for the selection of dogs participating in the PAT dogs scheme and I am sometimes involved in this process. It can be a demanding task, and we have to beware of biased breedism when, for example, disproportionate numbers of Cocker Spaniel and German Shepherd Dog owners present their dogs for the scheme. The important principle is that PAT dogs should be drawn from all breeds and cross-breeds, so that all tastes are catered for.

Other working functions are being developed for dogs: witness the growth in numbers of sniffer dogs used for the detection of the subtle chemicals in explosives. There is a vast international trade in naturally- and laboratory-derived drugs, and sniffer dogs are the principal weapon by which society is protected from this evil. Detection or failure to detect these chemicals can have major consequences for individual law-enforcement agencies, sometimes for whole societies. For the sniffer dogs, neurotic breakdowns can sometimes occur when they are exposed to excessively demanding training or working regimes. In Beirut, for example, the government is endeavouring to train dogs to detect blast bombs left by militia-men in the midst of densely populated streets. All too often, dogs going into this work will pay with their lives; the vehicles are left with unstable mercury switches attached to the explosives, and the detector-dog that enters such a vehicle will inevitably blow itself up.

In my experience, policemen don't like to be embarrassed in public any more than animal psychologists. Those who use dogs in police work are especially self-conscious because it is still only a recent tradition, mostly since World War II. Other policemen can be either patronizing or downright critical, despite the impressive evidence of the usefulness of dogs in finding and holding fugitives, detecting narcotics and so on. Police dog handlers rightly take immense pride in their animals' ability; they like to show off their training skills at public fêtes and then enjoy the companionship of the dog when off-duty at home. But a police dog has to conform to certain rules, like being quiet on the job. Starski was a dog who gave criminals advance warning that he was on his way.

Starski, a German Shepherd, was the responsibility of PC John X from a police force in the north of England. They had been working together for the last two years and John had become very attached to him. Although he could be ferocious in pursuit of a criminal, Starski's general temperament was gentle and friendly, especially towards John's wife and children at home. The problem was his excess of enthusiasm: he let out extraordinary howls at the prospect of police work. Whole neighbourhoods knew when John and Starski were approaching to answer an emergency call. When searching buildings, Starski also gave a continuous vocal talk-back on his rating of scents and clues. John's colleagues were not sympathetic to Starski's vocal eccentricities which to them reflected badly on his master's competence as a handler. They had already been sent on a specialized police training course which, remarkably, Starski had passed with flying colours. He could discriminate very well between real-life exciting drama and mock-up training exercises.

However, Starski had been criticized by training instructors for his excitability whilst on duty. Their remedy for his problem was to apply physical violence in the form of a harsh well-timed whack or check on his choke chain. John was unhappy about this advice, preferring a kinder approach. He had already tried, with some initial success, to calm Starski down by distraction rather than brute force punishment. Starski was a dog seemingly oblivious to pain who howled even louder when reprimanded.

All this trouble with Starski had battered John's self-esteem at work, so he came to me as a private individual rather than through official channels. Starski was a big, long-haired dog who looked like a bear but probably weighed under fifty kilos. Mostly black, he would surely strike terror into any miscreant contemplating escape. And yet I was touched by the obvious affection that existed between man and dog; I knew that I was going to learn a thing or two that evening.

I felt rather pleased to be invited to join John and Starski on their night patrol: it was like a fantasy fulfilled. We put the dog in the back of the van and went through the factors which elicited the worst howling. It was already fairly obvious to me: rapid acceleration of the vehicle, changing down to third gear, driving above fifty miles an hour and the sound of sirens on other police and emergency vehicles. After five minutes waiting outside a transport cafe in a typical Lancashire drizzle, a call came over the radio summoning us to attend a fracas at a pub. The instant John turned the van around and increased speed, Starski began pacing and howling.

Sitting uncomfortably with my paraphernalia of tape recorder and sound-generating devices, I experimented with ultrasound, a Dog Stop Alarm and titbits through the grille of the van. Starski was out of his mind with excitement, circling in his crate and literally screaming. It was a sound I have rarely heard from other dogs and then only from German Shepherds in situations like this one. I did not have a free hand in selecting therapy for Starski, for the practical realities of police work are not always compatible with the psychological approach. Moreover, permission for any course of behavioural therapy I might suggest would have to be obtained from John's senior officer, and we were at that time working off the record.

We arrived at the pub with Starski almost matching the sound output of the police sirens. In the confined space of an unlined Ford van the decibels made normal conversation impossible and there was no way John could speak on his police radio. Nevertheless, Starski cleared the pub of Friday night revellers by a couple of woofs and just by being there. It was getting late and I was tired and cold. Policemen who work Friday and Saturday nights are heroes, I thought, as I was taken back to my Murvi van for a sleep whilst John and Starski carried on together through the night.

We deferred formal therapy until I was in the north of England again, the following week. We met at an empty warehouse adapted for training police dogs and their handlers in 'man work'. On this occasion, I was to play the 'man', a criminal swathed in a protective hessian 'bite suit' which gave me more the appearance of a Michelin-man than of an average-slim psychologist. John cheered me up by explaining that Starski nearly always held his man by the right arm and I must be sure not to fall or he might bite my unprotected feet. And I wasn't allowed to carry a Dog Stop, or titbits or any of my other protective quick routes to a dog's heart.

I chose to hide on the third floor of the four-storey building, amongst pallets of empty cardboard boxes. After the agreed delay of five minutes, John and Starski came into the building. Starski's vocal outpourings made it easy for me to know where they were. I back-tracked to the second floor after they had 'searched' it and declared me absent. After reaching the fourth floor without finding me, Starski went silent, but carried on searching and eventually cornered me in my hidey hole on the second floor, giving a train of excited, yapping barks before grabbing my right arm. I had to stand still patiently whilst John called Starski off and rewarded him by a play routine with his favourite rubber toy. We had elucidated the critical factor which stimulated howling: anticipation of a successful find. Reduce the expectation of a find or delay fulfilment, and Starski was dumb.

Away from the police and public scrutiny, John and I devised a plan to modify Starski's behaviour. He had already been taught to 'speak' or bark on command, which was his party trick at home with the family. I advised that this should now be the only permitted sound in Starski's repertoire. How could we suppress or interrupt howling? I did not want to use any unpleasant punishment on this dog, knowing that it would offend John's humane feelings and might serve to undermine the positive esteem in which the general public hold the police dog section. I wanted John to try a quiet and passive 'punishment' technique: to introduce a time delay before the excitement of release to 'work' at the scene of a crime. On training runs, John was to elicit howling by speeding up his driving, changing gears and so on. The moment Starski sounded off, he was to stop the van immediately. There would then be a variable interval or delay of ten to sixty seconds, after which 'punishment' ceased and the journey could resume.

In theory, this could involve an unduly long delay between being alerted to an emergency and arriving at the scene: potentially good news for criminals. Always flexible, I agreed to my rules being bent in the actual pursuit of law and order. However, everything in John's manner during training had to be the same as when he was on service: the same uniform, radio contact and the like. It seemed to me that once John had proved to his sergeant that he was making progress using this technique, he ought to be allowed to employ it whilst on active service.

The next phase of therapy was training Starski not to whine or bark whilst making a search. We fitted him with a headcollar attached to a long running line. At every excited yelp John stepped back three paces, requiring Starski to return to his side. If he was quiet, they could proceed. There was never to be admonishment by voice; John's manner was always to remain flat and unexciting.

I received beautifully scripted records of progress and setbacks over the following two months – would that my own records were so tidy! The trend was clear, however. By the end of the second month howling occurred only when there was a cacophony of sirens and bells from other police vehicles. Within days of instituting the new training technique, the search behaviour became almost mute. Importantly, it was Starski who penalized himself by howling, whilst John retained his role as the dog's best friend, a source of pleasure not punishment. We were employing the psychological technique of instrumental conditioning in just the same way as Professor Barry Skinner had with his rats. Most pleasing of all was the nice letter I received from John's wife, who explained how much her husband enjoyed his work, yet was as sentimentally attached to Starski as anyone else could be to a family pet.

Most working dogs lead full and interesting lives, especially if, like Starski, they can combine it with tucking up by the fireside when off duty. Unfortunately, that privilege is not usually given to Greyhounds, kept in their thousands to support the compulsion to gamble.

At the end of my seminar to Greyhound breeders and trainers, I was approached by a thick-set gentleman who asked how his dogs might be practically encouraged to chase the lure or 'hare' on the racing track. This was a problem that I had not really considered, generally wanting to avoid involvement with the dog-racing industry because I knew that such a high proportion of their 'failures' were either neglected, rehomed or killed. My curiosity was, however, roused by the welfare implications behind the question. Greyhounds that do not chase are useless for racing and so may die young. If we could encourage a higher proportion of young Greyhounds to fulfil their primary purpose in life and chase the lures more reliably, the present over-production of Greyhound puppies might perhaps be reduced. Accordingly, I agreed to attend the man's breeding and training establishment in Hampshire, to spend a little time watching, listening and learning about their business.

In fact I spent half a day there, so fascinated was I by what I saw. This was quite a palace in terms of dog care and training. Thirty adult dogs were used either at stud or as brood bitches, an annual production of 150–200 puppies. I was shocked to find that fewer than a third of this number graduated to race on the tracks, the surplus generally being put to sleep. Even the successful dogs might not have a long natural life; if they did not perform they could only go downhill to a 'flapper' track where conditions were anything but ideal for the care of these sensitive dogs.

I watched young puppies being introduced to rabbits' tails tied to a string – sometimes flicked from the end of a stick like a fishing rod, at other times dragged through the grass by a kennel lad. Whereas some puppies ran after the rabbit tail, others just ran after their brothers. These were the followers and not the chasers: the 'after you' types who would never win a race. I noted that training was conducted as a group exercise for the litter, with little focus upon individual puppies. I suggested they change the procedure to encourage puppies to chase the lure either alone or, at most, in pairs.

Then there were the older dogs, four to six months old and beautifully proportioned half-sized Greyhounds. A home-made lure was moved by a contraption which hauled in the string attached to the lure. Groups of six or more juveniles were permitted to chase the lure across a large field, by now wearing light muzzles to prevent them scrapping. About half the dogs showed little interest in the lure, preferring to sniff underground animals, play with one another or chase birds. Following the normal practice of the Greyhound racing industry, these dogs would not live long. The final phase of training was to race for real. The dogs were usually taken to a small local track and participated in a pretend race. Again, there were casualties who failed this last hurdle in the selection process.

I was surprised to find how infrequent were their training exercises; once a day, sometimes less than that and involving only a few minutes of running by each dog. I suggested that less time be spent on sprucing up and polishing the establishment and more on individual contact and handling for the young dogs.

It was late afternoon and the autumn light was drawing in as we gathered in the kennel kitchen for a round-table conference with the proprietor and his staff. Most of them were school-leavers keen for any job with animals, no matter how ill-paid. The keenest of all were lads from Ireland, farm boys who had themselves trained and lived with Greyhounds as members of the family. In Ireland dogs are a much more personal affair, not something for the big business, mass production approach I was seeing here. My off-the-cuff suggestions about a more individual approach to the care and training of puppies found a warm reception among these lads. One of them then threw me a hard question. In Ireland, he said, he trained his dogs like a Lurcher on live rabbits; they were better racers because they had had the thrill of a kill. Was that the fault with these English dogs, who rarely tasted blood and only played at chasing a stuffed lure or model hare? I could see the reasoning behind his arguments but did not want to pursue this line on the grounds of rabbit welfare!

When I arrived back at my office on the farm, I was sniffed from top to toe for new smells by all our free-roaming canine helpers, who do more or less as they please during a typical day. I began to harbour uneasy feelings about being on this particular assignment with racing Greyhounds. I had no doubt that I had already given them useful tips, just by getting them to think about their own situation and the time-honoured practices of the trade. But I knew too much about the other side of it – especially about dogs leading unstimulating lives with little future beyond being kennelled, muzzled and then dying young – to wish to become more involved.

The uncomfortable facts have been placed before me by a remarkable lady, Celia Cross, who founded an organization called 'Greyhound Rescue', which takes on the throw-outs from this enormous industry. Greyhounds make the loveliest of pets, calm and majestic creatures until aroused by the passion of a chase. On a lead, perhaps on an extending lead, they usually plod harmlessly on walks past the temptation of cats or rabbits. I have never known a pet Greyhound to bite its owner intentionally. They bark but don't bite visitors, they don't require marathon walks but they do like to be loved.

I was first introduced to the delights of Greyhounds as pets by a physically disabled lady who rules her pack of three with a feather. They are ideal for her because she can use them as props to pull herself out of her wheelchair or from the floor in case of a fall. They are also sufficiently large for there to be no danger of her tripping over them, and sufficiently sure-footed not to crash into people. They are the ideal assistance dog for paraplegics, or for anyone else seeking the quiet life with a devoted friend.

Celia Cross has had me assist in the rehabilitation of many an ex-racer and she herself has become quite an authority on the subject, using a combination of intuitive understanding and kindness. Her organization runs on a shoestring budget but achieves big results for the benefit of these unfortunate creatures, both in the UK and overseas.

I doubt that the people who bet money on dogs, sometimes just on a name in *Sporting Life*, have any concept of the cruelty and waste which lies behind the glamour of Greyhound racing. Many small-time owners of racing Greyhounds wax sentimental about their dogs and go to visit them frequently when they are in licensed racing kennels. Such dogs have to remain in authorized trainers' kennels throughout their racing careers, after which a few exceptional ones are finally taken home to be with their owners when they retire from the track. Many more end up with Celia Cross or are killed.

Even the process of racing with Greyhounds utilizes only a small part of the animal's overall capacity for intelligent behaviour. One might have thought that selecting only for fast chasing might affect their problem-solving capacity. I have seen no evidence of that in the Greyhounds I have worked with: they are sensitive and clever animals in bodies perfectly sculptured for stamina and speed.

Looking at Sam, I should really include him as a working, professional dog. He comes with me every day to the farm, not flinching from the sometimes unpleasant business of meeting our patients. He performs with unfailing zeal on TV shows, sings in radio programmes and poses for any cameraman or journalist prepared to hear his story. Of all the working dogs I have administered to, I don't think I have found one who would match his all-round excellence at making the world a happier place. I was delighted that he shared with me the honour of being voted Pro Dog Man/Dog of the Year in 1988; he earned it.

10

Hobnobbing

An endearing feature of the way animals relate to people is that they do not discriminate between rich and poor, smart and scruffy, fat and thin. Dogs are not impressed by aristocratic ways and titles: it is what we do rather than what we are that is important to them. As social animals they bond to us because we are available to them. We give them our time, we are active in play like hunters in the wild, we are susceptible to blackmail over food and affection, and we probably have an approved body odour. In return, the need of human beings for the company of animals is a universal trait which bears no relation to social position.

In the still class-conscious society that is Great Britain, our love of animals cuts right through barriers of race, sex, accent and income. That is a particularly satisfying element of my work: I would not wish to be catering only for this or that category of owner. Social class is a concept I have always found alien and unpleasant, principally because I regard myself as being classless, coming as I do from a farming background that does not easily fit into the conventional groupings so beloved of market researchers. Nevertheless, I am always curious about the British and their ways and my job provides a wonderful opportunity for people-watching.

My first very rich client was the multi-millionairess wife of a Norwegian businessman living in London. Their problem was a lovely Old English Sheepdog, Schnip, who chewed carpets when left alone. There was nothing remarkable about this case apart from the fact that Schnip focused her destructive energies upon priceless antique Persian rugs, doing up to £10,000 worth of damage on each binge. Their London apartment lay just behind the Albert Hall, in a 'good' part of London's Knightsbridge. The scale of affluence was then strange to me, the country boy up from Devon.

Schnip had plenty of Persian rugs to choose from on the walls and floors, and if she tired of their texture she could always move on to old clipped Chinese ones. The cost of the damage had no effect upon the advice I had to offer in helping them to overcome the problem: it was a straightforward separation anxiety case, presenting no more or less professional challenge than could be found in the case of an ex-Battersea mutt destroying the council flat of its owners in Tower Hamlets.

I left my Norwegian client for my next call to a gentleman on the Embankment. I had been asked to visit him at the request of the police and also by the Salvation Army, after his dog had attacked a policeman. The message from the Salvation Army was that John James could not be admitted to their hostel so long as he was accompanied by his dog Bison, who fearlessly protected his master against anyone wearing uniform. After dark, Bison was reputed to become the 'devil under the arches' amongst the other dossers inhabiting the twilight world beneath Waterloo Bridge. Everyone except the police had learned to give John a wide berth during their night-time drinking and socializing.

John had had several close run-ins with the law over his dog and after each bite he was obliged to move on with his few scrappy belongings to a different refuge for London's homeless. Fortunately for him there was no central police record of these incidents so he was safe so long as they kept moving. The Salvation Army believed that John could be helped to take up a stable life again, especially as his drinking habits were not so serious as many of those around him. He was well-educated, was not a junkie and definitely wanted to break out of the terrifying cycle of poverty and hopelessness into which he had sunk since the acrimonious break-up of his marriage.

John had been warned the previous week that he should expect a visit from 'the Dog Doctor' and he was asked to have other residents in the underground complex near the Royal Festival Hall look out for me. I arrived late in the afternoon, and it was already cold and damp in the gloom beneath the arches. The stench was just awful. A small amount of light percolated down from the streets above, the residents were visible only in the glow from their cigarettes and occasional flares from burning newspapers. I soon found John James in the place where I had been led to expect him by the Salvation Army. I was wearing my scruffy Barbour jacket, which Bison reckoned was near enough to being a uniform to warrant a hefty vocal threat, but not an actual attack. I tossed a chunk of cheese onto the pavement in front of Bison which thankfully changed his opinion of me.

John was embarrassed at having no money to pay me, but I explained that I was there for my education, both to learn about his remarkable dog and about his lifestyle. But John was very firm that there had to be some payment for the professional service that he wanted of me, so he asked me to come back next week, by which time he should have collected social security payments due at his last fixed address. I protested that money wasn't the main thing in life and that perhaps he had some small thing that I would find useful in return for help, that maybe he would even be glad to be without. Spying the cache of cider, cheap wine and two bottles of Guinness in his open pantry (a cardboard box) I suggested that a fair exchange for my professional services would be a bottle of stout. Honour satisfied, John, Bison and I assumed a normal client-patient-behavioural therapist triangle.

I was offered the luxury of a tea chest to sit on, but asked that we move into daylight where I would be able to read my notes. The smell of the place was also getting to me. By this stage, Bison was on an incongruously smart leather lead, which I took hold of whilst John followed with my case. He told me that he had picked up the lead in Hyde Park – probably left behind by some well-heeled Knightsbridge Poodle, I thought. In the open-air pedestrian precinct near Waterloo Station, I was at last able to see Bison and watch his behaviour towards the passing throngs. He was the size of a small Labrador, rich brown with pretty white flecks on his head. Bison seemed to focus upon men more than women but hated to be stared at or touched by anyone except John. The positive feature of his behaviour was that he would accept food, first from me and later from passing 'stooges' whom I roped into the evening's therapy session.

Bison turned out to be an extremely responsive dog and after a single session we made life beneath Waterloo Bridge considerably safer for the million or so people who walk that way every day, to and from the Station. John took enormous pride in Bison's appearance and did his best to look after him by scrounging, begging and sometimes buying food for him. He was regularly washed in the horse trough at Elephant and Castle, a friendly vet nurse in South London sprayed him for fleas and he could be sure of a well-padded bed in a dry, draught-proof cardboard box. For a dog, that rough kennel could be a palace and his master a king.

A couple of years after helping John for a bottle of Guinness, I had a telephone call from a veterinary surgeon in Windsor. He explained that he had a client with several dogs that had begun fighting: could I suggest ways in which to tackle the problem. I ran through a host of variables which might affect the outcome of treatment and started asking questions about the breed of dog, how many dogs, the occasions on which fights occurred and so on. The vet quickly came to the point: his client was Her Majesty the Queen, the dogs were of course Corgis, and would I please be prepared to take on a royal assignment if that was what Her Majesty wanted. At that time, our practice was only three years old and my reputation, though respectable amongst veterinary surgeons, was barely known to the public at large. I imagined that it was entirely unknown to the Royal family! The Queen's vet said that he would speak to his client and find out what she wanted to do.

The next day he phoned back with the news that the Queen would be grateful if I could call as soon as possible. She had heard of me through the Princess Royal because I had adapted our Halti headcollar for use by the Riding for the Disabled organization, of which the Princess is Patron. We checked diaries and agreed on the next day, but not before I had had a briefing from the vet on etiquette and the need to maintain strict confidentiality. I asked if I could share the secret with my wife Vivienne, whom I could hear coping with our toddler daughters at meal-time next door. Permission granted, I gave Vivienne a good tease on 'Guess who might be my next client?'

Vivienne is better versed than I in the rules of social etiquette, particularly those relating to royalty. She even produced a dusty old book on the subject which I was instructed to read (but never did). She particularly emphasized that it was not the done thing to greet Her Majesty with the statement, 'Pleased to meet you, Ma'am'. I listened dutifully and checked for soup stains on my one decent suit.

The next day, I teamed up with the vet at his premises, where I was again told the Who's Who of the Royal Corgi clan. There had been an ongoing line of Corgis in the Queen's life since she was a child. I went through their clinical histories, noting that their most frequent reason for requiring veterinary attention was because of dog fights. Otherwise, the seven purebred Corgis and three Dorgis (Dachshund cross-Corgis) appeared to be a healthy pack. Fights had occurred at Windsor Castle and in the grounds, in a car and at Buckingham Palace, but curiously not with the dogs' foster caretaker, with whom they stayed when the Queen was abroad. Given that all the males were entire, I expressed the opinion that it shouldn't be surprising if there were the occasional scrap. It was explained to me that these were not just mild scraps: blood had been spilled.

I was shown to the practice Daimler, quite a relief since my motor of the moment was a battered, fourteen-year-old estate car which I considered would definitely have looked out of place in a castle. I was happy to be a passenger in the Daimler; and the guardsmen stood to attention as they whisked us through police checks and round to an inner courtyard that the public never sees.

This was a home visit with a difference: I don't normally have the benefit of the referring veterinary surgeon escorting me to his client. I was more than grateful on this occasion, because he is not just a knowledgeable veterinary surgeon, but also an accomplished social guide who would help me through the challenge I was about to face. We were taken by an equerry to the royal apartment, up such a warren of stairs, corridors and doors that I would have no chance of escaping if I committed some awful *faux pas*. Even after my student experience of oral examination, I don't think I had ever experienced such a stressful build-up to a social encounter.

I really needn't have worried. I was greeted by Her Majesty warmly, we shook hands and, of course, I replied, 'Pleased to meet you, Ma'am'! The ground should have opened up beneath me, but the Queen seemed not to notice and went on to talk about veterinary matters. I got on with the business of dogs and took their histories again, the human and canine lifestyles together with the clinical history that I had already been given by the vet in charge. The dogs, it seemed, spent a lot of time in the car, travelling between the several Royal houses and especially between Buckingham Palace and Windsor. I asked if there had ever been a fight during such a journey and was told that though there were squabbles, none had actually erupted into a major battle.

I asked to be introduced to my patients who were waiting downstairs in the gardens of the castle. We went to meet them. When the dogs were brought out from a side door they immediately broke loose and rushed in greeting towards the Queen. At first they barked at the vet and myself, but we were soon able to play roly-poly with Myth as she came up to have her tummy rubbed in classic Corgi fashion. They so much reminded me of my childhood Corgi, Rusty on the farm in Devon, where he earned his keep by fearlessly swinging on the tails of cows who were slow to come in from the fields. That is what Corgis were bred for: especially to dive under the kicking angle of cattle-hooves, and nip the poor beast on the frog of its foot. Any sensible cow would keep moving for fear of such

Left: The Carr family, with complex human-animal interactions to unravel. There were five children (not in picture) and 30 animals of 8 species in a London town house (*Alistair Morrison*)

Below: Business at the Kumars' grocery store in Southall was down because of Mangal. Loyal slave to his family, but terrorist to customers and any other living creature. Sam and I are making small headway (*Alistair Morrison*)

Left: I offer my body to Sherpar, a Tibetan terrorist, after checking that the safety equipment of extending lead and headcollar were well secured. Mine is a job that keeps me nimble (*Alistair Morrison*)

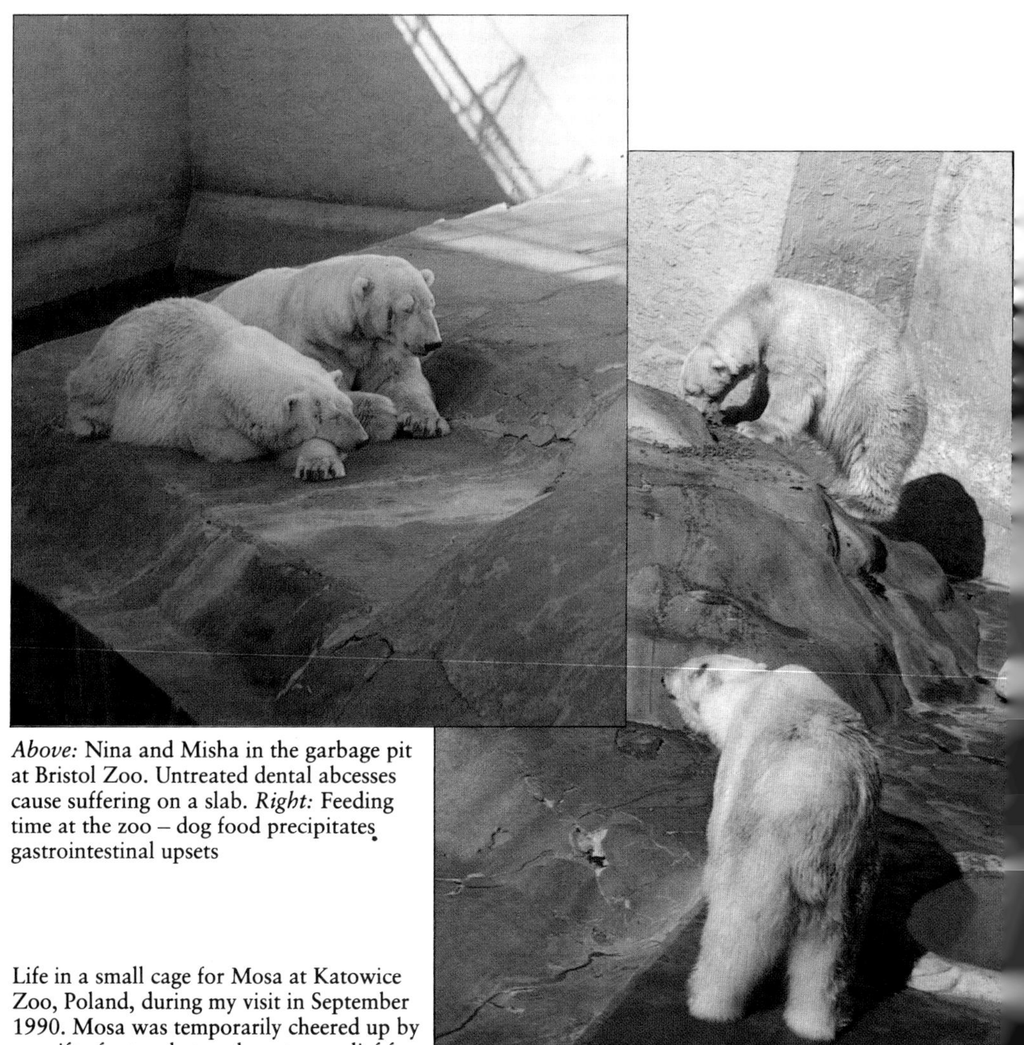

Above: Nina and Misha in the garbage pit at Bristol Zoo. Untreated dental abcesses cause suffering on a slab. *Right:* Feeding time at the zoo – dog food precipitates gastrointestinal upsets

Life in a small cage for Mosa at Katowice Zoo, Poland, during my visit in September 1990. Mosa was temporarily cheered up by my gift of a toy, but no long term relief for this British bear is in sight

Left: Tina, an angelic-looking guide dog showing no hint of her wilful ways

Below: Carl Boyde and Afterthought at Hardwick Court Farm. Vet and dog tamers extraordinaire

Left: Jamie, constant companion to Brenda Elsoffer, would literally never leave her side

Below: Emily, my daughter, being roped in to test the stopping power of a Halti on this Shire dog (*Alistair Morrison*)

Above: Snoopy and Spot Oppenheim-Barnes take to Sam in Regent's Park

Left: Ed Stewart and Wellington come to terms with the power of Afterthought. He always wins

Below: Rula Lenska, Silky and Lacy

an under-foot attack, but the swinging-on-tail technique was also there as the weapon of last resort.

That working trait also tends to get pet Corgis into trouble nipping people's ankles, as it had done occasionally for the Royal Corgis in the past. We watched the dogs interacting and I noticed that disputes and rivalry between them often centred upon closeness to Piper who was liable to pester Chipper, the oldest male and traditional top dog of the group. Otherwise, all seemed like peace and harmony in the Royal pack, and I complimented the Queen on their behaviour.

It was 4 p.m. and time for the dogs' meal, when problems may have arisen between them. We returned to the apartment where a tray was brought in with ten bowls for ten dogs, together with their rations for the day. When the volume and contents of each bowl had been adjusted by Her Majesty, a topping of gravy was added. Then she looked across to the semi-circle of quiet but salivating dogs congregated a few metres away and called each one in turn to take his or her food. There was never a growl or rude look between the dogs and I was amazed at the harmony which reigned indoors at this theoretically high-risk time. The Queen explained that she had always been strict in requiring good manners amongst the dogs at feeding time and each was obliged to wait his turn, the eldest to be fed first and youngest last. It struck me as a useful exercise for other owners to follow: establishing consistent rules for the pack which favoured the development of stable relationships between the dogs.

I reached for my notes and again went through the precise events leading up to the three serious fights which had occurred between the dogs. Over an hour had elapsed since the consultation had begun with the Queen and it was time for me to start pulling together the threads of what I had seen and heard to create a workable strategy for the future. I knew that to run a pack of ten tough Welsh hill farmers' herding dogs takes formidable skill and will-power, which the Queen undoubtedly possessed. However, she did have other responsibilities in life apart from being chief of this dog pack. One dog in particular became our focus for attention, and his future had to be determined between us. This dog had, it seemed, for some time been the subject of family jokes, for his ostentatious machoism. I targeted him as the main instrument of social disharmony, and suggested that he be rehomed.

The subject of protection and safety for those involved was then explored. Muzzling of one or more dogs had to be rejected, even as a short term arrangement because fights were few and far between and never predictable. I had already had ample experience of dog fights amongst other patients, and knew that some would continue battle almost to the point of death no matter what the distractions. In other words, dogs can become completely insensitive to all 'normal' stimuli like screams, kicks, a bucket of water or a blanket thrown over them. Sometimes only direct physical intervention to lift or pull fighting dogs apart is effective. In a tailless breed like Pembroke Corgis, there isn't much to grab hold of apart from their scruffs, which can bring vulnerable hands too close for comfort to flashing teeth.

I was interested in loud noises as a stress factor for dogs and wondered whether we could harness certain sounds to make fighting dogs attend to we humans. I had recently seen a pair of Jack Russells for whom the only stimulus which stopped their fighting was the dramatic clang of a dropped dustbin lid. But where could we discover a sound-stimulus which was loud, portable and tuned to the more sensitive upper hearing range of dogs? I outlined my ideas for an aural dog-fight interrupter to the Queen and she was keen that I should develop or procure such a device for use on the Corgis. I had already heard of anti-rape or anti-mugging aerosol alarms in the USA, but had not at that time (1984) had the opportunity to try one out in our practice with dogs. The idea eventually took the tangible form of the Dog Stop aural alarm.

Back with the dogs, an action programme had been agreed and it was time to go. We had been with the Queen for something over two hours; the time had flown because her company was so pleasant, intelligent and revealing. I transferred from the upholstered luxury of the Daimler to my own, decrepit car, with its seat-springs poking uncomfortably into my body. Driving back from Windsor past the Windsor Home Farm, I came to the conclusion that I would greatly prefer to be governed by this monarch than our contemporary band of democratically elected politicians. I was in excellent humour and, knowing I would do no more consulting that evening, took Vivienne our to dinner to celebrate.

The disruptive Corgi was duly dispatched to Princess Anne at Gatcombe, where apparently he was kept in hand by her Lurcher. Perhaps it was an attraction of opposites, but these two dogs developed a respectful and relatively peaceful relationship which would have been impossible within the Royal Corgi pack. The good news was that until recently there were no more serious scraps. Then, in 1989, there was a disastrous fight in which, sadly, the little Corgi Chipper suffered fatal wounds. No-one could intervene in time and the Dog Stop alarm we had developed for the Royal dogs was probably in someone else's coat pocket at the time: out of reach and of no use.

The story about my involvement with the Queen's Corgis hit the tabloid press in 1986–87, after an interview with Princess Anne in the *Sunday Telegraph*. Until then, I had not breathed a word about my consultation to anyone. However, now that my secret had been let out by a member of the Royal family I was bound to acknowledge that it may have been true, but thereafter I offered no comment. Since then, there has been a lot more press investigation and comment, much of it making fun of the Queen's supposed inability to control her dogs. As my story illustrates, nothing could be further from the truth.

The passion of the British Royal family for animals is not unique to the House of Windsor; witness the tireless work on behalf of dog welfare by H.S.H. Princess Antoinette de Monaco, or the consistent support for the World Wide Fund for Nature by members of the Dutch Royal family. Many others of the world's royal families have come to see us with their pets, and again we are struck by the constancy of people's love for animals, be they rich or poor.

An Italian Count recently brought his sheep-chasing Labrador to see me, though the Count was not so likeable as other well-connected visitors to Hardwick Court Farm. He seemed genuinely upset not to have received the red carpet treatment to which he had presumably grown accustomed, and in a short while he had succeeded in offending all of my patient and usually tolerant lady colleagues. I alone succeeded in remaining correctly polite!

A Princess from the House of Saud needed my help with her several Siamese cats. She was in London to complete her education and had fallen in love with felines, contrary to her upbringing and the ways of her family back in Riyadh. I went to see them at their luxurious fourth-floor penthouse flat, where most things that an indolent Siamese might wish for were provided. In return, they gave the Princess Saud a non-threatening, unconditional affection that was hard for her to find in Britain. The cats' only problem was about use of the litter tray, and mistakes were causing anxieties about propriety and health in the Princess, as well as amongst visiting compatriots whom she could not trust to keep her secret from the folks back home. I learned that cats do not enjoy such a high status in Saudi culture, and would be unlikely to be in the home, let alone on the bed, where these cats usually slept with their Princess. I sympathized with her being caught between two cultures, though I believe that her's was a generation fast catching up with our more tolerant and humane attitude towards pet-keeping.

The deadline for the Princess Saud was the imminent visit of her father to London: could the smells and the marks on carpets be eliminated in time? She would pretend to her father that the cats were kept as a hobby in an unused bedroom, well away from the main living areas and certainly well away from her bedroom. I advised on a straightforward litter-tray-training programme, where first we determined the preferred material that the cats would use for toileting. It was not to be a proprietary brand of litter from the supermarket, rather leaf mould and beech mast, which contained smelly fungal remnants that pose a real temptation to cats. I learned about the especially attractive properties of decomposing plant material and biologically active soil in my childhood days, where our farm cats would reliably head for freshly cultivated soil or a well-manicured seed bed. I brought bags of Surrey leaf mould to the Princess the next day and the cats performed as predicted. I did not ask for the contract to keep up the supplies! In fact, after a few months, she was able to dilute leaf mould with regular clay cat litter and the problem was simply solved. Father came to London and then returned, not knowing about his daughter's feline bed mates, nor about their excretory habits.

The world of showbiz brings many patients to us, perhaps because writers and actors lead such uncertain lives that they develop an especially close bond with their animals. The writer Carla Lane is always active on behalf of many deserving animal causes, and her home is more or less given over to seventy-two birds, seven cats, frogs, a dog and any other animal that needs a safe haven. I first went to Carla's home to treat her nervous Irish Wolfhound, Maximus, a quivering giant of a dog. He was purchased from a breeder in haste when her previous Wolfhound died; a year-old show dog that had spent all its life in kennels. I pointed out that Maximus's nervousness derived from his chronic lack of early stimulation, like a child raised in a barren orphanage. We devised various play and therapy programmes to reinforce extrovert behaviour, and he seemed to adapt to a varied, stimulating life of part Liverpool, part London. The family coupé was upgraded to a Range Rover so that Maximus could lie comfortably on car journeys and all manner of dog sitters and walkers were found to care for him when Carla had to be away from home. By any standard he was a lucky, loved dog.

Despite his underlying fears, Maximus accepted his mistress's world remarkably well. Visitors like me who remained calm and passive would be given friendship after receiving a considered sniffing, but noisy extroverts were shunned. The rehabilitation of Maximus was entirely due to the patient kindness of his mistress, then last year I received an urgent phone call from her. There had been a family gathering at Carla's house beside the Thames, during which there had been a lot of Liverpudlian warmth and a little wine in circulation. Maximus was ill at ease, even growled and Carla tried to take him from the small front room where everyone was gathered. He resisted with his immense body bulk just as Carla's brother-in-law slipped his footing and crashed down upon poor Maximus. In panic, he snapped at the man's head causing a nasty wound, though a wound that from an average to small dog would have been only minor. On my emergency house call, I conducted a behavioural *post mortem* that identified several clear precipitating factors to Maximus's biting: a small room, wine, noisy family, Carla commanding Maximus to leave, then the fall. Since these were mostly avoidable circumstances, I argued that Maximus should continue in his world with sensible precautions being instituted by his people.

Maximus the gentle giant, beloved by all the animals in the Lane household, lived only for a few more months. Carla found him one evening in desperate abdominal pain from a condition later diagnosed as gastric torsion, a twisting of his stomach to cause an intestinal blockage. Maximus died that night in Carla's arms as she was trying, single-handed, to lift him into the Range Rover. He deserved an emergency home visit from a vet but, inexplicably, none would oblige that night. Country vets will turn out for a horse, a cow or a dog in distress, but Maximus was unlucky to be in London.

A few grief-stricken months without canine companionship elapsed after Maximus died, before Carla at last succumbed to the charms of a wilful Lurcher puppy, Igor.

He is a bold, playful spirit in total contrast to the restrained habits of Maximus, tweaking at other facets of Carla Lane's complex personality. She remains, in her own words, 'the biggest animal nut of them all', tirelessly working for animal sanctuaries and stimulating more humane attitudes towards animals. 'Remember me for helping animals, not for what I write.'

Rula Lenska's views about zoos, conservation issues and animals in general are also similar to my own. She and Dennis Waterman came to the farm in 1989 with their two slightly unruly Mongrels, Silky and Lacy. Lacy, a sort of Alsatian-cross-Collie-cross-something had been rescued from a pub, whilst Silky had been found wandering on the motorway. They looked to be in heaven amongst the many temptations of the farm, but that wasn't why they had come to see me. Lacy had just disgraced herself by biting the postman, but she also chased cars, raided dustbins and bullied other dogs. She rushed over to Sam with hackles up and tail bushy, but Sam instantly went into courtship-distraction mode, turning potential aggression into sexual invitation. This amused Rula and Dennis, but suggested to me that Lacy wasn't really a psychopath; she just needed more active supervision and schooling. Although the consequences were often serious, her misbehaviour was largely motivated by a clumsy attempt at social investigation.

Silky, I guessed, had had a Rough Collie for one parent, perhaps a Bearded Collie for the other. She was appropriately hirsute but also inherited the Collie fear of loud noises, such as the guns that were forever being fired around their Buckinghamshire home. I prescribed a distraction technique to tackle this problem, with over-the-top play to block fearfulness. Since their visit, Lacy has given up her pursuit of postmen, indeed has almost become a non-biting pacifist. Both dogs have been affected by emotional developments within the Lenska/Waterman household but then so are all pet dogs.

The media person I have had most laughs with is probably Ed Stewart and his family, who own a Great Dane, Wellington, together with a highly competitive German Shepherd Dog, Buster. I first met Ed in his Radio One days, and later when he was on Radio Mercury; but now I was in a different role, as therapist to his dogs. On arrival I had Sam in the car who, gauging himself to be both outnumbered and out-bodied at the Steward canine residence, wisely chose to stay there. Wellington's bark fair put terror into Sam, though I doubted there was real aggression in its tone.

It was a hot summer's afternoon which was an excellent excuse for taking down the case history with a glass or two of wine on the patio, whence we could see the absurd goings-on between the two dogs. Buster was always top dog, any attention to the younger Wellington producing a frenzy of jealousy. But Wellington was in many ways a more lovable and better adjusted dog than the obsessive German Shepherd, so it grieved the Stewarts that Wellington always had to be the one who lost out. Fortunately, Buster was also obsessive in his chase behaviour: one way to foil his competitive psyche was to throw a ball to the far end of their garden and whilst he searched for it in the bushes, we could be nice to Wellington.

Apart from Wellington's barking, he also had a problem with urinating indoors, and the dogs tended to scrap. I noticed large cracks on the outside walls of the Stewarts' house and wondered if they were perhaps caused by Wellington's barking, a sort of Walls of Jericho effect. On the other side of their large garden, the Stewarts had neighbours who, though tolerant, must have had some negative thoughts about Wellington's vocal capacities. Apart from urinating indoors, he also occasionally stole food, which from his one-metre plus vantage height meant there were few places where food could be safely stored in the Stewart household.

I asked Ed and his wife Ciara what had brought things to a head now: why had they called me in today rather than a year ago? I was told that Wellington had come to them only recently, from an antiques dealer acquaintance in London who could not offer him a suitable life: he had had to be shut up in a shop or backyard for long periods alone and was given no formal training. Ed had taken pity on Wellington, even though Buster the German Shepherd remained his favourite. But their busy lifestyle did not allow much time to rehabilitate someone else's disaster. Nevertheless, they had made enormous progress, especially by giving Wellington more confidence in human company.

Because feeding time was such a mess of crumbs and saliva, the dogs were usually fed in an outhouse, a rambling double garage full of clutter. I suggested that they might also be confined to the garage at times of potential crisis like meals or during parties when Wellington tended to steal food from the guests. Ed was worried about Wellington's barking, and feared that if left alone in the garage the dogs might also fight. I expressed doubt that they would fight and asked them just to try it. I told them how to interrupt Wellington's barking using the thrown-can technique, after praising and rewarding him for giving the first warning bark. Then there was the urinating – which for a dog like Wellington could be almost as big an operation as for a camel that had just quenched its thirst. Since he only did it by the front door on a small patch of carpet, I recommended that this area become the night-time sleeping quarters for the dogs. Buster could continue to be a proficient guard dog and sentry for the household and Wellington would be unlikely to despoil his own sleeping zone. The new arrangement worked immediately and well.

The Stewart children, Francesca and Marco, accompanied their parents with both dogs to a test session with the sheep on our farm recently, because there was always a slight possibility that Wellington might chase and maul livestock. I kitted him out with a headcollar, and off we went over the hill and down towards the

M25, where Mr Boyde's flock of sheep had sensibly retreated. Wellington quivered with anticipation of the joyful chase ahead, having already noticed that I was treating him in a liberal fashion, giving no macho commands and only lightly restraining him on a ten-metre long line. He spotted Sid the psychopathic goat in the flock and made for him. I let him run to within a couple of metres of Sid and then hauled on the line. Poor Wellington spun around, just as the Dog Stop alarm fired off from Ed, a tin can with pebbles was thrown by me and worst of all he was attacked by Sid the goat. Sid looked dignified in danger and tried to head-butt the now depressed Wellington. We introduced the dogs to the rest of our attack-trained flock of sheep and I was able to give both dogs a clean bill of behavioural health. Certainly the relationship between them had settled down since Buster had been clearly appointed top dog, and given rights and privileges that were not shared with Wellington.

Besides Royalty and media folk, the other group of famous people our practice seems to attract is politicians. My first MP with a disturbed dog was Andrew Bowden, who came to see me when I still practised from our house with my wife as assistant. He brought Tammi, a little West Highland White Terrier bitch with a propensity for growling and snapping. Tammi was a 'rescue dog' who had been badly treated, regularly hit on the nose and inadequately fed during the early part of her life.

Andrew and his wife Benita adored Tammi and organized their lives around her needs, even with the hectic schedule imposed by British politics. A lesser man than Andrew might have bivouacked through the week in London and just come home to his wife and dog at the weekend. Not so Andrew, who commuted from Brighton whenever his political duties allowed so that he could be home for a late night or early morning walk with Tammi. Our job was to find out what it was that provoked Tammi's fears and made her growl.

We considered that her early mistreatment, combined with confinement, restraint, fear and frustration were the principal factors which made her lash out. Westies have a deserved reputation for being snappy: they are action dogs designed to catch and kill a rat faster than the poor rodent can extricate itself from danger. Tammi's behaviour was bound up with that inheritance, so we designed some gentle handling exercises. She was not even to be scolded for growling. I asked Andrew and Benita to soothe her until she stopped. Tammi's problems had only recently got worse so I did not want anyone to over-react to the situation, nor was there any need to limit the Bowdens' indulgences or to ask them to be unnaturally dominant. I also asked that Tammi be given a change of diet from a high protein tinned brand to a home-prepared low protein regime.

Tammi changed significantly under the impact of our therapy to the extent that after consulting their veterinary surgeon, Tony Cowie, the Bowdens decided to make her a mother. Vivienne and I were invited down to a dinner party to meet her offspring whom we diagnosed as adorable.

Andrew Bowden is a politician whose choice of political issues reflects his own deeply held convictions. Fortunately for animals, he passionately believes in the importance of pets to people and he actively protects the rights of all pets and pet owners in the House of Commons. He is a member of the National Advisory Panel of Pro-Dogs. He fought the introduction of Draconian control measures against dogs in Northern Ireland and an attempt by Dame Janet Foulkes MP and others to introduce dog registration and generally stricter limitation and control of dog ownership in the United Kingdom. Andrew believes pets bring out the best in people and that dog ownership is much more often a success than a failure and it should be neither unreasonably taxed nor discouraged.

Jim Lester, MP for Broxtowe, Nottinghamshire, also lets his beliefs about animals colour his political thinking. I first met Jim, his wife Merry Lyn and his daughter at a National Canine Defence League do, an animal charity for which he works as their parliamentary affairs adviser. They had brought along their Bearded Collie bitch Ziggy, who was agoraphobic. I was invited to visit Ziggy at home where her anxieties and neuroses would be more obvious than in a crowded, open-air setting.

Whilst Jim Lester was participating in a parliamentary welcome for the President of Italy, Roger Mugford was consulting with Ziggy. She was the hairy watchdog for a block of flats throughout the week, all the other residents being MPs and all except the Lesters dogless. Ziggy was liked by the inhabitants of the flats because of her cute looks and even more acute hearing. She barked only when there was a visitor or potential intruder: otherwise she was friends with everybody, and introduced a note of sanity and fun to the relatively high-stress occupation of being a politician. Ziggy disdained walks around the congested streets of Lambeth, an eccentricity that could be lived with since she could always do her business in the pocket-handkerchief garden.

Merry Lyn was the most conscientious of mistresses and after packing the kids off to school drove Ziggy five miles south to

Dulwich Park, for a scamper over the vastness of that wonderful urban green lung. The trouble was that Ziggy would go just so far, then freeze and scoot back to the car. If she couldn't find her own car, it could be any car. She had once leapt into the vehicle of a complete stranger and caused great embarrassment, eventually mirth. Regular dog walkers in Dulwich Park were justifiably amused that I was being consulted and awaited the outcome of my therapy with curious scepticism.

The treatment I chose was the simple system of behavioural 'flooding', using the well-established extending lead technique to force Ziggy across the boundary of some imaginary, fear-evoking precipice. The technique could not be used when she was off the lead because she might just bolt for home, through any number of dangers. Merry Lyn's voice had a tremendous effect upon Ziggy's behaviour: if she used a 'jolly hockey sticks' tone of voice Ziggy would usually respond positively and follow, but if her voice was either excessively firm or sympathetic, she would either take no notice or bolt. The various 'no-go' points in Dulwich Park were identified and approached, then crossed on a systematic basis during walks. We devised pleasant experiences for Ziggy at each place where previously she had been spooked, and she gradually overcame her fears.

As we were taking her through this process, Sam was haring around the park in joyful pursuit of birds, squirrels and assorted wildlife at the bottom of a particularly muddy pond. I was obliged to take a few embarrassing minutes out to recover my disgustingly mud-caked Setter and commit him in disgrace to the back of my car. One always hopes that Sam will be a perfect example of canine conformity in front of a famous client but he rarely pays me that compliment.

One odd feature of Ziggy's behaviour was that she would only turn to the left when being reluctantly taken for a walk. As coincidence would have it, some six years previously I had seen another Bearded Collie, who had exactly the same problem, even the same name! It is a breed that is extraordinarily prone to forming neurotic phobias, but the probability of finding two Bearded Collies with the same weird trait and name are remote in the extreme. I have never encountered this quirk in any other breed of dog but Beardies, who are known at the farm as 'Weirdie Beardies'.

Somehow I have also attracted a disproportionate number of pets belonging to Cabinet Ministers during the Eighties. Mrs Thatcher's own attitude to animals was established in my eyes when she was reported to have suggested rehoming the No. 10 Downing Street cat, Wilberforce, to Chequers with the excuse that, at sixteen years old, it was time he retired. Perhaps on the advice of her several animal-loving ministers, he stayed on at Downing Street to enjoy the lifestyle that he had always known.

The former Minister of Consumer Affairs, the Right Honourable Sally Oppenheim, is a Jack Russell freak, and consulted me years ago when her two young male terrorists, Spot and Snoopy, were experiencing temporary difficulties in adapting to London life after a Gloucestershire puppyhood. They grew up to become confident city types, popular members of the Regent's Park canine fraternity, with a fairly indulgent life at home.

Two years later I was called to see the Oppenheim Jack Russells again because they had taken to menacing certain large dogs in Regent's Park; they could quickly acquire the reputation of midget gangsters. Their manners had begun to deteriorate eighteen months before, when Spot was savagely attacked by a Weimaraner. Now other tall, Weimaraner-like canines were a potential target for the Oppenheim twins, on or off the lead, usually males, in city parks or rural Gloucestershire. Fortunately there had been no real damage or blood spilled amongst their victims but Mrs Oppenheim's concern was that they might one day get into trouble with the law or even be 'eaten up for breakfast' by a bigger dog. An MP can hardly afford to be emblazoned across the tabloid press as having imperfect dogs.

My second consultation was like a meeting of old friends, the dogs having fully indoctrinated their mistress into the right way to treat a Jack Russell. In her words, 'We only live with the dogs, they don't live with us.' My report was a long one, given the potential seriousness of the consequences. I explained my simple but reliable technique of recall training and of a hormonal treatment which might be a preliminary to surgical castration. I emphasized the importance of being strict in the dogs' management, enforcing all commands. I was dealing with such an indulgent character in Mrs Oppenheim that I knew that this would be particularly hard advice to follow. Finally, I equipped her with a Dog Stop alarm, which they were to fire off if the dog's attention needed to be grabbed. Snoopy, the top dog of the pair, urinated as he escorted me from their house: he was definitely not as impressed with animal psychology as his mistress.

A few days later I received a letter from Mrs Oppenheim telling me that Snoopy, the one with the brains, had had a run-in with a horse's hoof and the hoof had been harder than his head. It had been Snoopy and Spot who had run after the horse so the injuries were entirely self-inflicted. Snoopy had suffered concussion and probably a cracked skull, but he had proved the truth of the countryman's saying about Jack Russells: 'You only improve them by kicking'! I hasten to add that I disagree with this, but Snoopy did become a reformed character after recovering from his injuries. Since Spot was Snoopy's underling, it was likely that he no longer received underhand instructions to be a thug. Castration was permanently postponed and the dogs settled back to live happily amongst other dogs.

More recently Mrs Oppenheim told me that the personalities of Snoopy and Spot continue to evolve and that they have taken to indulging in bizarre sexual orgies in public. In summer 1990, their proud mistress entered them in a dog show at an agricultural fair in her Cotswolds constituency. In full view of too many people who knew that she was their owner, Spot and Snoopy proceeded to rape all around, whereupon the hapless exhibitor was requested over the public address system to remove the spectacle from view. Be sure that when your dogs let you down, they will choose the most embarrassing time possible.

The famous people I have mentioned are in most ways indistinguishable from my other clients apart from certain key elements in their lives. Being famous may place restrictions upon freedom of lifestyle because of legitimate concerns about security and privacy. The public expect famous people to be different, to be special, to be witty, to be busy, to be able to cope better than ordinary people and so on. In my experience, none of those differences really exist and the company of animals remains the greatest social leveller of them all.

11
Dogs at law

A woman's body had just been discovered and the only witness to her death was the dog she was walking at the time. I was given this information in a telephone call from Surrey Police Headquarters at Guildford. It was murder, but by whom? I was somewhat startled to be asked to make my way to the station 'for a conference'.

At Guildford Police Station I was greeted by an affable, overweight Detective Inspector who was heading the inquiry into the mysterious case of Glenys Coe. He seemed to know too much about me for comfort: he knew that I had said some critical things about Burmese cats at a lecture recently (I later discovered that he bred them!), and that I had spoken out against the use of police dogs to perform tricks like jumping through burning hoops to entertain the public at fêtes. What else did this man know about me? I had no reason to be anxious: it was his way of putting me at my ease, letting me know that he regarded me as a professional and ever so slightly flattering my ego. We were there to do a job of work, and quickly. The details of the case were explained to me by his colleague.

Glenys Coe was a young teacher, attractive, single, living alone but with at least two boyfriends: it wasn't certain whether each knew of the other's existence. The partially stripped body had been discovered a week earlier, on 29 August 1984, beside railway sidings near Guildford Station; the victim had been strangled and sexually assaulted. It was believed she died at around midnight, a time when she habitually took her Old English Sheepdog bitch Tara for a last walk of the day from her flat nearby. What was puzzling the police team was that her body bore scratch marks that seemed to have come from her own dog. The mystery deepened when the dog was found at home the next morning inside the apartment by one of her boyfriends, Mr X, who then raised the alarm about Glenys being unaccountably absent. Her body was discovered soon afterwards.

Because Tara was found in the flat, it was assumed that the murderer had taken the dog back after the crime, put her in the flat and then left. This could only have been done by someone known to the victim, and the boyfriends, Mr X in particular, became prime suspects. He had been interrogated for several days and insisted upon his innocence. The police had been unable to establish any motive for him to murder his girlfriend nor to have sexually assaulted her. Was it possible that Mr X had found out about the other man in Glenys's life?

I asked where I came into the case. The question was put to me: why should a dog attack its own mistress? Would Tara walk back with a stranger to be let into her apartment; indeed would she have gone off with a stranger at all? Was there any way we could 'get inside' Tara's mind and find some clue as to what she had witnessed and done just before the death of her mistress? I discounted the latter, protesting that I was not a latterday Dr Doolittle who could get Tara to speak up! However, I explained that I had great faith in the consistency or honesty with which dogs respond to repeated stimuli and situations. Could we, I asked, run a mock-up of the murder, using actors, and film the proceedings so that we could closely study Tara's reactions? This drew an enthusiastic response from the police team and we planned on setting up our grisly experiment the next day. I requested that the whole proceedings be videoed and photographed and that I have the assistance of at least one policewoman. Tara had been looked after by a former boyfriend of Glenys Coe in the week after her death, and the dog had formed a close attachment to him. I requested that he and the WPC be the 'victims' in the mock murder to follow.

Three days later, we gathered at the railway station during the afternoon, not at night because of the difficulties this might cause in recording Tara's reactions on film. I was taken to Glenys Coe's home, a neat ground-floor maisonette with Habitat furniture, trendy cushions, a Marilyn Monroe poster, piles of exercise books from her pupils and assorted keep-fit gear. Tara's needs were well catered for: biscuits, tinned dog food, bowl, combs and a cute hand-made quilt for her to lie on beside Glenys's bed. I left feeling much affected by the tragedy that had befallen this lady, but the visit had provided me with a useful first insight into what we should do in the experiment to come.

I said I would prefer not to meet Tara until after all our preparations were complete. I wanted her to be taken along the track last walked by Glenys Coe, across a wide expanse of cinder, up a bank and into the thick grass where she was believed to have been attacked and raped. The police believed that Glenys was then dragged back to the railway siding across the cinders, a distance of about a hundred metres, and that she was probably murdered there. The scratches from Tara's claws were impregnated with cinder dust, so the police surmised that they were inflicted during these last few moments of her life.

There was another mystery about this awful incident. When Tara was found in the flat, she had heavy grease patches around her muzzle and elsewhere on her head. She may have ingested some of it and the vet who had examined Tara was asked whether a dog was likely to lick grease. His opinion was the same as mine, that dogs usually hate petroleum products. I was asked to demonstrate and prove the point by the conscientious Detective Inspector.

It seemed to me that we had three priorities. The first, and this was my role, was to establish Tara's reactions to her owner or friend when she was attacked by a stranger. Secondly, we needed to see what Tara made of the heavy grease that had been left behind by railway workmen, and finally, we had to determine whether Tara could possibly have let herself back into the house without human assistance. By now, a fair crowd of police had gathered at the scene and they were asked to stand back so that we could begin our trials. The video camera was in place, and Tara was brought to the scene, her first visit since the murder two weeks before. Would she show any signs of fear and run off, or be the usual bold Tara at a place she had been to on hundreds of previous occasions. She seemed happy and showed no particular interest in the point where Glenys's body had been found. Then she walked on up the bank to the point where her owner had been first attacked. Remarkably, she sniffed at that spot then urinated upon it; perhaps a chemical sign of possession and awareness of her former mistress's presence.

The former boyfriend, Tara's present caretaker, was instructed to retrace Glenys's last steps with Tara at his side. Right on cue, I leapt out of the bushes, kitted out in my thick Barbour jacket in case Tara decided to attack me. The ex-boyfriend screamed, pretending to put up resistance, whereupon the most extraordinary thing happened. Instead of attacking me, Tara attacked the boyfriend. She leaped up, barking hysterically, tail wagging, treating the whole event as a boisterous game rather than a terrifying drama. When standing on her hind legs, Tara was almost as tall as us, and the way she scraped at the boyfriend's clothing fully accounted for the scratches on

Glenys Coe's body. I emerged from the brief encounter unscathed but satisfied with what we had learned about Tara's behaviour.

We then enlisted the WPC to replay the role because of her uncanny similarity to Glenys Coe. Tara attached herself to the policewoman, but again became excited and joined in when she struggled or screamed.

I often have to stage mock attacks upon the owners of my canine patients whilst investigating the role of victims in eliciting territorial attacks. Usually it is German Shepherds or Rottweilers that are the subject of litigation between the owner and the victim of a dog bite. On only two previous occasions had the test dog attacked the owner rather than the villain (myself) and in each case his behaviour was directed by cries from the owner. Indeed, my own dear Sam will do this as a party piece if I leap about screaming.

I concluded that poor Glenys cried out when she was attacked, but that her screams did not bring her the help she needed. The police team were pleased with the results of our experiment, which had gone according to plan and more or less confirmed their hunches. Now, what about the grease? An old tub of grease had been found partially filled with water by the railway sidings. Chemical analysis showed that the grease on Tara came from the same tub; had it been smeared on her or had she contaminated herself? The vet who examined Tara on the day after the murder was certain that it must have been done deliberately. I produced two clean saucers on which to conduct an impromptu preference test. One was smeared with grease then covered with milk, the second just had the milk. Tara confounded all predictions by first drinking from the greased saucer, then from the clean one, eventually licking both clean.

The police team were beginning to get bored and I suggested that only the former boyfriend, my Detective Inspector friend and the film cameraman return to the house, to look more closely at how Tara might or might not have let herself into the maisonette. The front door was on a strong self-closure spring of the sort used on fire doors in hotels or offices. It had seemed to the police that the spring was too strong for Tara to have operated on her own, and that someone must have pushed it open for her. They had already determined from both boyfriends that it was Glenys's habit not to slam her front door locked because she was given to losing the Yale key and was afraid of being shut out all night. She had not been worried about being the victim of violent crime. I watched as Tara walked in and out of the open door, then we closed it and encouraged her to push it aside. The former boyfriend was in the house, Tara and I were outside. She just shoved her nose into my face and licked my ears. I fell over laughing. I asked the boyfriend to call her, and eventually she squeezed the door open with her snout and went in. I then had to try and establish how a frightened Tara might have reacted when confronted with the closed door. I activated an ultrasonic bleeper behind her which had the effect of making her dash through it. This time it slammed closed behind her and had she been a dog with a tail it would most certainly have been trapped. But we had proved that there was sufficient energy in the self-closing mechanism for the door to lock itself, thus resolving the apparent mystery of the dog being alone in the house the next morning behind a locked door.

It was an important new angle for the police, who had not considered this possibility. My view was that Tara must have been under great pressure, even terrified, to have pushed through that door. Of course, the alternative possibility was that the boyfriend had put Tara back and closed the door himself before returning later to raise the alarm. I was told that there was other evidence to incriminate Mr X and that he would continue to be held in police custody. However, Tara's evidence had been most useful in exercising the detectives' minds about possible alternative killers.

I didn't hear anything more about this inquiry for months, and I was curious to know what had happened, so I telephoned Guildford police. They said that they continued to believe that he was guilty of the crime. In all probability, they told me, it would be coming to trial and I would be required to appear as a witness. But that is not what happened. A man was later arrested in Essex on a rape charge and during police interrogation admitted to the murder of Glenys Coe. He had been working in Surrey, near Guildford, had watched her leaving her house to walk the dog, and followed her. He admitted to having raped and murdered her before driving away. Confirming the results of our behavioural experiment, he had not put Tara back in the flat: she had run away and let herself back in.

Poor Mr X had been held in prison for almost a year on suspicion of a murder he did not commit. The case is still unresolved, and likely to come before the courts as a civil action over wrongful imprisonment.

A few years passed after this, during which I was involved in cases of someone suing someone else over a dog at least once a week. However, none of them were quite so shocking as the Guildford case. Then matters took a dramatic turn with a call from the West

Midlands Police, about a woman who had been seriously injured after being raped in Handsworth, Birmingham. It was explained to me that the case involved quite horrible mutilation of the victim Mrs M, who at the time was accompanied by her Staffordshire Bull Terrier dog. Would I please attend to examine the dog and advise them on its behaviour? I didn't dare ask too many questions of the caller, because I already felt quite ill at the prospect of what I would be required to do. I took along a colleague, Stephen Corben, who had just joined our practice, thinking that this would be a good chance for him to find out whether or not he really had made the right career move.

Handsworth Police Station is a barn of a place, with high ceilings, bare walls and long corridors. There was no hint of art or humour to leaven the stress that those who work in the building undoubtedly experience. I was given only the briefest outline of the criminal charges laid against two men who were being held for the attempted murder of Mrs M: to know too much might have coloured my interpretation of the behaviour of the dog. They wanted to know whether it was likely that Mrs M's dog would have torn at her body and eaten her skin and flesh whilst she was unconscious. The accused men had admitted to raping Mrs M but had claimed that her subsequent injuries were caused by the dog. We left to visit Mr M and his dog in sombre mood.

Mr and Mrs M lived in a neat brick-built terraced house in a road like a film set for Coronation Street. We were introduced to a shy, friendly Irishman, and literally bowled over by his enthusiastic fat Staffie dog Skipper. When I explained who I was and that we had just come to do some tests on his dog, Mr M relaxed. I had been warned not to say too much about the case in front of him, since at that stage he did not know about the horrible treatment his wife had suffered. It was painful information he had no need of at that time, just a week after the crime. We were invited to sit on the settee and Skipper overwhelmed us with his podgy little body and warm licks. He acted like a puppy, though he was eight years old and extremely overweight.

I took the detailed history. Skipper had been bought by Mrs M as a present for her husband from a breeder in Birmingham. He really only enjoyed eating meat and scarcely ever ate anything else. He liked exercise, though he was a bit 'iffy' with other dogs. Mr M understood the tendency of Staffies to get into fights and never permitted or encouraged him to threaten other dogs. Skipper was a keen walker, though currently he suffered from arthritis which was being treated by his vet with Butediazole. I was interested in his physical health and suggested we go for a brief walk. It was also a good excuse for me to get some fresh air as I felt a touch of nausea coming on.

Poor Mr M most definitely did not know the whole story of the attack upon his wife, believing she had been raped and that the physical injuries she had received were relatively minor ones. He told how she had returned to bang on the front door late at night, then collapsed in his arms. He noticed a little blood, but had inquired no further before an ambulance took her to hospital. Mrs M had been seen by her husband earlier the same morning, before he left for work. He knew she had a weakness for the bottle and imagined she had gone drinking with friends after the pubs closed in the afternoon. She was prone to doing this, falling asleep in an alcoholic haze and returning later in the evening.

The walk with Skipper and Mr M was uneventful, but I took some photographs and complimented him on the dog's fitness and fine looks. Skipper was all eyes on any passing dog so I gave routine advice on how that unwelcome habit might usefully be curbed. But that was not the purpose of my visit and we returned home for the all-important tests. My colleague Stephen produced some fresh butcher's meat, which he offered to Skipper.

Skipper grabbed it precisely, skilfully avoiding Stephen's fingers. My turn next, and I held the meat between finger and thumb for Skipper to drag from me. He showed no aggression or frustration at this, but gently and persistently dragged at the meat until he had extracted it from my hand. The final phase was to cup the meat into my hands, with only the smell of blood to direct his struggles. Struggle he did, but always gently. He nudged my hands, looking appealingly at me. Then he tried gentle pawing, but not enough to scratch me. Finally, he took to nibbling between my hands and fingers, never bruising or hurting me. Here was a dog highly motivated to recover meat, with every reason to bite into my hands and recover what was his. But remarkably, his proprioceptive or touch-receptors on tongue, lips and gums were so sensitive that he knew just how far to go without breaking my skin. A millimetre further or a little more pressure and he would have broken into my flesh and done what he was alleged to have done to his mistress on the night of her rape. But I was now certain that Skipper had not damaged his mistress and all present were most relieved to hear my conclusion.

The significance of this test was that the two men accused of Mrs

M's attempted murder could no longer use the Skipper story in their defence. There was every reason to suppose that Skipper would eat chunks of human tissue thrown to him, from his mistress or from any other source, since meat is just meat. However, he had proved that he would not have ripped it from her live body.

A further component of the men's defence was that Skipper joined in their sexual activities and that they had had difficulty in restraining him from doing so. I chose my words delicately as I asked Mr M about Skipper's sexual proclivities. He explained that Skipper was not sexy and had never known a lady dog. I asked if he would mind if I tried to prove the point. Permission granted, we stimulated Skipper's penis manually, but there was no interest: this dog was so overweight and food orientated that sex took a low priority.

The case came to trial in July 1989, nine months after my visit. Courtrooms are usually awesome places, but the Crown Court at Birmingham is a remarkably attractive building that tempers the horror of the tales told within. At this stage I still did not know the whole story behind the two men who were on trial, because expert witnesses like me cannot listen to the proceedings until they have been called to give evidence themselves. When my time came I was led in to the courtroom and shown to the witness stand. I noticed two untidy-looking men in the dock. I had given evidence in Court on many previous occasions but this was certainly the most frightening: after all I was participating in a process which might deny these men their freedom for many years. It was important that my evidence, though only a small part of a larger story, be offered accurately and without prejudice.

My ordeal in the witness box lasted for an hour in which I explained my background, qualifications, what we had done with Skipper, our interpretation of the results and so on. After a basically sympathetic line of questioning from the barrister for the prosecution, there came much more hostile questioning from Counsel for the Defence. First my professional qualifications were queried, then I was asked how I could possibly claim to read the mind of a dog. I was handed photographs of Mrs M's abdomen, showing the mutilation, and asked to comment upon the details of injury. I was told to look closer, and in all some dozen photographs in gory technicolour were placed before me. The courtroom was silent as I went through this hideous pack of photos.

I was then asked by the Counsel for the Defence whether or not I thought these injuries could have been caused by a dog. I replied that I was certain they could not, that the line of injury to the abdomen was too neat: dogs tend to grab and tear at their prey and leave untidy puncture wounds with strips of flesh remaining. I was having to examine evidence of a brutally scientific carve-up by a person, not the actions of the chaotic Staffordshire Bull Terrier that I had examined. Despite more and more hostile questioning on this point, I did not concede that Skipper could have been involved in injuring his mistress in any way, though I did admit that he would probably have licked his mistress's wounds and ingested blood and tissue if these were detached from her body.

I couldn't understand the significance of this line of questioning until afterwards, when I spoke to a detective outside the courtroom. He explained that a police surgeon who had examined Mrs M after her attack stated that scratches on her buttocks could possibly have been caused by a dog's teeth. I asked whether the distance between these scratches had been measured. They had, and were spaced differently from the distance between Skipper's canine teeth. The police and another forensic surgeon agreed with me that Skipper had nothing to do with Mrs M's injuries.

Skipper's role turned out to have been vital to the case and the next day Kuljinder Bhachu and Harbhajan Mahil were found guilty of rape, indecent assault and causing grievous bodily harm with intent. The Judge found them guilty of acts of 'abominable depravity' and sentenced them to a joint total of thirty-one years. Tough punishment for a ghastly crime.

I had met Mr M at the Court. He had been steadily rebuilding his life with his wife when she had suddenly collapsed and died in March, just six months after the rape. Her death was not directly connected with the injuries she had sustained in Handsworth. She had gone to Ireland for a funeral and had imbibed too much during the wake: her kidneys could no longer take the strain. Meanwhile, Mr M spoke fondly of Skipper and of the comfort he had been in the awful year just past. Members of his local community in Handsworth, Irish, English and Asian alike, had all been wonderful to him, supportive to the end. Whereas a lesser man without such social support would have become depressed and lonely, this man seemingly went about life as normal, resuming his job as an interior decorator, going for walks with Skipper – but never into a pub.

The reader will be forgiven for thinking by now that I only represent the police, the forces acting for law and order. However, in forensic work that is not always so, and I have to do my honest best for whoever appoints me.

The case of Hyke, an American Pit Bull Terrier, found me on the other side because his owner, my client, Ivan Dume, had the police ranged against him, with a charge of assault with intent to cause grievous bodily harm to a policeman. I was asked by the solicitor acting for Mr Dume to assess Hyke's temperament and to determine how he would have reacted when he was confronted by policemen in a raid on his owner's flat.

At this time, 1986, American Pit Bull Terriers were just becoming a part of the South London underworld scene. From a brief telephone conversation with Mr Dume's solicitors, it sounded at first as though I might be working for a less-than-deserving cause. However, I kept my prejudices to myself and duly drove to a vast council estate in Clapham. I was accompanied by a somewhat nervous solicitor as we ascended the bare and seedy stairways to the fourth floor and Mr Dume's flat.

Hyke had heard us coming the moment we entered the building and his barking echoed down the uncarpeted chamber. Daytime visitors were uncommon and it was obvious that Hyke provided a protective look-out function for the other residents: front doors on to the landing opened a crack and curtains moved in the flats opposite. On the fourth floor, I found a cheap, 1950s green panelled door, much splintered, jemmied and patched, presumably from the altercation with the police two weeks earlier. As we reached the last flight of steps, the door opened and Ivan Dume invited us in, with Hyke straining at the leash to do who knew what to us. He stopped barking and just fixed us with small beady eyes, mouth in a wide panting grin, tail wagging. His body language could have meant anything: friendliness or imminent attack. I could feel myself being pushed forward by the now petrified solicitor, who was keen to bring up the rear; after all, I was the expert, this was my moment. Ivan told me not to worry about a thing; that Hyke liked me because I was introduced as a friend and, as soon as I sat down and had been sniffed over, we would become inseparable.

His predictions were correct. The moment I sat down in an armchair, Hyke walked all over me, sniffed every detail of my clothing and licked my face. I had carried titbits with the idea of making friends, but in the anxiety of the moment I had quite forgotten to produce them. Hyke found them for me and nearly tore my jacket apart by shoving his head into my pocket. The solicitor laughed self-consciously and marvelled at my confidence. If only he knew. I had already had a detailed statement forwarded to me by him, which nearly said it all:

'My full name is Ivanhoe Constantine Tolisford Dume. My date of birth is 8th May 1955. I have been charged, I think, with causing grievous bodily harm to a policeman by setting my dog on him. I will plead not guilty.

'The series of incidents which led to my arrest really started when my wife, Winifred Dume, and I had a serious argument. That was three or four days before my arrest. The police were called on that occasion. There was a great deal of shouting which ended with my wife packing her belongings and property. She then made some sarcastic remarks which set tempers going. I started unpacking her things. The eldest child and the two younger children were there at the time. I wasn't getting any answers from them so I lost my temper. I told her that if she took anything I would smash everything up. We were shouting at each other. She can generally outshout me. I picked up a baseball bat and started smashing crockery and plates which had been placed in a box. I threatened her with the bat, but I had no real intention of striking her. I then calmed down a bit because I realized that I wasn't getting anywhere. I went out of the front door and sat on the balcony cooling off a bit. Then I saw a van arrive and a whole lot of police coming up. I believe they were telephoned by the eldest child, who had gone down the drainpipe to do so. I returned inside the flat and closed the front door which I had opened to let myself out on to the landing. I was still holding the baseball bat.

'The police came up and knocked on the door. They asked me to let them in. I told them to go away because it had nothing to do with them. I said that nobody was being hurt and that there was no call for the police. The police then asked my wife if she wanted them to break the door down and come in and she said no. She was standing next to me. I heard the police outside with one of the children asking if my wife and I were married or were we common law husband and wife etc. I think at one stage my wife certainly did ask me to open the door and I said no.

'The policemen asked my wife to move away from the door, "luv". Then they started kicking the door down. I had my left shoulder against the door, I think. I was half leaning against the door and half facing it trying to keep the door shut. I had the baseball bat in my right hand. Then the door started coming in. I realized that I could not stop them. I leaped back to avoid being crushed against the wall by the door and went back down the corridor still carrying the baseball bat. The dog, Hyke, leaped out through the door at the police. Hyke is a good watchdog. He will normally not allow anyone through the door unless a member of the household is with him. Hyke must have been behind me while all this was going on. I didn't see him and I don't recall whether he was barking or not. There was a lot of noise and I may not have noticed it because Hyke often barks even if you knock on the door let alone try to kick it in.

'As I moved the dog went towards the police and out of the door. I didn't see what happened. The dog went through a gap in the door and went outside. There was a lot of commotion and I heard someone say "Get the dog off him" or something like that. I said nothing to the dog at all. I think he attacked them. I went back to the door and opened it to call the dog back in. The police were in a circle beating and kicking the dog. He could not move at all. I had the baseball bat in my hand. I swore at the police and told them to leave the dog alone. One of them shouted something like "Get the shields in there." I was calling the dog but he couldn't move because every time he did so he was beaten. Then the police rushed towards me. I ran back into the front room. They followed with shields in front and batons raised. I remember rushing for an ornamental sword which was in the corner of the room. I had intended hanging it up. It is not a sharp sword but was pointed. It does not have an edge. By the time I turned round I was overborne by numerous police. I was flung backwards across a couch which smashed, and was pinned down. There were large numbers of police on top of me. I did not have a chance to struggle. The house was full of policemen. I heard one of them say "You black bastard, I'll give you setting a dog on a policeman," and I felt a blow over the head. I remember feeling hot all over and I think I blacked out. I was getting kicked and batonned. The reason I think I blacked out was because the next thing I knew I was face down on the floor with my hands cuffed behind me. I was being kicked about the body and felt a kick to the face. I was struck on the left ankle and on the shin. The police lifted me up and took me outside. I was put on the floor of the van and one PC placed his foot in the base of my back and pushed me against the seat railings. I was taken to Clapham Police Station. I was not interviewed but did see my solicitor.

'I was mostly shocked at the way things had developed. I was doing no injury to anyone, although I realize that my behaviour might have been frightening. I never struck any of the policemen and definitely did not set the dog on them.'

As you will gather, my client was in serious difficulty, because to be charged with causing grievous bodily harm to a policeman is a major offence usually punished by a spell in prison. Did Hyke attack the policeman on command from his master or was he just naturally territorial? The fact that we visitors had a relatively uneventful first meeting with Hyke tended to support the police case that this dog was a trained guard dog acting on commands. It was my job to establish how much control Ivan did or did not have over Hyke.

It quickly became clear that he had almost none. Hyke developed an instant and overwhelming passion for me and began to mount my legs. I was uncertain about pushing him away and laughing commands from his master had no effect whatsoever. When Hyke grabbed my jacket to obtain a better grip on my knee I felt that enough was enough, and anxiously requested that he be extracted. He had to be lifted away bodily, by Ivan holding his thick studded leather collar and his tail. Hyke then turned his amorous attentions to the luckless solicitor, making rather obvious thrusting movements in the region of his armpits. Again, Ivan was the saviour!

We went outside to continue our observations. I learned that Hyke was basically a free-roamer of the neighbourhood, able to take himself off to the nearby Clapham Common across the horrendously busy A3 road, and he always returned unscathed. Everybody seemed to know Hyke: he was a local celebrity. Children we passed on the estate smiled and said, 'Right on', 'Be good to that dog' and so on. The story about Hyke had travelled on the community grapevine and there was no doubt as to which side was favoured, Ivan's rather than that of the police. Hyke was just then making sexual advances to a lady's small Poodle and I suggested that it might be sensible to call him away. Ivan called and called to a seemingly deaf dog. We put him on the lead and he pulled in this and that direction – clearly leads were an unaccustomed experience for Hyke. I even tried to have him sit at the kerb: I gave the command then offered a titbit. Hyke just leapt up to grab the food from my hand!

I concluded that Ivan was truthful in his testimony about Hyke: this was an untrained dog and I could see no way that he might either encourage or stop him in the act of attacking somebody entering his property. I had to be sure on this last point, so I asked Ivan to keep Hyke on a lead whilst I came along and attempted to attack his master. I rushed towards Ivan and pushed him by the shoulders, dragged him by an arm and pretended to hit him. I was amazed at the speed with which Hyke collected himself and changed from a mood of apparently good-natured tolerance to one of homicide. Fortunately, I was ready for him, and hopped sideways rather than backwards. He cruised past me like a spent missile, giving me time to freeze and throw titbits in his direction. We were soon back to being friends again. Ivan then told me how serious were the injuries the policeman had suffered from Hyke: he had been badly bitten around his genitals and his calf muscles were seriously damaged. Small wonder that the police were angry – though by now I was certain they were wrong to bring a prosecution against Ivan.

I prepared my report, which simply described what I had seen and emphasized that I did not believe the account of the incident which had been given by the police. Hyke was too undisciplined to attack on command: he was simply an excitable, territorial American Pit Bull Terrier with formidable jaws. I did not reveal my misgivings about the casual way in which Hyke was owned and permitted to run around the neighbourhood. Ivan told me that after he was arrested by the police, no efforts were made to secure his flat against burglars or to find the dog. They just walked away, leaving the house open and Hyke homeless. I thought the case was fairly clear-cut and didn't doubt that justice would prevail.

Ivan's case came up six months later and, remarkably, he was found guilty. I had not been asked to give evidence personally at the trial and Hyke's side of the story only came from my two-page report. The solicitor acting for Ivan was surprised and distressed because he, too, had come to like his client and believed in his innocence. Chaotic though he was, unlucky in life though he had been, Ivan was also a decent person trying to get his life together after a deprived childhood. I phoned Ivan's girlfriend, Karen, to express my distress at Ivan's imprisonment. She was going to see him in Wandsworth Prison and promised to pass on my support and friendship. Meanwhile, could I possibly do the family a favour by offering Hyke a home, as he was becoming too much for them to handle without Ivan?

I put it to my wife Vivienne, who looked at our daughters Ruth and Emily and gave a definite but well justified 'No'! 'Aren't you getting too wrapped up in this case?' Vivienne asked. She was right, of course: in spite of myself, I had become emotionally as well as professionally involved. I could not help thinking that if I, a white Englishman, had been in Ivan's position the courts would have treated me more leniently than they had treated him. Ivan's choice of breed may not have been ideal for his circumstances but he was kind and well-intentioned towards his dog.

I phoned Karen back and gave her the bad news, but promised

to try to find Hyke a temporary home with the National Canine Defence League, who provide a service for prisoners whose pets need boarding. This is one of the several valuable services which this charitable organization provides for dogs in distress. I was to meet Karen the next Monday, and we would take Hyke to the NCDL Petersfield kennels for the eighteen months that Ivan would be locked up. Hyke's welfare was apparently causing him a great deal of worry.

Monday afternoon came but no Karen. I phoned the solicitor to inquire what might be the problem. He told me that Ivan had just been released on bail pending an appeal. Thankfully, the case was eventually dismissed and the sentence quashed. After eight sobering days in Wandsworth, Ivan was once more out and about with his dog.

That Christmas, we had a lovely card from Ivan and Hyke, from a new address. I went to see them and found that he had moved in with Karen and her children. Hyke was looking just fabulous. His wide leather collar had been exchanged for a brass-decorated leather body harness, and his muscles rippled under the sheen of a perfect black coat. Ivan was in good shape too. He had resumed his former job as a swimming-pool attendant and saw no more of his wife. There was much back-slapping and mutual congratulations as I left, but I was struck by his complete absence of bitterness towards the police and our system of justice. He was sorry that a policeman had been hurt but carried on with life as usual: a survivor no matter what misfortunes life throws at him.

Quite often it is not a person who is on trial, but a dog. I have now been involved in many such cases and they are always fascinating. I only ever give evidence if I am quite certain that the charges are unjust, that the dog is not a continuing danger to society and that it should be allowed to live out its natural life. That was certainly my view of Billy Jones, a remarkable English Bull Terrier from Enfield, Middlesex. Billy had only one enemy in the world: the neighbour's miniature Yorkshire Terrier. The feud between the two dogs had been going on for almost eighteen months, since Billy was a puppy. The Yorkshire Terrier regularly barked and snapped at him and sometimes physically attacked him. Eventually, Billy grew up to be a big Bull Terrier and began to bark back at the Yorkshire Terrier. On one occasion the worm in Billy turned, landing him and his owners in court.

As on several previous occasions, the Yorkshire Terrier had escaped from its house and attacked Billy, who was on his lead in the street. The little dog was injured as Billy picked it up in his gigantic jaws, but this time the Yorkshire recovered sufficiently to fight yet another day. That day came in August 1989, when Billy escaped through the front door into the street, where he attacked and killed the Yorkie. Mr and Mrs Jones were definitely not to blame: they had always shown a conscientious attitude towards controlling Billy, but on this occasion builders had left the front door open.

Billy's case was due to be heard at Enfield Magistrates Court in February 1990 and we had less than a month in which to prepare his defence. I invited them to visit the farm, where we would put Billy through his paces. He met Sam, he met Jasper and everybody in the office fell for him. He was quite the most social dog we had seen for many a week, and my colleague Elizabeth, who is mad about Bull Terriers, would happily have kidnapped him. Billy was all power but no malice, tail wagging and eyes searching for mischief. He was an excellent specimen of his breed, tri-coloured with an eye-patch, and a frequent winner at dog shows. Most of all, I was struck by the caring attitude of Mr and Mrs Jones towards Billy, who to them was a child, a friend and more. They had no children of their own, though there were lots of nephews and nieces who were also in love with Billy but never endangered by him.

I wrote an impressive (I thought) report detailing the various tests we had performed with Billy on cats, poultry, dogs and people, and how he had passed them all with flying colours. I emphasized the importance of Billy to the happiness of his owners, the pleasure that he gave to them and to others. I explained that a feud had been going on between these two dogs and that sadly, with the imbalance of body weights, the smaller dog had not survived a duel which had occurred outside the reasonable control of his owners. It was a terrible accident and in future Billy would be kept on a lead at all times. I concluded that there was really no need to issue a destruction order against him.

The police were being encouraged to make an example of Billy and were pressing for the maximum penalty, death, because the case came within the scope of the 1989 Dangerous Dogs Act. This legislation significantly strengthened the courts' powers to deal with violent dogs, and at the same time there was a strident press campaign highlighting a succession of awful cases in which large dogs had attacked people and animals. Billy could not have chosen a worse time to tangle with his Yorkie neighbour.

February 8th 1990 was the first day of Crufts Dog Show, where I was running a dotty dog clinic for charity, but I also had to be in Enfield Court at 2.30 p.m. With difficulty I beat the traffic from Earls Court across London, arriving in the nick of time. There were crowds of witnesses and defendants blocking the corridors in what is obviously prime time for prosecutions. Eventually, I found the Joneses huddled in conference with their solicitor. It seemed as though half their street had turned out in support of Billy, along with their supportive veterinary surgeon, Moira Wilson. It was she who had first put the Joneses on to me, thinking that a character statement from me would help Billy when his case came up. The only character missing was Billy himself.

We knew that something strange was going on. There was much discussion between the police prosecutor and the solicitor acting for the Joneses. The defence lawyers were demanding an adjournment on the grounds that the police had brought their prosecution under criminal legislation, when it should have been a civil charge. Everyone agreed that there was no question of the Joneses intending that their dog should attack and kill the little Yorkshire Terrier. The police solicitor had to leave and take advice from higher authority. We were left waiting for an hour, the tension wearing down Billy's anxious owners and friends. At long last the prosecutor returned and conceded the point. Remarkably, Billy was a free dog!

It was a close-run thing, only on the legal technicality of the case being 'out of time'. The police have six months in which to bring any prosecution and in this instance Billy was saved by two days: there was no possibility of their bringing fresh charges. There was a party that evening in Enfield and the Joneses received piles of mad, Spuds Mackenzie cards by way of congratulations. I telephoned them the other day, just to be sure that Billy hadn't committed any more crimes. He has not re-offended, and he continues to be a friendly entertainer to everybody he meets. Mrs Jones is expecting their first baby and looks forward to the event without any anxieties about what Billy might do. Justice was done.

The present government is proposing to strengthen the law regarding the control and care of dogs and perhaps this is justified by present circumstances. Meanwhile our society is becoming increasingly litigious, people are less tolerant of their neighbours and less prepared to accept that accidents do happen from time to time and that sometimes they involve an animal. Accordingly, more dog owners sue other dog owners because they have been bitten in a dog fight, sue their veterinary surgeon because their 'valuable' show dog died under anaesthesia during a traumatic caesarian operation, or sue their neighbour because his dog barks at six in the morning.

I may or may not sympathize with the appellants in such cases but I have to do my best for them and their dogs when called upon. These days, I am asked to give evidence on behalf of the dog who is accused of a crime as often as for a person who has been bitten, injured or inconvenienced by a dog. Cases are now numbering one a week and a new scientific discipline, forensic animal behaviour, is well-established in legal circles.

12
The perils of pedigree

It is not so tough to breed dogs: they have conducted their sex lives without human assistance for a good long time now. It has always seemed to me that the main challenge for breeders is to *stop* their animals from breeding too frequently or with the wrong partner. Dogs are usually so promiscuous that a 'successful' mating can't be all that difficult, or do much for the self-esteem of owners, even if they do style themselves as 'professional breeders'. By contrast, the breeder of a rare Amazonian Parrot or a near-extinct butterfly must feel tremendous satisfaction that they have pulled off the job successfully. For dog breeders, the payoff has to lie simply in producing better puppies than those that have gone before.

I have always had a strong respect for the way in which natural selection has matched wild animals to their environment: evolution always maximizes 'fitness' in the natural world. How can man improve upon natural selection? Essentially, only by playing at God, and especially when trying to breed better dogs. There is certainly an enormous moral and philosophical responsibility to be borne by those engaged in 'the sport' of dog breeding. I use the term 'sport' because it is so widely used by the dog-show enthusiasts, though it is not a word I like. To me, it implies that breeders are somehow doing it for fun, that their satisfaction is of greater importance than the production of viable, healthy progeny who will go on to bring happiness to their prospective owners.

My main concern is to bring about an improvement in the role that dogs play as companions to human beings. I am not alone in this view: most dog breeders whom I encounter sincerely claim to share these aims and do not willingly or knowingly produce physical or mental weirdos. The fact is, however, that the technicalities of genetics are so complex and the organization of the dog-breeding and showing fraternity so chaotic that mistakes do happen. There is no central authority governing the world of showing and breeding dogs, and the Kennel Club argue that their responsibility is principally to maintain a register of dogs – a stud book.

In my opinion the future of an individual breed of dog should rest with the members of a dedicated breed club in each country. The problem is that these clubs are usually organized along fairly democratic lines, and as in all democracies no one person may possess the power that is necessary to take the hard decisions that are needed. The official breed standards often represent the lowest common denominator of agreement that can be achieved between members of a club, and the only physical attribute on which one can be confident of unanimous agreement is that 'male animals should have apparently normal testicles fully descended into the scrotum'. Rarely is there a professional geneticist on hand to guide the selection programme for breeds: it is entirely dictated by amateurish, if well-meaning judges, applying their particular fashion to animals they encounter in the show ring.

Personally, I find dog shows repetitive and starved of action, with little to entertain except the bizarre habits and expressions of the judges as they peer into eyes, count teeth and grab the poor animals' scrotums to ensure that they contain the requisite number of testicles. On such occasions I often find myself wishing that the whole process could be mechanized, so that the dogs could be left at home to splash about in muddy ponds or chase seagulls. However, one of my punishments in life is to attend dog shows and I never miss the annual jamboree that is Crufts Dog Show, where I man an advice centre for exhibitors and any other dog lover who comes along. After attending a number of shows it became clear to me that the more candid of breeders were finding behavioural problems in their dogs that were similar to those I was treating in pets of the same breed. Conversations with the breeders of my patients justified a cynical view that 'good temperament comes from good breeding' and 'bad behaviour is caused by bad owners'. How, I wondered, could I get at the truth, which probably lay somewhere in the middle of these extremes, and how could I use my speciality to help judges at dog shows select in favour of better behaviour?

I wanted to devise a simple test that measured aspects of canine personality in a practical way and which related to the behaviour of pet dogs. I also wanted to be fairly scientific in my approach, so that others could repeat the trials at other shows and in other countries, to confirm or deny my conclusions. The year was 1984

Above: Therapy for Dick in the Bois de Boulogne, with an amused audience on the bench

Right: Dr Patrick Payancé and Strychnine: do as I say, not as I do!

Left: Rules consistently applied by the Queen.
Above: The Windsor dogs – adoration of a lady who knows about canine psychology (*Sir Geoffrey Shakerley*)

Above: On the streets, poor dogs and children in Baltimore, USA. My friends had immense pride of possession in a world where pride is a rare commodity

Below: Professor Joseph van Heeren playing cool with African Wild Dogs

Above: After our escape – the dogs regretting that Mugford is not on the menu today

Dogs in rural Africa and at a coal yard in Soweto. The dogs have a life no easier than that of their people

Right: Litmus, a Yorkie in charge of Bill and Ben: an overwhelming smell of urine pervades this spot

Below: Daley and Thompson, agoraphobic Labradors in harness to Mugford and Erica: the struggle is over

Above: Maurice, a Boxer with an inconsolable fear of thunder, for whom ear plugs were the simplest and most practical solution

Left: Bella, formerly afraid of garbage trucks, now desensitized

at Crufts, and I was fortunate in having the able assistance of a young psychologist, Amita Senn-Gupta.

We could not walk into the show ring and conduct our tests, since this would have interfered with the proceedings as well as raising formidable problems of classifying and recording the data. In the actual show ring, there would be considerable interaction between dogs and their handlers, and it would be well nigh impossible to compare the performance or reactions of a breed in one ring with those in different rings elsewhere at the show. Accordingly, we chose a simple 'stare and touch' test of dogs sitting on the benches, alone and without their owners present. With hindsight it was perhaps cheeky of us not to ask the owners' permission to examine their dogs, but we thought it essential to work anonymously. All the dogs we tested were either tethered or caged, none was interfered with, and the results have remained confidential. I could certainly not do such a trial nowadays because I am too well-known in doggy circles, and I would attract curious onlookers who would interfere with the outcome of our tests.

I carried the stopwatch and recording sheets and lucky Amita was the stooge or test stimulus. First, she had to squat and stare at the chosen dog for twenty seconds. The dogs usually gazed back in a friendly way, wondering perhaps why this stranger did not come closer to be licked. A few looked disconcerted and retreated, whilst a few more dashed forward and tried to bite Amita's nose. I was always on hand to warn her to jump clear at the critical moment!

The second phase of our trial was distinctly more dangerous for Amita, but she survived her assignment unscathed. She had to offer her hand to be ignored, sniffed, licked or be bitten. Most of the subjects did sniff her hand and were friendly, others seemed terrified and only a few were aggressive. My interest particularly focused on the latter two responses because such behaviour in a pet dog would obviously be unacceptable, even dangerous. Was the behaviour of dogs at Crufts to be a preview of the types of behavioural problems I would one day encounter in pet dogs of the same breed?

Most of the dogs we tested proved remarkably friendly and temperamentally sound: Golden Retrievers, Irish Setters, Labradors, Old English Sheepdogs, Cairns, Long-haired Dachshunds and English Bulldogs were all fine and friendly. Other breeds did not fare so well. A cacophony of barking began as we rounded on the Smooth-haired Dachshunds. Seventy-eight per cent of twenty-one Smooth-haired Dachshunds tested were aggressive and barked. There was little possibility of Amita touching these dogs without losing a finger so I pencilled in 'presume would bite', based on past experience of these little fellows. Just three weeks previously, I had had a miniature Smooth-haired Dachshund as a patient who had narrowly missed severing his master's jugular vein when he lunged for his throat. We were amazed at the intensity of aggression that these dogs showed, knowing that they are popular pets for elderly people. Dachshund breeders tell you that they are ferocious from their history of use in badger-hunting, and need powerful jaws to grab those unlucky creatures. Fortunately, badgers are now well-protected in law and perhaps it's people who now need protection against the former tormentors of old Brock. A former Dachshund breeder with inside knowledge later confided to me that the rot set in in the 1970s, when a popular kennels produced a succession of champion smooth-haireds from highly in-bred stock.

We moved downstairs to the German Shepherd Dogs or, as the British relabelled them after World War I, Alsatians. These big, unhappy dogs perched uncomfortably and silently in relatively small stalls, staring anxiously at passing people and dogs, hoping that one was their returning owner. Their reaction to the stare was usually to freeze, avoid eye contact or even retreat, never to make a friendly, forward approach like the hound breeds. Forty-seven per cent retreated uneasily, fearful of Amita's proffered hand. We were able to watch these same dogs being judged and they often had to be coaxed and cajoled by their handlers to stay still and accept handling by the judge. Without this trained restraint, there was no doubt that the dogs would have bolted into the streets of Earls Court and made for home. Fear is the great problem in German Shepherds: many are nervous of outsiders and it is a difficult aspect of temperament to modify, except by using psychoactive drugs. When German Shepherd Dogs bite, they usually do so out of fear, combined with loyal defence of territory and their master.

I felt sorry for these beautiful dogs with their superficial likeness to the wolf, but what imperfect animals they are! German Shepherds have always featured high in statistics for congenital hip dysplasia, congenital epilepsy and digestive problems, and they are always top of the league for biting people. German Shepherds have also attracted more 'professionalism' than any other breed: from well-intentioned dog trainers who use them for military, police and civilian work; from dedicated geneticists like Dr Malcolm Willis (who has pioneered many genetic improvement schemes within the breed), and of course from veterinary researchers who have endeavoured to find cures for the painful, degenerative conditions from which they often suffer. It is as though the harder man tries to improve upon nature, the greater his failures.

Finally, we went to the Cocker Spaniels, with which I had already had disastrous experiences within my practice. Some of our observations about the characteristic Cocker Spaniel temperament had been the subject of publicity in the newspapers and the dog press, and I thought I might find the same growly, place-possessive reactions in the Cockers I saw at Crufts as I found amongst our patients. How great was our surprise to find that all of the Cockers were friendly with none of them showing any signs of aggression. This finding is consistent with the defensive claims by many Cocker breeders and their puzzlement at my description of problems which pet owners sometimes experience with their dogs. My explanation is that the better-known Cocker Spaniel breeders tend to keep packs of dogs, often in kennels outside the home where bad behaviour may either go unnoticed or is inhibited. A kennelled Cocker cannot hoard paper tissues, steal food, 'possess' one person in the family or stake out no-go zones beneath chairs and tables.

My awareness of temperament in Cocker Spaniels began one Saturday in 1979, just before Christmas. It was to become a crusade that has ultimately had positive results. In 1979 the practice was still only six months old and I was learning more every day about the strange and eccentric habits of dogs. None came stranger than Buzzy, a beautiful eighteen-month-old Red Cocker belonging to Lord Charles and Lady Sally Setrington. I visited them at their trendy studio off the New Kings Road, where Buzzy was the centre of attention for customers and family alike.

Buzzy was a beauty whose long blond ears were constantly fondled by an adoring circle of fans. He may have looked like a dog on a calendar or a chocolate box but in the last three or four weeks he had started to act strangely. Some days he looked frightened and disturbed and wouldn't come forward to be petted by Sally. When he was given food he would stiffen and seem anxious, as though he had been teased and had his bowl removed, or been punished whilst eating. He had always had a passion for paper tissues, but previously he would give them up as part of an attention-seeking game; now, he hung on to them for dear life.

Then there were his mood changes in the evening. As the light diminished he would transform from Buzzy the affable Dr Jekyll into a monstrous Mr Hyde. He would try to hide from the light, retreating under an old armchair, and resist all pressures to bring him out. Both Sally and Charles bore bite wounds to prove that it was most definitely best to leave a growling Cocker alone at such times.

I was uncertain as to how as to proceed, having had no previous experience of what, to all appearances, was a dramatic, intermittent dementia: a form of canine schizophrenia. I hate such labels, but the parallel with psychiatric disturbances in humans was obvious. As it happens, the following week I was hosting a prominent psychiatrist from the United States with experience of working with hyperkinetic children, so I asked Sally if I could bring him with me on my next visit.

Professor Samuel Corson from the University of Ohio had earlier published a report on a disturbed, hyperkinetic dog called Jackson. Jackson, a black Cocker Spaniel-cross, had responded remarkably to the stimulant D-amphetamine by becoming calm and friendly; most dogs, like most people, become more active when on amphetamine. Some hyperkinetic children show similar paradoxical calming or improvement in their behaviour when administered amphetamine and it struck me that Buzzy might also suffer from such a neurochemical disorder in the brain. Professor Corson was keen to join me on my rounds and especially to see Buzzy.

Buzzy had not changed during the week between our visits: he displayed the same tendency of food and object guarding, and had bitten Sally again. Her dear friend was degenerating into a demon. The kindly professor of psychiatry, with his Russian-American accent and his well-groomed nanny-goat beard, struck quite a contrast with the trendy young English aristocrats who were my patient's owners. But they got on well and Professor Corson diligently went through Buzzy's behavioural checklist, comparing it with the one he had done for Jackson, who had resided in the research wards of his psychiatric hospital back home. He pronounced that the similarity was very close indeed and that Buzzy was definitely a candidate for the amphetamine treatment.

The Setringtons received this news with some satisfaction, feeling at least that Buzzy's problems were now receiving serious and competent attention: in Professor Corson we undoubtedly had the world authority on the subject. Buzzy's breeder had given them the 'It must be your fault, you're too soft with him' line, and other such carping 'I know best' talk. A great burden of guilt was in the process of being lifted from their shoulders by our diagnosis that Buzzy suffered from some serious organic brain disorder.

I contacted my vet friend Kevin Sullivan, whose patient Buzzy was. He agreed to negotiate with the authorities to obtain a small quantity of D-amphetamine, which amazingly he succeeded in doing. We were still living on the farm in Devon then and as Christmas was almost upon us I could not get to London for two weeks. I would like to have been present when the amphetamine was first administered but I had to give the go-ahead on the phone. With some nervousness I phoned the next day to discover Buzzy's reaction to the drug: he was no better, no worse, the same demon dog. Professor Corson had returned to Ohio and was not contactable for a couple of weeks, so I asked that the amphetamine treatment continue for a week. Still no improvement; indeed, if anything Buzzy was becoming more violent.

There was just a possibility of some dietary allergy, so over Christmas I suggested to Sally that they keep him away from the canned foods which often contain food colorants, indigestible gelling agents to bulk water, and other nutritional negatives. I devised a homemade hypo-allergenic diet for Buzzy, who probably ate better that Christmas than his humans. I called again over New Year – still no improvement. I also asked that they be more strict, aloof and dominant with him, but Buzzy's roaring rages happened regardless of the Setringtons' behaviour: it was as though he suffered from brainstorms yet he remained fully conscious. Buzzy did not present signs of *grand mal* epilepsy but I nevertheless felt it was worth treating him with an anti-convulsant drug, Mysoline. This medicine has a general calming effect on behaviour as well as suppressing fits.

Thankfully, the Mysoline had the hoped-for beneficial effects and Buzzy's rages became bearable, though he was still grumpy in the evenings. The Setringtons persevered with him for another five years until babies came into their lives and the risks of a bite became unthinkable. Sadly, we had to agree that Buzzy's quality of life and the safety of Setringtons justified his being sent to the great kennel in the sky for disturbed Cockers. He was put to sleep in December 1985, leaving behind happy memories overlain with grief and anger at his mental suffering.

The next Cocker Spaniel I saw was even more disturbed than Buzzy: a black dog called Nero who belonged to a nurse. He was so affected that all concerned agreed that he should be put to sleep immediately, without attempting behavioural treatment. I broached the subject of our examining Nero on post mortem, a suggestion that may have seemed in poor taste but which appeared warranted by the extent of his disturbance. Conversations with veterinary surgeons and dog breeders pointed to the existence of many more Cockers like Buzzy and Nero; indeed, they were rapidly acquiring a reputation as eccentric, disturbed dogs. Thankfully Nero's owner agreed to his body being sent to Cambridge University for examination by a vet specializing in neurological disorders, but no brain abnormalities were found. Nero's problem may have lain in some subtle neurochemical defect which would only be revealed on detailed electrical and chemical examination of his brain, an expensive and time-consuming operation. Did the problem justify so much effort?

Sadly, ten years and several hundred afflicted Cocker Spaniels later, we are no nearer to understanding precisely what causes this behaviour in some Red or Black specimens. Whilst the dogs afflicted are always of solid coloration, they can be male or female, young or old; some develop the condition slowly, for others the onset is sudden. In 1984 I published a study based on fifty disturbed Cockers which provoked great interest amongst scientists and veterinary surgeons, but which got us no nearer to devising an effective therapy. The only way forward, I felt, was to alert the public to the dangers whilst also encouraging breeders to try to be objective about the temperaments of their bloodlines and the progeny sold to pet owners.

The first approach was easy: after a hard-hitting investigative article in the *Sunday Times* there was a long and sometimes vitriolic debate about our findings in the dog press. One prominent veterinary surgeon accused me of breeder-bashing, while breeders accused me of being a sensation-seeking self-publicist. They could both have been right, though in reality I was motivated by the frustration of having to deliver bad news to my clients with such depressing frequency: for Cocker Spaniels make endearing puppies and are usually joyful companions. To lose such a dog is truly a tragedy for the families I have seen and sometimes they are single people for whom their dog may be almost everything. Cockers were becoming my *cause célèbre*, and I began to relish the battle.

The public debates were getting out of hand, but a chance to raise the level came with an invitation to speak at a meeting of the Cocker Spaniel Club of Great Britain, in summer 1984. I was to share the platform with a lecturer in veterinary neurology, Geoffrey Skerritt: he would cover the medical aspect whilst I dealt with the behavioural. The billing for the meeting varied from 'Dr Mugford called to account by us dedicated Cocker breeders' to the more detached 'Temperament and Breeding in Cocker Spaniels'. I really worked hard on preparing for this meeting, instead of my usual strategy of last-minute panic. We had by now collected 200 pedigrees of affected Cockers, which enabled me to calculate their coefficient of inbreeding. We had identified three bloodlines which occurred in over half the patients that I had seen, and our sample contained a seventy-to-thirty ratio of males to females. I had data on the usual diet of these dogs: every variation was represented but with a bias towards tinned food. I also knew the age of onset of this condition – from six weeks to eight years – and the usual outcome of treatments: no fundamental changes or improvements in the dog's behaviour, but more effective avoidance behaviour by owners as a result of counselling.

All too soon the Sunday afternoon meeting time came and I was on stage. I had already picked up the gossip that some of those present hoped to reveal terrible things about me and have me commit behavioural suicide. Others with a kindlier disposition made it clear that they had been working for years to expose and correct an unsatisfactory situation, without much support from the Cocker Spaniel breed establishment; they were pleased that their lone voices were now joined by mine.

I delivered four case studies that together summarized the nature of the problem, then went through my data. I also had some positive suggestions, even solutions. They were to revolve around the breed club operating a strict temperament-testing regime on offspring which breeders had already sold to pet homes, when they were six, twelve, twenty-four, and thirty-six months old. Test matings of dogs that would be used at stud would be required, just as progeny-testing is commonplace amongst cattle breeders. As soon as reports returned that one or more offspring of parent Cocker Spaniels showed bad behaviour, there would be no more breeding from that combination, perhaps from neither mother nor father. I recommended that before one could propose a dog or bitch for breeding, its ancestors and relatives belonging to other breeders and in pet homes must have passed the test of having good temper.

My plan required a high degree of central control by the breed authority, and would mean that many of the dogs currently being used for breeding and showing would be disqualified. The precise mode of inheritance of the condition still had to be determined: was it due to a single recessive gene which occurred in the homozygous condition in affected individuals, or was it a condition requiring the action of several genes acting together? The bottom line of my presentation was that the traditional, democratic, cottage-industry and free-market approach to breeding Cocker Spaniels could no longer be allowed to operate. As was nicely pointed out to me by one dedicated breeder, Cockers have had 'iffy' temperaments since

Victorian times, viz. Robert and Elizabeth Barrett Browning's problems with their celebrated Cocker, Flush. The principal difficulty raised by my proposals was the shortage of good bloodlines unaffected by the deleterious genes for temperament.

The meeting degenerated into ill-tempered arguments between members on the floor with occasional rejoinders aimed at me. An enormous tension in me drained away as a structured Question Time became a free-for-all against the Kennel Club, vets, profit-seeking behaviourists, a biased press and so on. A collective persecution complex was revealed in my audience and I began to find amusement in the irony of my dangerously exposed situation. I knew that my friend Geoff Skerritt would do a good obituary on me if I succumbed to the violence which simmered just below the surface. Eventually however, the meeting broke up without any definite decisions being reached. The situation is still unresolved.

In the intervening six years, however, there has been a marked decrease in the popularity of red and black Cocker puppies, and the diminished market has offered an opportunity for much more careful genetic selection. Along with the length of the Cockers' silky ears, the glow of their coats and their perky stance, breeders must now be alert to the important behavioural factors of possessiveness, guarding and general temperamental stability. Even without a formal scheme such as the one I proposed, the breeders, and more importantly the judges, are probably now being more honest with one another. We still see a few disturbed Cockers, but not so many as before, and I think that there has been a genuine and continuing improvement. With hindsight, it just seems unfortunate that it was so long in coming and that so many of my owners have been denied a normal, satisfying relationship with their dog.

Whereas the attitude of the Cocker Spaniel breeders towards my efforts has vacillated between hostility and childishness, the situation in other breeds has been markedly different. I try to direct my fire at the breeds which I see most often in my practice. German Shepherds are the most commonly referred, followed by Labradors in second place and Cocker Spaniels and Golden Retrievers equal third.

Golden Retrievers are fascinating because in general they live up to the reputation so nicely depicted by 'Goldie' and now 'Bonnie', the stars of *Blue Peter* on BBC children's television. The sad truth is that some of the worst attacks we encounter are from Golden Retrievers, and the victim is usually a member of the dog's own family. Dramatic mood changes occur in these dogs which offer their victims little opportunity for avoidance or self-defence. In some ways, these dogs present a similar profile to Cocker Spaniels but they differ in the savagery of their attacks, which can be repeated and prolonged. With their greater size, the wounds sustained by their victims can be dreadful.

The Golden Retriever breed is of course numerically large. They are more popular than Cocker Spaniels and they are often owned by families with children. Even before our practice became established I realized that some new and quite scary developments were occurring when I was approached by some conscientious Golden Retriever breeders about what they believed was a localized problem in the South-West of England. That was in the mid-1980s, and in just four or five years the concern has become national, if not international. Jason, an early case, illustrates what we are up against.

Carla came to our Wednesday clinic in Bayswater, London, where I used consulting rooms at a centre for veterinary specialists in Alexander Street. The nurses outside were making a tremendous fuss of Jason because he was such a proud, nice-looking dog, friendly with everyone. He was in his prime at two years old and his mistress, a young divorcee, wasn't so bad either. She had been to the Alexander Street clinic before with Jason, to see a dermatologist colleague: the dog had apparently been suffering from a chronic itchy skin problem which had been resolved by a combination of flea control, drugs and dietary changes. That had been a year earlier, and he had now reverted to a regular dog food diet.

Carla told me that on three occasions Jason had made savage attacks, once upon her and twice upon her boyfriend. The attack upon the boyfriend, in which his ear had been partially severed, had taken place two days earlier. The ear had been successfully sewn back on by clever micro-surgery, but it had been a close thing and Jason had a big question-mark over his future. The previous incident had occurred when Jason was sitting between Carla and her boyfriend, and the boyfriend bent down to pat the dog. Unknown to either of them, Jason was sitting on a tiny portion of biscuit, and he went for the boyfriend. He had not previously shown serious signs of defending his food, though they had avoided giving him bones because even as a puppy he growled when anyone approached to take it away. On many occasions previously, the boyfriend had been near Jason when food was about and he had not reacted aggressively.

After rushing her boyfriend and his ear to hospital, Carla had returned home intending to have Jason put to sleep. She cried and cried because Jason represented an important link in her life, between her recently dissolved marriage and her new career as a freelance photographer. Jason was Carla's constant companion, in some respects more constant than men had been, and they had spent many hours together on the road and in hotels. Her vet appreciated the dog's importance in his mistress's life and referred her to me on the understanding that she would take my advice and have Jason put to sleep if that was what I recommended. One side of me, of course, was strongly of the view that Jason should be put down whilst another part longed to help this damsel in distress.

I spoke to my skin specialist friend who had seen Jason earlier, and went through the dog's clinical history. I was interested in the correlation between temperamental behaviour in such Golden Retrievers and a greater-than-average tendency to skin complaints, diarrhoea, listlessness and mood changes. I'd seen this pattern of cases evolving in the previous two years with them, which in the early 1980s formed only a tiny proportion of our total patient load.

Acting on a hunch after a chance remark made by another dermatology specialist at a Scandinavian Veterinary Congress in Oslo, 1984, I began treating Golden Retrievers by adjusting their diet. I had had a few successes but I wanted to find out why it was that these dogs should improve when we removed them from their customary tinned dog food and substituted a diet of lightly boiled mutton with rice. In view of Carla's commitment to Jason, I decided to ask her if she would allow us to take blood samples and make an overall detailed clinical examination. After that, we would change his diet. Except at times when he needed to eat, Jason was to be muzzled, even in the house and especially when Carla was alone with him.

The tests revealed that Jason had elevated liver enzyme levels, pointing to a chronic impairment of liver function. However, with careful attention to diet it was felt that Jason could remain healthy. The reason why his liver was not functioning was never established: it may have been due to a faulty blood supply to the liver, he may have suffered from infectious hepatitis, or perhaps Jason had just been drinking too much! Whatever the reason, he probably experienced a marked rise in plasma ammonia levels in the few minutes after feeding, which would give rise to symptoms not unlike a severe migraine in people. The technical term for this condition is hepatic encephalopathy, which has been experimentally induced and studied in dogs and also occurs in people. People report feeling poorly and irritable, though they are rarely as aggressive as some of my Golden Retriever patients.

I had already established that changes to their diet improved some of these dogs, and now perhaps we had a clue to explaining why they improved. Jason seemed to like the new diet, became less moody and all was well for six months. Carla dropped me a postcard full of praise and thanks.

Imagine my distress when I received a tearful phone-call six months later. There had been another horrible incident in which Jason had mauled a child relative. As Carla and her niece walked into the kitchen, she saw that the garbage bin had been turned upside down and its contents chewed over. Before being called out to collect her niece from the station, she had cleared out her refrigerator and thrown all sorts of food into the bin. Jason was lying under the kitchen table on their return, and it's likely that he sensed the possibility of a verbal reprimand from Carla. However, on this occasion he didn't attack Carla but her niece, whom previously he had known and been friendly with. The attack lasted at least half a minute and it was only Carla kicking that made Jason let go. The poor girl received many bites which thankfully have not left disfiguring scars.

So much worthwhile progress had been made, but just one breakdown in control had led to disaster. It certainly proved the point about dietary management of Jason, but the situation was too risky to be allowed to continue. I spoke firmly and directly to Carla and told her to take him to the vet's immediately. I telephoned him from the farm, and Carla was allowed to jump the queue of patients so that Jason could be quickly euthanased.

We have since undertaken extensive research into the clinical aspects of affected Retrievers, the predisposing factors in their breeding and upbringing and the substantial influence of diet. We have shown that some canned dog foods dramatically worsen the behaviour of the few dogs that are vulnerable. Any high-protein diet, especially if the protein quality is poor, can have the same effect.

Our early hunch about the benefits of a low-allergenic rice-mutton diet was productive not because of our choice of sheep meat as a protein source, but because of the improvement in protein quality and the lowering of total protein intake to meet established nutritional requirements. It is as though the liver, the body's main powerhouse and destruction plant, could cope with only so much protein which, either in excess or with amino acid imbalances, can literally poison the body. Nowadays, there are a number of veterinary prescription diets that also offer a combination of low-protein levels with high protein quality. We are now focusing our research efforts on testing the suitability of these prepared diets as alternatives to the home-prepared regime.

The Golden Retriever breeders could not have been more helpful, and two of their members are even collecting and collating genetic information from our patients and from affected dogs given to the breeds' rescue society. And whenever I speak at a meeting of Golden Retriever breeders, I am received warmly. Even their physical appearance is appealing – they are nice, outdoor types, tolerant and fun. They keep their big soppy breed of dog because they believe in the value of dogs as companions; they are not in it just for the money or prestige. Indeed, it is always difficult to make breeding dogs pay, given the many outgoings and overheads associated with it. It may sound attractive to sell each of eight puppies for £200 or more apiece, but the keen show person has to spend a fortune on travelling to and from dog shows, on vets' bills, on a breeder's licence from the local authority, not to mention the cost of food and advertising.

If you breed Rottweilers, you most definitely will not now be making money, unlike the situation during the mid-1980s when the breed was at the height of popularity. Rottweilers became the dog of the 1970s and 1980s, culminating in a spate of horror stories when a few dogs attacked and in some instances killed young children. In the early 1980s, I often remarked on how placid and well-behaved were the Rottweilers that I was then seeing, so different from their image in literature and film as the 'devil dogs'. The specimens I saw in North America and Germany were not so pleasant as their British counterparts who, living on an island protected by strict quarantine laws, had benefited from a policy of active selection for good temperament. Unfortunately, this rosy view of Rottweiler behaviour did not last, as more and more dogs carrying an arrogant and unpredictable quality were imported. Sadly, I can now demonstrate that too many Rottweilers cannot be safely stared in the eyes because they have no fear when threatened by a potential assailant. Excessive courage can easily become arrogance: the reason why some male Rottweilers have suddenly turned without prior warning or apparent provocation.

The body signalling of these dogs seems to be subtly different from the reliable wolf system we see in other breeds. Because little warning is given, the victim of a Rottweiler attack is more vulnerable to injury: he has no opportunity to take avoiding action. I have often spoken on TV shows and at open breeders meetings about my concern over Rottweilers, and generally the reaction has been more like the one I get from the Cocker Spaniel breeders than from the Golden Retriever fraternity. Recently, at Granada TV studios in Manchester, I was beseiged by twenty Rottweiler breeders and enthusiasts after I had supported the need for tighter ownership restrictions. I had suggested that males should be routinely castrated and dangerous individuals muzzled in public places. There were howls of protest at the castration idea with plaintive cries from the floor along the lines of 'The breed will die out!' and 'How do you proposed to create the breed's replacement stock?' No comment from Mugford!

The rise and fall in popularity of Rottweilers says much more about the psychology of human beings than it does about dogs. There have been ups and downs in the popularity of many breeds in the past, and there is always a high risk of a breed being genetically damaged at its peak of popularity. When there is increasing demand for a particular breed of dog the discipline of rigorous selection for positive health and behavioural attributes tends to diminish, as breeders step up their output of puppies to meet the demand. This is not necessarily a criticism I would direct at all breeders: many responsible individuals take a long-term view of their favourite breed and try not to exploit a sudden rise in popularity.

Whether it is commercially-minded puppy farms or one-off amateur owners of a first bitch cashing in on the demand, if the British Kennel Club cannot enforce discipline or control upon its members, only market forces remain to sort out the mess. Meanwhile, this amateurish world creates considerable heartache for professionals like myself on the behavioural front, and research staff at our veterinary schools spend too much in terms of time and resources treating congenital physical abnormalities.

Changes in the status of a breed can often be quite rapid, as illustrated by Golden Retrievers and Rottweilers. Doubtless there will be more such awful behavioural anomalies unless the world of dogs and dog breeders is somehow changed. I was depressingly reminded of the inevitability of such fluctuations in the fortunes of particular breeds in a scientific paper presented by an eminent Swedish geneticist at a congress in Monaco in 1989.

Dr P. E. Sundgren went through his data on the relatedness and degree of inbreeding in thirty popular breeds of dogs in Sweden. In this respect, Sweden is somewhat like the United Kingdom, being cut off from the larger international gene pool by anti-rabies measures. Dr Sundgren examined the genealogy of dogs through past generations and found a remarkably high and consistent level of inbreeding, which makes most breeds vulnerable to the rapid spread of deleterious characteristics, that can come from mutation, unwise importation of an affected individual from outside Sweden or for some other reason.

To avoid the danger of such inbreeding, Dr Sundgren calculated that in an ideal genetic world, about twenty-five per cent of all the male dogs in the population should father puppies in the next generation. This figure contrasts with the reality of our super-stud system of breeding from just the selected few 'best' dogs at the top of the show-dog pyramid. As things stand today, there are unavoidable problems of inbreeding and consequential genetic disasters are bound to befall pedigree dogs.

This problem of having reproduction concentrated upon a small minority of inbred individuals is recognized in farm-animal breeding. The agricultural and horse-racing industries maintain a tightly regulated and computerised stud book, which ensures that optimum levels of outbreeding are maintained. The British Kennel Club has computerised its stud book, but it does not have the power – perhaps the willpower – to direct which dog shall be mated to which bitch. When we humans act as God and take over from natural selection, we need to be more than usually dedicated to the science of genetics.

Bearing in mind Dr Sundgren's work, it is easy to see how far from his optimum model we have strayed. At one stage in the 1960s, one famous English Bull Terrier sired nearly half of all litters in that breed. He was the unbeatable champion, the 'best' Bull Terrier ever encountered, fêted everywhere. In the few years since this dog achieved such fame, the realization has slowly dawned that it carried dangerous genetic qualities: the English Bull Terrier breed has become bouncier, and is too easily stimulated into hysterical, out-of-control behaviour patterns. In other Bull Terriers, the symptoms of this change included tail chasing, which can be initially amusing but is ultimately self-destructive for the patient. Now we see too many of these whirling-dervish Bull Terriers, all seeking manic activities with which to stimulate release of endorphins. We have had to create special therapeutic toys to keep these dogs preoccupied and devise complex management strategies to keep their behaviour more or less on an even keel. I do not mean to imply that the 'top breeders' of the 1960s intended this to happen: Bull Terrier breeders behaved like others in a system which consistently disregards genetic wisdom.

Dog breeding is not all doom and gloom: most breeders responsibly fulfil a necessary task and overall, an investment in a pedigree dog usually brings worthwhile returns. Pure-bred dogs are usually a relatively predictable commodity, which can reduce the risk of a mismatch between man and dog. Whilst Mongrels have very many endearing qualities and are usually good-tempered, you can barely guess what a cross-bred will grow up to become as an adult. Of pure breeds, I marvel that we never see Flat-coated Retrievers with aggression problems, yet to an unsophisticated eye like mine, Flat-coats are only black versions of the Golden Retriever. I have a long list of prejudices in favour of other breeds of dogs: Norwich, Norfolk and Border Terriers, Airedales, Irish Setters (Sam please note), Greyhounds, Deerhounds, Poodles in all their varieties. I could construct a comprehensive list of breeds that rarely come to see us with behavioural problems. Unfortunately, if I did that I might also be sealing their fate by encouraging too rapid a growth in their popularity. I understand that that is already happening to Flat-coated Retrievers. The value of a gemstone lies principally in its rarity.

13
Trainers and training

You often hear it said that when we domesticate animals they somehow lose their sharpness, their native cunning, their intelligence. These theorists don't make the same assertions about Man's development from hunter-gatherer plainsman to the settled socialized creature that he is today. In fact, the scientific evidence contradicts the view that the domestication of, say, rats, sheep and dogs, brings about an automatic impairment of their intelligence. Most domestic dogs can piece together complex clues to find the solution to a whole range of everyday problems, in just the same way as their ancestors did in the wild. Part of the pleasure of my job is in discovering the extraordinary feats of which dogs are capable, and in observing the reactions of their owners. Some seek an explanation in mystical and unscientific notions about 'sixth senses', others just take their bright dogs for granted. Sadly, many more imagine that their dogs are dimbos and don't encourage or permit them to develop their full potential.

A few days spent tracking and observing wolves or African Wild Dogs quickly persuaded me that there is much more to our domestic dogs' minds than some trainers would give them credit for. Just imagine your pet dog roaming over an area of a thousand square miles, sometimes alone, at other times joining up with relatives to visit any one of twenty home sites. These dogs acquire an extraordinarily detailed knowledge of their territory, for instance knowing where all the best ravines are over which to drive herds of antelope or caribou, learning where to avoid dangerous predators such as man, and in autumn moving to areas where the sweetest ripe Persimmon bushes grow. Wild Dogs learn about the habits, habitats and vulnerability of all their prey species; they exploit scent, light and sound in hunting. Then at home, we rattle our pet dog's lead and are pleasantly surprised when he rushes forward with tail wagging.

We plod about the park together, return home and that's it for the day. The poor dog's social and mental requirements have been satisfied, or so we think.

The learning capacity of dogs was well illustrated to me in 1973, when I spent a happy week studying feral dogs on the streets of Baltimore, Maryland in the USA. Bazzer was an especially pretty bitch about the size of a small Beagle, an all-round Collie mix. She was introduced to me by Nelson, one of the many black residents of Baltimore, who 'adopted' me as the eccentric limey who photographed dogs in their neighbourhood.

Nelson assumed proprietorship over Bazzer, but then I met three of his neighbours who also reckoned they owned her. She moved all about town, covering at least ten kilometres a day across busy streets, down alleys, over railway tracks, from the central dock and dangerous city centre to the surrounding mostly black, residential suburbs.

I had great difficulty in getting closer than ten metres to Bazzer, which puzzled me because she was fine with my local black acquaintances. Why was she friendly to the residents but not to me? It was quickly explained that she had had at least three run-ins with the city dog catchers, who tended to be white. On the last occasion, just a month before I arrived, there had been a major altercation between the dog catcher and Nelson, in which fighting had broken out during the course of Bazzer's liberation. Nelson's case was coming before the courts soon after my visit, so I gave him a character reference which suggested mitigating circumstances.

I took a particular interest in Bazzer, following her every move for three days. She had produced a litter of puppies two months before, though now all but one had been taken over or adopted by members of the Baltimore SPCA. Just one of the puppies remained to follow her about town, though at other times the puppy was 'lodged' in a derelict building frequented by hobos. There were particularly good pickings to be had from the garbage in a hospital complex, into which Bazzer gained access through a hole at the base of the surrounding fence. She would rush in, eat large amounts of food waste, carry what she could and return to her puppy. Then, she would reach over and vomit for him as he pestered the edges of her jaws. What I saw in Bazzer was a delightful example of primitive behaviour rarely seen in pet dogs: et-epimelectic vomiting to carry food from the 'kill' back to the litter. Nelson showed me where Bazzer had been trapped by the dog catcher, using a wire snare not unlike that employed by hunters to catch rabbits in England. They are dreadful devices, causing terrible pain and rapid asphyxiation. Bazzer was never seen again on that particular corner of the street, nor did she fall again for cheating white men like me holding out a chunk of meat.

In the hot afternoons, Bazzer disappeared from view until I discovered her beneath the air-conditioning unit of a barber's shop. The drip-drip of water from the air-conditioner, together with the draught from the fan, kept her cool and provided her only source of clean water.

At sunset, Bazzer became more active and went out on the hunt. Some children told me they had seen her with her puppy hunting rats at the edge of a municipal garbage dump. It is not only Terriers that like to hunt rats: hunting is a general trait of wild dogs and their domesticated derivatives. My time with Bazzer set me thinking about the general principles of how we might go about training dogs and providing a more enriched and dog-like approach to pleasing them.

My introduction to dog training had been a bad one. I had taken along my first Irish Setter, Bip, to a training club in the nearby town of Grantham in the 1970s. It was run by a police dog handler on a Wednesday; on Thursdays and Fridays he ran martial arts classes in the same hall. He was one of those teachers who did not vary his technique according to the subject under instruction. It was explained very clearly to me that I would need the 'right' equipment, which for an Irish Setter meant a galvanized iron chain with links as big as those we had used to tether bullocks on my parents' farm. Wanting to conform to the trainer's instructions, I purchased the said chain and dutifully applied it to my scatty Irish friend.

I joined the twenty or more other dog owners in a circle and listened to a diatribe about how to 'check' and 'sit' the dogs. Then there was an enormous eruption from the instructor which frightened the wits out of all the dogs except the one to which it was directed. 'LEAVE!' he bellowed. He was addressing a chaotic little Mongrel that had run ahead of its mistress to sniff the bottom of the dog in front, thereby flouting the rules.

I took a seat to the side of the hall and pleaded illness, insanity or something. Bip in any case was unhappy with the venue, having difficulty in maintaining a grip on the slippery varnished floors. In common with some other breeds of dogs, Setters are prone to growing hair between their footpads which makes it difficult for them to stand on smooth surfaces. This was my first-ever insight into dog training and it was even worse than I had feared. And yet I supposed, like the other owners at the class, that this man knew what he was doing and that perhaps it was ultimately in the dogs' interest to be treated in this way.

Seventeen years later, I can say that I was given a fairly typical insight into dog training practices on that evening with Bip. In that time I have given a hundred or more lectures to dog training clubs and trainers from Detroit to New York, Romford to Glasgow, Geneva to Utrecht. There are always instructors in my audiences like our English policeman, with only the vocabulary to demand 'Heel', 'Sit', 'Leave', 'No!', 'Down!' and so on. Dog trainers also tend to insist on using the 'right' equipment, whatever that might be.

Mrs Woodhouse insisted upon a particular style of choke-chain to train a dog. In tests I have run with the Barbara Woodhouse-recommended choke-chain, it pinches and garottes just as nastily as any other design of chain. A much-talked-about pair of dog trainers from the USA, Joachim Volhard and Gail Fisher, insist that trainee dog owners use a simple design of soft fabric choker and metal-spiked 'pinch' collar. I was amazed to see the choker being worn high up around the dog's ears, where most pain would be caused to the sensitive bones behind. The pinch collar has sharp spikes which bruise or penetrate the dog's neck, yet these authors seemed unaware of the psychological and even physical damage which such devices can inflict.

From the moment I formed our practice, I found myself questioning these previously unquestioned gospels of the dog-training trade. Much of contemporary dog training is based upon the military methods of Konrad Most, who started the heavy-handed ball rolling around the world in a standard book on the subject that was first published in 1910: *Abrichtung des Hundes, Individuell und ohne Strafen*. It contains little gems about where and how to beat dogs, the importance of a guttural voice, the theory of compulsion or enforced compliance to commands and so on.

Another doyen of traditionally-minded dog trainers was a post-World-War-II American dog enforcer, William Koehler. Some of his methods, which are still widely employed, are remarkably brutal, like suggesting that a live chicken be connected to an electrical shocking device, so that as it flaps, a dog being taught not to kill chickens will attack and itself receive a shock. Small concern for the welfare of chickens or dogs in that approach.

The intellectual and moral basis of dog training needed to be examined, I believed. To quote Most's narrow view of dogs' mentality: 'Dogs cannot speak or understand language. They are unable to form ideas and, therefore, have no conception of orders, obedience, duty, guilt, blame and punishment, praise and reward. They have nothing to do with any kind of morality or with good and evil'. I beg to differ!

How could I stop the widespread abuse of dogs in training and raise both the knowledge and emotional sensitivity of dog trainers?

My first target had to be Barbara Woodhouse, who in the early 1980s was still the darling of the media, the voice of British dog training. We were on a TV show together in the West of England and I had a chance to talk to her over dinner about her 'way' and her feelings about dogs. I had just read one of her books about how to break bad habits in dogs that also referred to the common problem of their killing chickens. It so happens that I am very fond of chickens, am a supporter of the pressure group 'Chicken Liberation' and wouldn't like to think of any dog hurting poultry. But Mrs Woodhouse's method was so bizarre, so bloody and also so impractical that I had to discipline myself to not protest my disagreement with her in public. In her book *Training Dogs My Way* she advocates chopping off the head of a live chicken, letting the dog on a choker and long lead chase the headless bird and at the psychologically propitious moment jerking it hard to frighten the dog. Just imagine the scene!

Apart from her eccentric and sometimes cruel methods, Mrs Woodhouse struck me as a sincere and caring person whom I don't believe seriously appreciated the suffering her 'corrective' methods had caused. All her life had been coloured by the belief that she was right, a born winner. She spoke genuinely of her own extraordinary powers of perception and her acute understanding of animals, and was always impressed by how quickly she could get any animal to conform. It didn't seem to matter to her whether the subject being trained was a child, a dairy cow, a horse, a pig or a dog. The basic technique was always the same: first show that you are the boss, and thereafter, offer a well-timed mix of rewards and punishments, accompanied by jerks on the choker and a special tone of voice.

I did not want to spoil our dinner by being rude to Mrs Woodhouse, but weakly suggested that the secret of her success must lie in the consistency and timing with which she applied rewards and punishment. 'Amateur' dog trainers might, I suggested to her, be less willing or able than Mrs Woodhouse to inflict pain on the animals they loved. She put me right immediately, saying: 'There are far too many soft people in this world who don't deserve to have dogs in the first place.' I also learned that chickens don't feel pain: she quoted Koehler, I changed the subject.

Shortly after that TV programme Mrs Woodhouse was filmed by the BBC at one of her training sessions, yanking and then lifting a Yorkshire Terrier off the ground by its choke-chain because it had pulled to yap at the dog in front. There was an immediate public outcry at this cruel display and I learned from cameramen present at the scene that the owner of the Yorkie stalked off the programme in disgust.

My chance for a reply to Mrs Woodhouse came soon afterwards, on another TV programme, when I chopped a marrow in half with one of Mrs Woodhouse's choke-chains, using the same action as one might when slicing cheese. To confirm the point, I yanked at my own neck with the device, regrettably using too much muscle power and leaving an unpleasant red ring at the point of self-inflicted punishment. I was criticized for being negative about choke-chains: where, people asked, was the alternative and improved 'Mugford' way? I have always insisted that Mugford does not have one way, rather an overall philosophy of sensitivity to the individual animal's needs and mental flexibility in the approach to caring for and training animals.

I was obliged to refine this philosophy when lecturing before an invited crowd of trainers at a Dog Academy in Ohio. I had already been given the royal treatment when I was being shown around this outfit that took in 100 dogs a month for training in attack and guard work, together with other dogs just destined to be 'better canine citizens'. The staff of twenty were mostly male and middle-aged; all had well-developed biceps. A cacophony of barking came from kennels arranged in a long, featureless line across a field, on either side of a concrete road. I gazed into the kennels and felt profoundly sorry for the inmates. They were in bare concrete and wire runs – no toys, no soft rags or beds from home. This was their lock-up for twenty-three-and-a-half hours a day, sandwiched between half-an-hour of 'professional training'. That consisted of being dragged about on chokers as an instrument of classical conditioning: the Unconditioned Stimulus of pain from the choke to accompany the Conditioned Stimulus of a shouted command. Thus to learn to 'heel' was to avoid a whiplash jerk of the choker should the dog fail to come back and join the trainer's ankles in time.

All this was a form of highly traditional dog training, undoubtedly effective in the hands of these Americans, but I wonder if the owners knew what their beloved pooches were going through? I had a chance to speak to some of the clients of this dog-training academy, and found that what they wanted more than anything was a pet who did not embarrass them in front of their neighbours, who did not jump up, who was not, in their words, 'too much trouble'. They had read somewhere that a trained dog was automatically a happy dog, and as husband had a career to pursue and wife was weary from children, why not get the professionals to do it for them? After all, you have a professional mechanic to fix a car, why not a professional trainer to educate your dog?

I was surprised at how well my lecture went down that evening: I did my usual role-playing act. I 'impersonated' a dog receiving their sort of training. I contrasted that with what dogs did in free-roaming and wild situations, and asked that we consider harnessing the species' 'natural response tendencies' during training. The trouble was that the dog-training gospel according to Dr Mugford was not yet comprehensively documented, though it was obviously effective against specific acts of unwanted behaviour like aggression or chasing cars.

I have talked to literally hundreds of trainers and psychologists about my developing ideas in relation to behaviour modification, but they have only recently come together in a systematic approach. Better training of trainers is obviously the way forward, integrating scientific theory with practice. That is why I give frequent lectures and courses to dog trainers, some of whom change their spots, stripes and even their names.

One such lecture was to the Hammersmith Dog Training Club in 1985, when an HM Prisons trainer of guard dogs, John Fisher, came up to congratulate me for doing such an excellent demolition job on conventional dog training. I was flattered. He seemed a nice chap and I was pleased to wean someone away from roughness. John became a frequent visitor to the farm, was keen to learn and to demonstrate what he regarded as the better side of Konrad Most, such as throwing choke-chains at dogs that misbehave or ignore commands. I introduced him to using headcollars and he became an enthusiastic convert from chains to brains. John has now teamed up with other dog trainers of the same view who refer to themselves as behaviour consultants or behaviourists: a good illustration of the impact which my criticisms about dog training have had, both upon the public perception of trainers and how trainers have learned new ways to market themselves.

The Mugford way of dog training may not yet be writ on tablets of stone but I have probably learned enough to devise some key principles that can influence dogs' behaviour simply and rapidly. First, I will pose four key questions followed by four key rules that can become the basis of a structured, individual approach to dog training, and then I'll illustrate my general strategy with a recent case study.

1. List the behaviours that you most admire in your dog.

2. List the behaviours that you most dislike in your dog.

3. Observe your dog carefully, and record the places, times and frequencies with which the admired and disliked behaviours are performed. In addition, note those events which tend to precede the occurrence of each behaviour.

4. What activities does your dog himself like or dislike performing? These preferences can become the basis for systematic reward or punishment during training.

Rule 1. *Exploit your dog's likes in a systematic way, to increase the duration of performance or to increase the frequency of performance of the behaviour which you admire.* Very often, this will be no more than a friendly gaze from you, as opposed to looking away from your dog when he does the wrong thing. More tangible rewards might be a titbit, a tickle, a one-minute play session with a favourite toy, being invited on to your lap or released to the garden for a rapid patrol.

Rule 2. *If you punish, never allow unpleasant events to occur when you are near the dog.* This policy automatically rules out your use of choke-chains because inevitably it would be you that would have to yank the lead and hurt your dog's neck. If you have to use some form of punishment, consider noise: for instance, an empty soft-drink can with a few pebbles inside dropped on the ground.

Rule 3. *Try not to compel your dog to adopt a posture which he will take up naturally without extra persuasion from you.* Every puppy and dog will, from time to time sit, lie down, walk beside you (i.e. heel) or come towards you. Watch your dog and especially your puppy doing all of these things and time your commands to accompany his spontaneous adoption of the desired posture. Don't shout 'Sit', then yank his head up and push his bottom down. Rather wait for him to sit naturally and give the command when he just happens to have got it right. Then quickly follow up the command with a reward that you know turns your dog on (for instance a titbit or a stroke).

Rule 4. *Never use equipment on your dog which you would be reluctant to use either upon yourself or upon a delicate child.* Would you take a toddler for a walk in busy traffic with a hangman's noose around his neck? All dog accessories are concessions to the changed and dangerous world we have created for dogs. None are 'natural'. Ideally, the equipment you use on a dog should place no more restriction upon him than is needed to overcome danger and reduce errors in learning. That is why I so like using extending leads, which provide the perfect compromise between freedom and safety.

Rarely am I presented with a dog that offers the challenge to demonstrate each of these tenets of dog training. Reagan, a Mongrel from Rhodes, was one such dog to visit the farm recently. He was one of those short-haired, dust-coloured Mongrels one so often finds in Mediterranean countries: the resourceful *proto canis* that probably evolved as the basic village dog of the ancient world. Reagan had been a beach bum, living off hand-outs from tourists.

Sally-Anne was a London secretary on holiday in Greece who was befriended by Reagan – she thought just for a week, but it turned out to be for life. She was in a restaurant when she saw Reagan creep in through the door, hoping to beg or steal off the table of soft-hearted English, German and Scandinavian diners. Instead, he received an almighty boot up his bottom from the proprietor, having miscalculated the speed and potential violence of this gentleman in the congested space of a crowded restaurant. Sally-Anne protested at the patron's ugly treatment of a hungry dog, upon which she was treated to a diatribe about the nuisance that stray dogs were to his business. He had been trying for weeks to catch this dog and always it was too fast and clever for him. At last he had had the satisfaction of giving it the lesson it deserved.

Sally-Anne was bored on holiday, being in the company of her mother who was only interested in those of her own age who shared her passion for archaeology. Sally-Anne was more of a naturalist, but not much nature has survived on the Island of Rhodes. Reagan was in luck. He was adopted by Sally-Anne who inevitably, six days later, couldn't bear the thought of leaving him behind. He travelled by British Airways to Heathrow and thence to a quarantine station in Sussex for six months.

Sally-Anne had already discovered that Reagan did not respond to English word commands, though he was very responsive to the tone of her voice and to her hands. On weekly visits to the quarantine kennels she had discovered that a raised hand provoked retreat, open arms or a tap of her knee invited approach. But more important than any subtleties of Sally-Anne's body language was food. During the first few weeks of her acquaintance with Reagan he could easily be incited to leap six feet to steal a crumb from her hands. His table manners were none too good.

I heard about Reagan through a mutual vet friend who suggested that Sally-Anne come along to see me for a one-hour training session when he was released from quarantine. I liked that idea because Reagan's story was an interesting one and I am rarely presented with a dog which is so totally 'uncivilized' or unaffected by formal training. Sally-Anne drove on to the farm in her Volkswagen Bug with Reagan hopping from the front seat over her shoulders on to the tiny rear parcel shelf, barking hysterically when he saw the other dogs and animals at the farm. He was about the size of a large, long-legged Jack Russell, an entire male (castration is worse than death to a Mediterranean) and as fit as a flea. As she got out of the car, he rushed past her and after the flock of Hardwick Court feral bantams, who scattered into the trees and barns for safety.

I just prayed that I could capture Reagan before the sheep attracted his attention. This was his first breath of free British air after six months' confinement in quarantine kennels. I 'borrowed' a colleague's luncheon box and we sat down to rustle papers and munch sandwiches, just as a tourist might on a Greek beach. Old beggars never change and Reagan was instantly at our feet, posing on his hind legs. I slipped a piece of baler cord around his neck and off we went to my consulting rooms.

Apart from descriptions of life on the beach and in that restaurant, Sally-Anne knew very little about Reagan's past. We could only determine his strengths, weaknesses and propensities by test and patient observation. A notable feature of Reagan at the farm was his continuous pacing: he never settled down and hated to be restrained, perhaps because of the quarantine experience. And yet he would gaze motionless for minutes at a time, perhaps for an hour if there was any prospect of a crumb from some person or place. I interpreted the pacing as being redirected or frustrated hunting behaviour, rather like that displayed by a wild carnivore able to see but not to catch potential prey through the bars of his cage. Reagan's cage had been at quarantine kennels, and the current temptation was Mr Boyde's poultry.

I scratched a knife on glass and instantly had Reagan's attention. High-pitched noises clearly bothered him. I had established that we could use an ultrasonic conditioning device as a means of interrupting unwanted behaviour. Sally-Anne bent down and casually stroked him. He in turn only wanted to lick and investigate her hands, which seemed more important than direct contact of her hand on his coat. Reagan was a very 'chemical' dog who probably had not had so much manual stroking or gentling as normal pet dogs. What would his reaction be to hands, I wondered? I raised my hands rapidly in a threatening manner and he retreated in fright under the table. A slow lifting of my hands, particularly pinching forefinger and thumb as though holding a titbit, brought him instantly into a begging posture.

Reagan did not know his name and he had no concept of 'Sit', 'Stay', 'Down' or 'Come'. Everyone except me knows that old dogs don't learn new tricks, so it fell to me to prove them wrong.

Outdoors, Reagan went wild on a lead, veering to left and right, trying to escape. We guessed that there may have been unpleasant associations from people bending down to attach a lead to his collar, perhaps a dog catcher. Reagan was determined not to be caught again. I got round that simply by fastening a special collar I had designed which incorporates a retractable lead built in to the collar. In this way the dog wears the lead within his collar, so it is always to hand. Since Reagan had no concept of an appropriate walking position in relation to either Sally-Anne or myself, we decided to start from first principles.

Using the regular collar and lead whilst walking at a brisk pace, keeping his attention looking up to a piece of food in my right hand, we found that Reagan walked beautifully to heel on my left. If I slowed down to a normal walking pace, he walked ahead and tried to block further forward progress by coming around to face me. I resumed rapid walking, saying 'Heel' each time Reagan was in the correct body position, immediately offering him a minuscule titbit. He only received titbits when his nose was parallel with my knees. I handed the lead over to Sally-Anne who repeated the exercise. Note that I never gave the command in advance of his assuming the desired body-relationship nor did I ever have to jerk him backwards on the collar and lead. That would have been the conventional dog training way, classical conditioning rather than the more appropriate instrumental conditioning paradigm.

The next objective was to teach Reagan his name. In an enclosed arena at the farm, Reagan showed not the slightest interest in his 'handle'. However, when I sat on all fours in an odd posture and made a mewling sound like a lost puppy separated from its mother, Reagan was instantly beside me. This offered a means of building upon Reagan's natural curiosity, through his irresistible attraction to oddities like me and instinctive investigation of puppy sounds. I repeated the exercise six times, bending down on all fours, mewling, then calling his name as he approached. Arrival in front or near me produced either a small titbit or a rough and tumble game.

His tolerance of my manual handling was at first low: he was still terrified of two outstretched hands, who knows why? However, within minutes of finding that I was an easy touch for food, he began to tolerate my handling, which was slowly acquiring secondary-reinforcing properties by association with food. I suddenly backed away on all fours like some comical hunchback on a film played backwards. Now we saw the chase-play instincts come out in Reagan, like the hunter pursuing an injured wildebeest or rabbit. I kept it up, calling his name whenever he came within range. We then had a five-minute break for me to recover my composure and repeated the exercise. Immediately, Reagan obeyed the 'Come' command and looked up at his name.

I could now have proceeded to training the 'Sit' and 'Down' responses in the Woodhouse or any other dog trainer way. There is no doubt that to compress and force a dog down to the ground, at the same time shouting the command, works in practice. Dogs soon learn to comply, if only to avoid physical aggravation. But why use a heavy-handed method when a simpler and kinder way exists?

I fitted Reagan with a headcollar and did nothing but walk and play with him whilst he adapted to wearing it. After a while, I stopped and gently lifted Reagan's head a few degrees above his back, which caused him in turn to lower his bottom. As his haunches touched the ground and he adopted a classic sit posture, I said 'Sit' quietly, immediately followed by a titbit. I repeated this exercise three more times, then we played for five minutes. The next occasion, only the fifth time in the training sequence that I said 'Sit', Reagan immediately sat and again received his titbit. Finally, I went through the 'Down' training sequence in much the same way as for training 'Sit', except that I waited for him to lie down out of exhaustion or attraction to a comfortable carpet. On every occasion he lay down, I would say 'Down' and offer a titbit. It took seven repetitions of the command before I could reliably precipitate Reagan's lying down to the word alone.

It had been less than an hour's pleasurable effort for Sally-Anne and myself, in which she had carried out at least as many of the exercises described here as I had. We went out for a walk again to cheer up the poultry in the yard. Memories of the recent dash after bantams were still fresh in Reagan and he pulled ahead in excited anticipation. We do care about our bantams as we care about all the livestock on Mr Boyde's farm, and I returned to fix an extending lead to Reagan's headcollar, so that we could give him his freedom yet still protect the best interests of bantams.

He hurtled through the eight metres of his extending lead and spun around to face me, looking mildly confused. Now he had an indication of the length of the extending lead, and for the remainder of our walks he ran to and fro within six to seven metres of Sally-Anne or me. I walked towards the bantams: Reagan was ready for another chase and kill. Just as he was within a metre of pouncing on a bantam and her sole surviving chick, I hit the ultrasonic bleeper. Too late, Reagan was already in full flight and took no notice of the ultrasonic whine. I hit the lead-brake in the nick of time and felt a cad for having disturbed the bantam during her pride in motherhood.

I scrounged around the farm for a soft-drink can and popped in a couple of pebbles. We rounded the corner by the piggeries and stables to see a flock of ten bantams scratching on the dung heap. Away went Reagan again but this time the tin can flopped beside him as he was five metres from me, two metres from the bantams. He leapt back as though the ground had exploded beneath him, though in reality the can had not actually touched him. He returned to me and was offered comfort, praise and a titbit for resisting temptation and returning to my 'Reagan come' request.

Sally-Anne was then drawn to the horses hanging over their stable doors. She was stroking the nearest one when Reagan spotted them and made as if to do the same charge as he had at the bantams. Since these were livery horses belonging to people who paid a fee for the privilege of having them at the farm, I decided not to incorporate them into Reagan's therapy. Instead we went off to the fields, where a large herd of horses was browsing. These horses are rarely faced with the threat of having to work in carts or be ridden, because they were mostly bequeathed to Mr Boyde by now-deceased, grateful clients who knew that their beloved steeds would enjoy a long natural life at Hardwick Court Farm. Being a softie, Mr Boyde honours these bequests, so his farm is over-populated with sweet-natured, unworked old nags.

Reagan didn't mind. A horse was a horse to him and Mr Boyde did not mind my offering his horses a little extra stimulation in life if it was to the ultimate benefit of a Greek dog. The can plopped beside Reagan as he came to within striking range of a Percheron.

Again he returned to me and then to Sally-Anne, who called his name and the 'Come' command. An hour earlier none of this would have happened.

We soon found that we had an audience for our antics – from the farm and the Behaviour Centre. I long ago resolved to exploit any willing worker in the cause of animals and this audience was no exception. First I dragged out Stephen, who took Reagan on the standard course around the farmyard using the same commands that Sally and I had used. Next it was Andrew's turn, and finally Penny, my vet colleague who had just joined the practice and was still learning the ropes.

Reagan was a dog who, because he came uncluttered with previous training and mis-training, made it all look too simple. Most of our patients come with many previous hang-ups and associations, and so do their owners. We have had generations of dog trainers promoting this or that quirky method, many of them contradictory and all claiming to be the 'right' way. Much of everyday dog training is rooted in the distant past. For instance, it is deemed correct that every dog walks on the left of his owner; but in fact this has no more behavioural significance than that a cavalry soldier leads his horse on his left while carrying a rifle on his right arm. Today, not too many of my clients stalk about with a rifle when walking the dog.

I am a total optimist about the future for dog training and dog trainers. It is a pity that the very name 'dog trainer' now conjures up an image of cruelty and punishment, because that has not been my intention. I have merely had the privilege of contributing to the evolution and reform of dog trainers, first in the UK by attacking choke-chains, and now increasingly in the rest of the world. The reform is made easier by the entry of more women into dog training who tend to be less endowed with muscles and more influenced by Dr Spock than by Messrs Most or Koehler. Perhaps men are too much concerned with their image, with a desire to conform combined with a need to be in control. Personally, whilst I remain quite confident of my gender, these have never been my priorities in life.

The overall care and training of dogs will continue to improve as people learn more about the natural world in schools and on television. Puppies also need to learn appropriate behaviour and reactions before they acquire naughty juvenile ways. At our Puppy Playgroups we have created a specially sound-deadened room that seems to prevent the hysterical barking that one sometimes hears at dog training clubs in chaotic uncarpeted halls, and this in turn reduces the need for shouting. In a year or two we shall know whether the graduates of the playgroup really have become more socially competent, friendlier and more companionable dogs. I try to wear my objective scientist's hat when reviewing the questionnaire data that comes in from their owners, but secretly hope that my bias in favour of early training by non-compulsive, psychological methods proves to be the best way.

14
Around the world

It was my third weekend trip to Paris to work with Dr Patrick Payancé at his veterinary premises in Neuilly, close to the Bois de Boulogne. On the previous trips Patrick and I had run through our different approaches to animal behaviour therapy and clinical veterinary medicine, and visited some of his colleagues to tell them about the service we planned. I had also spoken to lots of French journalists about the eccentricities of British pets compared with their French counterparts. We were in France to introduce the concept and practice of animal behaviour therapy to that country, four years after I had started work in the UK. Patrick and I had been friends for many years. He shares my professional interest in the intricacies of feeding behaviour in animals and in the value of the bond between pets and people. We also share an interest in good food and company: Patrick is a *bon vivant.*

This particular weekend began at Heathrow Airport on a Saturday at the unearthly hour of 5.30 a.m. I had an action-packed weekend of interesting cases ahead: eight dogs and cats that had stymied either Patrick or other Paris vets. It seemed to me that our reputation might succeed or fail on how the next two days went.

I arrived in Neuilly in time for coffee and croissants at 8.30. Katherine, Patrick's wife, was already focusing on my desires for lunch and was relieved when I said I would eat anything she put before me. As it turned out, 'anything' was a marvellous rack of lamb, stuck with a profusion of garlic which made me glad I wasn't facing an Anglo-American clientèle afterwards. A gulp of coffee, a quick roll on the floor with Strychnine, the Payancés' slightly overweight softie Weimaraner, and off to work we went.

Patrick is no conventional character, his work premises being a mixture of homely delights and state-of-the-art veterinary medicine. Either way, it was a good environment in which to practise for me, in that it put both animals and owners instantly at ease. My only worry was whether my imperfect French would cope with the challenge ahead.

Our first patient was an eight-year-old Miniature Schnauzer, Lascar, accompanied by a Madame Robert. The Robert family were patient by any standards: for every one of the past seven years, Lascar had vomited any food placed before him. Usually it fell to a long-suffering maid to clean up the mess, but understandably she had recently left the family service and *malheureusement* it was now the responsibility of Madame herself. I was told that Lascar ate well: his meat was bought fresh from the butcher each day, and was boiled, seasoned, chopped and mixed with rice ready for the evening meal. In an attempt to find a cure, Lascar had been taken to all the local veterinary, homoeopathic and dog-training experts. Every imaginable homoeopathic remedy seemed to have been tried. Madame produced a bagful of bottles labelled with exotic names like 'Tinct Arnica', 'Phosphor 30', '*L'Herbe de Craint*' and so on.

I fingered my way through the bottles, wondering what on earth had been the rationale behind them. I soon learned that Homoeopathy is much in vogue amongst the French, for their pets as well as for themselves. It all looked hit-and-miss to me and Madame Robert seemed not to have been offered any scientific explanation by these 'alternative' practitioners. Her most recent visit had been to a local dog trainer, Michel Baron, who made the realistic assessment that he was out of his depth with Lascar and forwarded him to Drs Payancé and Mugford.

I thought we should attempt to reproduce the symptoms, so we opened a can of dogfood: *Canigou*. It is meant to be very palatable, but Lascar turned his nose up at it, being used to home-prepared *haute cuisine*. We asked Katherine if she could spare some meat from our luncheon rack of lamb, which was even then marinading in wine. Scarcely believing our request, she cut us a sliver, boiled and mixed it with puffed-rice pellets that are popular amongst French dogs. We presented the concoction to Lascar who wolfed it down, looking agreeably surprised at this early morning treat. He didn't vomit. My respect for him increased. As I admired his bijou collar, rhinestone-studded on hand-decorated leather with a felt lining, I was told that he had been to the *coiffeuse* for 'stripping' the day before in my honour. Even the dogs of France are more *chic* than their English counterparts, I thought to myself.

We went into other aspects of Lascar's life. He was walked just once a day to the local park from his home in a second-floor apartment in the *Rue de la Pompe*, in the fashionable sixteenth *arrondissement*. What was there for him to do at home, I inquired? The answer was that there were not too many demands upon Lascar's energies. He mostly just padded about, barking at the noise of the lift or people passing on the stairs. Monsieur and Madame were out for most of the day and because the maid was not too fond of picking up the dog's vomit, he was always permitted to re-ingest it, leaving just a small stain on the floor for her to remove. He did not appear distressed in the moments after vomiting and reconsumed his food with almost as much enthusiasm as he had the first time round. Lascar was a conservationist: he had invented a sort of gastronomical perpetual motion.

I was reminded about tales of Roman debauchery and gluttony, particularly the habit of bulimia. Here was a gourmandizing dog who had switched into the very same behaviour, and there were several factors that favoured continuation of the habit. Vomiting for dogs is always easy to do because their wild ancestors generally carried food in their stomachs from the kill to feed puppies at the den. This means that it can occur without any of the nausea that is usually experienced by human beings. For Lascar, this behaviour had the payoff of extending the duration of eating, an activity he clearly loved. The key diagnostic feature in the history of Lascar's problem was that he rarely vomited at the Robert's weekend country retreat. I surmised that if he had had more outdoor interests like hunting, he would have had less need to invent stimulating ruses indoors. As so often with dogs, boredom is the worst enemy of good behaviour.

My advice was simply to swap Lascar's rich diet for a more functional, high-fibre dry one. This was to be carefully regulated to 450 grams a day, either offered on an *ad libitum* basis or split into ten separate mini-meals distributed throughout the day. The hope was that with more frequent feeding, the relative significance of any one meal would be reduced. The low palatability and high fibre content of the dry diet should have made the process of vomiting and reconsumption less attractive and more difficult, because of the food's sticky, high-friction texture. I also strongly recommended that they clear up the vomit immediately after it was deposited. Lascar would just have to go hungry! I told them that I was unhappy that he had lost the company of the now-departed maid. It seemed that Madame Robert, tired of doing her own housework, had been trying to persuade Monsieur to hire a replacement, so I was doing her a favour by providing the clinching argument for more staff. Lascar was to be given lots of walks, games, more canine and human company.

Within four days, Lascar's eccentric eating habits had completely stopped, the Roberts reported to Patrick. They were amazed at how easy and simple it had been to cure him and were puzzled that so many other qualified professionals had pursued medical explanations of his behaviour when it so obviously mirrored a pattern of natural behaviour in wild dogs. I felt pleased with our first efforts because Lascar was just the sort of dog I like as a patient: well-behaved in himself but with a single problem causing a major headache for his owners.

Our next patient was Sylvie, a female Dobermann just one-and-a-half years old, who two months before seeing us had begun eccentric behaviour in the car. Like many Parisians, Monsieur Spanier and family took off to the country in summer and occasionally commuted between Paris and the south at weekends. In April, they had taken Sylvie to their cottage in the Midi and she had travelled well. Shortly afterwards they had had a car accident in which the dog had gone into shock and had sustained some damage to her eyes. She had needed minor surgery but the outcome had been successful. But on their next journey south, in August, Sylvie had been a disaster.

My Franglais began to fail me as they used longer and increasingly onomatopoæic adjectives to describe just what Sylvie did in the car. Hadn't I heard them driving up from Porte Maillot, three kilometres away? I suggested that we went for a short car journey so that I could witness it for myself.

They drove a Citroen Safari, which has a particularly spongy suspension that rocks about on bendy roads. With Sylvie dashing wildly from side to side, we achieved the swaying effect without even having to move off from the pavement. The noise she made was ear-shattering from the moment Monsieur Spanier took out his car keys. I could see and hear the problem very well so we quickly retired again to Patrick's comfortable consulting room, to analyse Sylvie's behaviour.

Sylvie was interesting because she had been hand-fed until she was about a year old on account of her finicky appetite. Suddenly after her first season, she began to eat normally. She was a very loving dog: she followed them about the house and could never be left alone or she would be destructive. They released her for walks in the Bois de Boulogne but she always stayed close to them and never played with other dogs, of which she seemed afraid. The car was used for all trips to the park because the Spaniers themselves did not enjoy walking and they lived more than half a kilometre from the Bois. So from an early age the car had assumed an exceptionally important role in Sylvie's life.

They had been to their regular vet, who had prescribed steroids of the sort I sometimes use for the treatment of extreme aggression in dogs. I was puzzled at the reason for offering these, as Sylvie had not been spayed and that particular drug is known to have the effect of provoking pyometra, a reproductive upset. I was confident that Sylvie's problem was not a medical one and that she was another ideal case for us to be treating behaviourally.

The advice I offered to M. Spanier was much the same as the advice I usually offer to owners of car-crazy dogs. Most important of all was a general reduction in the use of the car, especially for exciting trips to the park: I recommended that they walk Sylvie to the Bois from now on. M. Spanier was a stocky, well-fed Frenchman whom I guessed would benefit from the extra exercise! Then again, I suggested that they start taking Sylvie in the car when they were going nowhere in particular, to and from the shops, for instance. Where a trip in the car was unavoidable, she should be left in it for five to ten minutes before being let out for a walk. I demonstrated how she could be trained to lie down flat in the rear passenger footwell, initially tethered to the floor with just fifteen centimetres of head movement, thereby reducing her view of the world outside. If her behaviour improved, her leash could be lengthened by a few centimetres at a time.

I strongly recommended that they develop a more independent and dominant relationship with Sylvie because, encouraged by the early habit of hand-feeding, they had induced a state of learned helplessness and child-like dependence in her. Sylvie was no slimline Dobermann and a more robust lifestyle would definitely do her no harm. In the car, the punishment they should administer to her was denial of the rewards that mattered most to her. For Sylvie, that meant leaving her alone, slowing down or even stopping the car. M. Spanier was expressive in his thanks for my advice and voluble in his appreciation of our solidarity with the French during the war. Personally, I am not much interested in harking back to World War II, though I thanked him for his kind words and gave Sylvie a hug and a good talking to, mostly to stop her master becoming overly sentimental about the past.

By now it was time for lunch. My trips to Paris always bring home to me the dramatic differences between the French and the British when it comes to food. For me, lunch is just a five-minute scramble of sandwiches and water; for the Payancés, it was the full works, and the garlic did its job on my appetite. I can never understand why we British live as we do – frantic work and functional food – when we could live like the French. I politely declined the wine, but my half-heartedness was immediately sussed out by Patrick, who poured some for me anyway.

The first case in the afternoon, Patrick explained, was very special: a young lady who had seen us on TV two months earlier but who could not afford regular veterinary treatment for her pet. I expressed anxiety at seeing a case without formal veterinary referral and Patric was just agreeing that we should investigate further when Monique Picet arrived, accompanied by her boyfriend and Dick, their aggressive Labrador-like cross-breed.

Monique was tiny – four feet high at most – a delicate woman in her mid-twenties with a hunchback and lovely twinkling eyes. Her boyfriend was a black lad named Gilbert, seemingly no more than a teenager. They lived in a sheltered institution which seemed to have a liberal approach to liaisons between residents. Essentially, they lived together as man and wife, Gilbert being physically more capable and strong, Monique the thinker and talker. Dick had been acquired from the local kennels of the Dog Welfare Society about three years before. He came without a history, but they guessed that he was now about six years old. From the moment they acquired him, he had been very aggressive to other dogs but he was always loving to Monique, Gilbert and their friends. Dick was, however, anxious about being in a surgery; he seemed relieved when Patrick took off his white coat and stopped looking like a vet.

Dick was wearing a particular nasty, fine-linked chain which functioned just like a torturer's garotte. My war with choke-chains was already well underway in the United Kingdom and the United States and I thought that Dick provided a good opportunity to start my offensive in France. I explained how much it hurt by demonstrating its action on Monique's shrivelled little arm. I left a red weal around her wrist where it had sunk in and she looked shocked, expressing alarm that Dick may also have been damaged by this device.

We all piled into Patrick's black Mini and off we went to the park. We must have looked quite a sight in the Bois de Boulogne. It was May, so picknickers and families were all about with their children and pets. Dick became a tyrant, growling, stalking and lunging at any other dog he saw. At this time, I had not yet perfected the headcollar, so we were still using a slow, less effective socializing technique for dogs like Dick. First I discarded the choke-chain and substituted a wide collar which spanned at least two of his cervical vertebrae. To that we connected an extending lead so that Dick could have freedom to roam in the park and interact with other dogs. We quickly trained a *couché* (down) response using the rattle of the now redundant choke-chain and, *in extremis*, threw it at or beside Dick when he disobeyed the command. This was immediately followed by a titbit and another approach to whichever dog he had threatened earlier.

I had to teach both Monique and Gilbert the importance of good physical control and a stronger, more dominant attitude. The first thing I had to overcome was their habit of avoiding other dogs, dragging Dick behind them in retreat. I asked them to walk away from me with Dick and to try showing increased, positive interest in other dogs. Even from a distance of a hundred metres away, I could see the change in Dick's demeanour: one of frank astonishment that the rules had altered.

Although I knew we had another patient waiting, I felt that it was important we continue so Patrick volunteered to return to the clinic and start the next case whilst I stayed with Monique, Gilbert and Dick. The biggest challenge I faced was to try and instil in Dick's owners the conviction that they could succeed, and to persuade them to stifle their instinctive response, which was always to pet the dog at the moment he was being most hysterical and aggressive. I nearly exhausted my French trying to explain what I meant. It began raining and we had to give up, but I promised to see them on my following trip to Paris. In fact, they saw Patrick the next month and he reported a big improvement. He administered a hormone treatment and encouraged them to keep up the therapy. Later, of course, we sent them a headcollar, which meant that little Monique was able to assume effective control of Dick for the first time.

We shared a taxi back to Patrick's clinic to find him well into a consultation with Minet, a nine-year-old cat who was afraid of Madame DuPont's twelve-year-old son Stefan. The fear had developed suddenly, four months earlier. When Stefan was at home from school and at weekends, Minet would not come out from beneath Stefan's brother's bed. Brother Gérard was beginning to get annoyed about this since Minet had defecated on several occasions and he had a sensitive nose. Indeed, in the last few months there had been a general breakdown in Minet's behaviour: she had begun to defecate in the kitchen, but not beside where she was fed nor in the nearby litter tray.

Dr Payancé had taken blood and urine samples and was concerned to find elevated white blood cells and evidence of crystals in the urine. At the time she mostly ate dry cat food. Patrick believed Minet showed signs of feline urolethiasis syndrome (FUS), a worrying bladder disorder of cats which can rapidly prove fatal unless treated by a combination of veterinary and dietary changes.

I could find no obvious reason for Minet's collapse of confidence, except that perhaps some internal sensations of pain associated with the FUS had been unwittingly blamed upon Stefan, the noisy, active one in the family. He was not a cruel boy and I was certain he had not earned the fear of Minet, of whom he was very fond. It was clear that everybody was worried about Minet's welfare.

I counselled Minet's family not to over-react to her oddities and devised a conservative strategy which essentially involved playing for time, in case there were medical complications. There had been talk of drugs, or homoeopathic treatments, both of which I advised against. I recommended instead that they rebuild Minet's interest in Stefan's company by making certain obvious and positive events occur when he was about. The most tangible of these was that he should feed her; he was to do this five or six times a day, double the normal frequency. She was to be kept moderately hungry, receiving perhaps four-fifths of her normal *ad libitum* daily intake. By contrast, Stefan's mother and Gérard were asked to have as little as possible to do with Minet.

I was fairly confident that the internal house-soiling was not just a reaction to stress but was also due to the juxtaposition of the litter tray and the food. Nice cats, even ones like Minet, are reluctant to do their business close to where they are fed, yet placing food near the tray is perhaps the most common mistake committed by cat owners. I told them to establish a litter tray in the toilet and bathroom, where these things properly belong! I also suggested that Minet occasionally be fed under brother Gérard's bed where she had defecated in the past, and at other spots around the house. Then there was the question of cleanliness. There was no doubt that Madame DuPont was a house-proud lady but I nevertheless introduced her to the delights of biological, enzyme-based cleaners. Finally, I asked them to stop making such a fuss of Minet, to relax and generally try to build up her confidence. Patrick was pleased with the return of blood and urine health-indicators to normal and was confident that there was no medical basis of her problems. I received a warm kiss on the cheek not just once, but three times, and felt that we had had another useful consultation.

It had been a wonderful day. The Paris Behaviour Clinic concept was good for us all. It provided me with an insight into a different clientèle from my usual one, and it was an excellent training ground from which Patrick could launch himself into behavioural therapy. We were both exhausted but had to prepare our reports because I knew we would miss important details if I waited until my return to the UK.

Over dinner, Patrick, Katherine and I discussed national stereotypes, the French and English always liking to run the other down. First impressions of my French clientèle were that they were more up-market, more obviously bourgeois than the British pet owners who come to see me. Their veterinarians were more sophisticated than their British counterparts, more accustomed to referring cases for opinion and often backed up with the results of detailed clinical tests that helped make for reliable diagnosis. There was also the important matter of gastronomy. There is far more home preparation of meals for French dogs and cats than for their British or American counterparts. A country's treatment of its domestic animals provides a good sociological window on human attitudes, and there was no doubt that the Parisians I had met pampered their pets!

The next day started with an early consultation with a quiet lecturer in biochemistry, Professor V, who taught at the Alfort Veterinary School in Paris. He had brought Papyrus, a black miniature poodle to see us, leaving his wife and thirteen-year-old daughter asleep at home. Only academics and behaviour therapists are alive in Paris at nine o'clock on a Sunday morning. Papyrus sat on Professor V's knee for the first part of the consultation and whenever I asked him to put the dog down he seemed distressed and climbed back up again. This apparently was his normal behaviour at home.

Papyrus belonged to daughter Dorothée, for whom he had a special significance: in a sense he was the brother that Dorothée did not have. The two were inseparable but on occasion the V family had to leave Papyrus behind, and at such times he showed all the signs of a separation anxiety, particularly in barking. Having been trained as a clinician and not as a zoologist, Professor V had gone for the medical approach. Three drugs had been tried: imipramine, Trioxaline and megestrol acetate (Pruritex). The first two are often employed to sedate and relieve depression in people, and the latter is a non-specific steroid we sometimes use on aggressive animals. I could not understand the point of using them on Papyrus: his problem simply arose from an excess of love.

All drug therapies were ruled out and I recommended that the family develop a more detached, independent relationship with

Papyrus along the lines prescribed for our many other over-attached canine patients. When we had completed our consultation, Professor V expressed surprise that he had not thought it through himself in terms of causation, rather than trying unsuccessfully just to suppress the symptoms. He admitted that Dorothée would probably find it hardest of all to undergo the change in the relationship which was demanded because she herself had become so dependent on the Poodle. He was going to return home and have a father-to-daughter consultation. I joked that he would probably be better at it than me. We had also provided Professor V with an eye-opener about introducing his vet students to animal behavioural therapy. It is now on their curriculum.

Our next case was Charles, a middle-aged cat who had taken to attacking his owners, Monsieur and Madame Georges. His history was fascinating. Like Sylvie, he moved to the country at weekends where he was usually well-behaved. At their cottage he would hunt mice, birds and rabbits and was rarely seen until, miraculously, he returned just at the moment they were about to leave by car for Paris. There, life was entirely different, in a gardenless apartment with nothing to do but eat diced, raw meat three times a day.

Every other day in Paris a strange mood would come over Charles, when he could launch ferocious attacks upon people: hands and ankles were the usual targets, but on one awful occasion M. Georges' face was scratched. At first his attacks had been a joke but he had now begun to inflict serious damage with his teeth and claws and it had to be stopped. There were no children or aged relatives in the Georges household, otherwise I would very likely have recommended that Charles be put to sleep.

I concluded that he was showing an unusual response to being denied the possibility of expressing his normal predatory instincts. We only occasionally find cats like Charles: most adapt remarkably well to sheltered indoor living. My advice was short and simple: provide playful outlets for Charles' hunting instincts, especially catnip-scented toys. Catnip can stimulate expression of bizarre aggression in a few cats, but it is a rare side effect and we would just have to test Charles and see. Apart from making his life more interesting and fun, I suggested that he be trained to hop up onto a small table to eat food, away from Monsieur and Madame. Training was begun by a clap of hands, offering a signal to give up murdering masters and mistresses and think about feeding instead. The composition of his diet was changed from raw meat to a lower protein complete canned food. Finally, we told them to punish Charles by pouring water over him on his next ambush. Charles did not become an overnight pacifist, but at least his owners were happy that they understood the underlying biological basis of his problem, and to an extent could now control it.

The pleasures of Paris outside Patrick's clinic were beginning to call; we were spending too long indoors. I wanted to be out and about to see what the French really get up to with their pets. The opportunity came after lunch with a home visit to the Baron de W, who had a problem with two fighting Dachshunds, Toffee, aged thirteen years and William, then just eight months. Apparently they would be well-behaved if he brought them to our clinic, so would we please come to his home?

Our credentials were critically checked by the *concièrge* of the block, which was off the Avenue du Leclerc on the outskirts of Montparnasse. There is something about Edwardian apartments in Paris that is quite timeless. No concessions are made to colourful décor, nor to the provision of carpets or modern lifts. Instead there are stained wood and clanky rope-hoisted lifts with brass controls that would confound an airline pilot. Fortunately Patrick was able to figure out which lever to pull.

The Baron had quite a home. We could as well have been on a farm for the acreage of carpets that the dogs could spread over. And spread over it they did, tinkling it with urine at every corner and piece of furniture. All had been peace and calm until William came along, and things had got even worse when he matured sexually, about three months earlier.

The Baron was a rosy-complexioned person, I thought running a high risk of hypertension. He rang for coffee and cakes and deferentially showed us to the *grande salle*. The Baroness then made an impressive entry and we settled down to watch the dogs: the aged Toffee perched on the Baroness's knee, William on the Baron's. The couplings were no accident. The Baron liked the fearless quality of young William, who was friends with everybody and loved nothing better than rabitting and ratting at their 'small' estate in Provence. Toffee was more delicate, more comfort-loving, and definitely in love with the Baroness. He came off worse in fights, though the battle scars were not especially serious. However, they had been warned by their vet that next time, Toffee might not survive the encounter. He was already showing changes in his personality, even hair loss from what the vet believed to be a response to chronic stress.

To demonstrate the problem to us, both dogs were put on the

floor, whereupon William immediately froze and stared menacingly at Toffee. Toffee struggled to get back onto the Baroness's knee and when, at my suggestion, she prevented him from jumping up, took refuge under her chair. William slowly stalked Toffee, at which moment I pressed my sound alarm for fear that a fight was developing. They instantly separated but not before the Baroness had shrieked as though from apoplexy. I resolved to warn my clients from now on if there were any chance that I might need to use the alarm.

Coffee, cakes, fruit, a photo album of the dogs and much more were then wheeled in by the dutiful maid, who was promptly sent away again. Our eyes met and I thought I detected silent irritation at her exclusion from our conversations, which after all concerned her just as much as her employers. Of the seven French consultations so far, I had come across three families who employed full-time servants, all of whom were treated in a manner that would no longer be tolerated in Britain. Time for another revolution I thought.

We returned to Toffee and William. There were complications over the need to change the relative status of the dogs, in particular over subordinating the older dog. The Baroness could not contemplate that her beloved Toffee be treated as second in the important things of life, and certainly not that he be castrated. However, after a sherry had warmed her up she agreed to my suggestion, admitting that it would probably be in their best long-term interests.

The Baron enthusiastically agreed, knowing full well that this strategy was also in his and his darling William's best interests. However, he was not so pleased with my next suggestion, that William himself receive a hormone injection in an attempt to return his abnormal status to something like it had been at puberty. Would William be suitable for breeding, which was planned for him in the next year or so? I replied that I was sure he would be fine after the injection had worn off.

We then went through the procedures which would put both owners in control of both dogs, emphasizing the need not to provoke jealousies by having either dog fussed in the presence of the other. Like other clients I had seen that weekend, the Baroness had taken both dogs to alternative therapists, including 'mesotherapy', a form of acupuncture combined with homoeopathy. I was slightly embarrassed by Patrick guffawing at the wrong moment as the Baron and Baroness explained the theory of mesotherapy to us. I politely indicated my curiosity in the subject and expressed disappointment that I had had no personal experience of it. The Baron promised to send me details of where I might attend courses and thereby be the first to use mesotherapy on animals in England.

Patrick and I returned home well satisfied with our weekend, and joined a family party that was partly in my honour. Then it was off to Charles de Gaulle Airport with its techno-futuristic, materialistic images. This was the other side of the French – the love of things modern and mechanical. Many more weekends in Paris followed during the next three years, as the *Clinique Comportementale* turned into a monthly event. However, I was becoming increasingly involved in commitments to work in the United States and as my wife Vivienne sensibly pointed out, I could not be everywhere at the same time. By then, Patrick was more than competent at running the show and needed to consult me only on particularly difficult cases.

So it was that for the next two years I turned my attentions to the USA, often staying with friends in Westport, Connecticut, Doug and Bardy McLennan, but otherwise roaming the length and breadth of the States, speaking to veterinary symposia, welfare groups, to people in the pet trade and appearing on radio and TV shows.

My first patient in the USA was a Dobermann in Detroit. Nacho hated travelling in cars and had begun to quiver like a leaf at dog shows, which both he and his mistress Katie Bonner had previously enjoyed. He was fine if they walked to a show, but living ten miles out from the sprawl that is Detroit, this was not often a practical option. Katie lived with her mother in a large property that was mostly given over to the needs of four Dobermanns. They admitted they had an addiction to the breed. Nacho's fear of cars was not only affecting his attendance at dog shows: his whole quality of life was beginning to suffer. I chose to tackle his problem by applying a slow, careful technique of systematic desensitization, working in the Bonners' yard and using a Buick station wagon as the target vehicle.

First of all, we threw a toy for the other three dogs to pursue through the open-door of the station wagon. Nacho stood back watching as the mad trio, who were normally confined to the back of the vehicle, scrambled over the well-kept upholstery. I tugged on the lead and attempted to persuade Nacho to come forward, but he stopped fifteen feet from the vehicle and only force would have brought him closer.

I drove into the yard the gleaming black Jeep which my hosts in

Detroit, Rosie and David Welch, had lent me for my time in that fair city. Perhaps a Jeep would be more to Nacho's liking than a humble station wagon – and he did indeed prove easier to guide and lift into the back of it. I let him hop out again and gave him a titbit. We then unbolted the rear seats of the Jeep and placed them on the ground for him to lie on. We made it a game: he had to catch a ball, bring it back to us, and then sit and wait on the seats. He soon picked it up and became very clear, skidding on the dry, autumn leaves and ruining the upholstery on my friend's Jeep seat. (I borrowed some dry cleaning fluid before returning home to Rosie and David.)

As Nacho improved, we moved the seats closer and closer to the Jeep. Eventually we re-installed them, and adapted the game so that he was jumping in and out of the Jeep. We then turned our attentions to the Buick with the same objective in mind. In the meantime, I was beginning to comprehend the basis of the larger problem with Nacho: he was indubitably Katie's favourite, and she was forever petting and comforting him when he was fearful. When some noisy, half-drunken neighbours appeared in the drive, I saw the other side of Nacho. He could also be a territorial tyrant who succeeded in making the visitor beat it for home. But like most Dobermanns, Nacho was more talk than bite.

We eased Nacho into the Buick and went for short ride, whilst I monitored his heartrate. It did indeed race to well above normal, 150 to 160 a minute from its normal resting level of 100. I promised to contact her vet to suggest an anti-hypotensive drug, a beta-blocker that would slow down his heart. By a combination therapy of the behavioural shaping technique, changes in emotional attitude by Katie and the drug support, Nacho gained his CC in that summer's championship shows. That success impressed his owners even more than it impressed me.

Back in New York, I was accompanying a good friend and fellow animal psychologist, Dr Peter Borschelt, on a house call to a thirteen-th-floor apartment and a Shih Tzu with separation anxieties. When Leila was left alone, she simply panicked. Like other owners I have seen all over the world, Mrs Schindler tended to share her love at the wrong moments, like just before leaving home, and punished her dog when she least deserved it – upon returning to discover a mess or complaints about howling from neighbours. I was able to be a fly on the wall, not fussing Leila when Peter and her mistress left the apartment. We noticed that when she did so wearing indoor slippers (perhaps to go down to the basement to collect something from a storeroom), Leila was not at all bothered. However, when she dressed to go outside, the dog was overcome with anxiety.

We narrowed down the key event which provoked distress in Leila to Mrs Schindler's behaviour with keys and the door lock. If she turned the key just once, Leila was relaxed; if she turned it two or three times, and fiddled to activate the burglar alarm, Leila became panicky. This is a syndrome that I have recognized many times since: a predictable sequence of behaviour by the departing owner triggering panic behaviour in the dog.

I spent the next few days with Peter, tramping around high-rise Manhattan and the over-crowded Bronx. At street level there seemed to be endless danger, chaos and dirt, in strange contrast to the affluent, ordered existence to which high-speed elevators transported we street-weary therapists. My friend Peter does not have the benefit of green fields and safe parks in which to conduct his work, and many of his clients are not endowed with the natural understanding of animals that we tend to find in British and European owners. Mrs Schindler was like so many other American clients I have helped, both in the USA and as temporary residents of the UK. They have lost their rural roots and their dogs are treated like little people, indulged and adored so long as they conform to unrealistic role models: lover, child, policeman or spouse. The idea that dogs might actually think differently from people may come as a revelation to such owners. Fortunately, not all Americans make that mistake especially if they live away from the Big Apple in small town USA.

I was in Los Angeles to attend a veterinary convention and to meet up with old friends from my Devon farming days who had emigrated to Southern California. Before I left Britain, I had been asked by the manageress of Harrods' pet store to follow up on a couple of Jack Russell Terriers she had sold to Sam Bowman, Rod Stewart's road manager. I had already had a visit from Sam in London, when Rod Stewart was playing at Wembley Stadium, but I could only learn about Zik and Zak from photographs he showed me. Zik, at about three, was the older of the two; Zak, bought on another trip to London as company for Zik, was a year younger. In fact, they had always had company in the form of live-in Mexican maid Maria, a lady whose chief assignment was to care for the dogs.

Life was kind to Zik and Zak apart from the fact that their owner Sam was away on the road with Rod Stewart for long spells, but they could be sure of having regular postcards from 'Dad' and amazing presents upon his return. They never went off Sam's property, which covered a few acres outside and more acres of carpets and tiles inside. They could move in and out of Sam's bed as the fancy took them, have a drink from the chilled water dispenser in the kitchen, beg for fine food from Maria and then in the heat of the day, cool off on the honey-coloured tiles surrounding a gigantic indoor swimming pool. For a Jack Russell used to life on farms and bred to run down rabbit-holes, this must have seemed like the life of Reilly. But they did have a genuine behavioural problem: a penchant for digging holes in carpets.

Sam was one of those lovely owners who would never have dreamt of punishing his dogs and certainly not because they chewed or scratched mere carpets. Nevertheless, both he and Maria were getting restless at the trouble and the cost involved in repairing the many patches which appeared like mole hills, pockmarking a vast expanse of deep carpet. There seemed to be no rhyme or reason in why they dug holes here rather than there. Zik, it was decided, was the main culprit, and he only did it when Sam was away. When Sam was home, of course, life was much more exciting for all concerned. So I concluded that it was simply boredom that provoked their digging habits. My exposure to countless Jack Russells in their natural habitat – mostly in muddy English fields – gave me the authority to suggest that Zik and Zak were only expressing their behavioural inheritance, which makes them burrow to pursue interesting things underground.

It was my job to find an outlet for these expensive terroristic tendencies whilst retaining for Zik and Zak the indulgent and companionable aspects of their civilized, Hollywood lifestyle. Accordingly, I devised a programme which involved developing just a little more independence in the dogs, especially on the day or two before Sam left for a trip. I also advocated more outdoor life for the dogs on the Hollywood Hills which, although dry and sandy with hostile prickly plants, still represented a decent compensation for being away from rainy England. The gardener-handyman was roped in for the job of providing regular walks for Zik and Zak, because Sam did not have much enthusiasm for walking the dogs himself.

What about their digging? I recommended that Sam establish a large deep sand-pit, of the type my kids would love to play in, with one or more bones buried in it each day, procured especially for the purpose from a traditional butcher on Wilshire Boulevard. I was also worried about the absence of structured and social play so I suggested that therapeutic rubber toys be offered for the dogs to 'hunt', just as they would hunt rats in their native land.

What could be done with the carpets? I examined them closely for signs of animal life, and sure enough a silverfish, a small insect, was discovered. The Jack Russells, it turned out, were hunting tiny creatures in Sam's carpets as a substitute for chasing larger, outdoor creatures.

Sam became a good friend and before Rod Stewart's next concert in London he sent us four complimentary tickets. The deafening tomb that is Wembley Stadium during a rock concert seemed far removed from the peculiar lifestyle that Zik and Zak enjoyed in Hollywood.

The main purpose of my recent visit to South Africa was to go on a veterinary lecture tour, but it also gave me the opportunity to look at the social and cultural attitudes of the many ethnic groups in that country. If life appears hard for the people who live in a township like Soweto, how was it for the animals? Had the traditional attitudes of the black African people towards animals survived the process of urbanization and white influence? I was fortunate to be able to find out for myself.

The first part of my tour placed me before predominantly white audiences, both veterinarians and members of the general public. My talks were extraordinarily well-attended and I was surprised that so many people in South Africa had heard about our work. Question time produced a cross-section of the animal problems that I am used to dealing with in other countries, which always keeps me pinned down for a couple of hours after finishing a lecture. However, an unusual and recurrent theme of South African questioners concerned the attitude of white-owned dogs towards black people.

One lady described a vivid case which nicely summarized the problem. She had a Kerry Blue Terrier bitch which she said loathed all black people except her maid, who was allowed to enter the house to work. However, the dog never allowed the maid to leave the kitchen when the owners were out of the house: the poor woman became a prisoner in her employers' kitchen. The gardener, on the other hand, was disliked whether or not the white family were present. On one awful occasion recently, he had been working outside when the dog had darted from the house and grabbed him by his buttocks as he tried to escape over the barbed wire security fence which surrounded the property.

'What could be done to reverse this dog's anti-black feeling in the changed circumstances of the new South Africa?' The question had some tragi-comic elements to it which I could easily have exploited for cheap laughs, but I did not. I had already heard of similar situations confronting other dog owners in South Africa who, by and large, I did not find to be unpleasantly racist in their attitudes; most seemed genuinely to want to change their dogs' attitudes. I explained that wild dogs used many cues and signals to determine who is and who is not a member of their social group. In the wild they use a combination of visual and vocal signs and possibly a group odour or scent derived from sharing a common habitat and diet.

Amongst the different racial groups in South Africa there are also great differences of diet, clothing, and general lifestyle which domestic dogs would be well able to discern in addition to obvious differences in colour. The bottom line of my analysis was that dogs belonging to white people tend to treat other whites as being less strange, even members of the same pack, whereas blacks are treated as outsiders.

I asked for the opportunity to visit the questioner, which I did in an amazingly beautiful Johannesburg suburb the next day. It was a good learning experience for me and sadly, at the end of my visit, I concluded that the problem with this particular dog would probably never be safely resolved. Her hatred of the gardener and of any other black visitor was total and being a Terrier, she was unlikely to respond to the gently-gently techniques of behaviour modification. However, I did not wish the lady to despair; I wanted to reinforce her desire to be tolerant of all people, regardless of race. We kitted Tequila the Terrier with a muzzle and asked N'Guli, the gardener, to take her for a walk. He seemed very embarrassed at being asked to do this, but finally acceded to my encouragement, laughing in an infectious way so that the whole thing became a party. When he returned, we let Tequila off the lead again and watched her reactions to N'Guli. It was nasty and he became terrified, despite the dog being muzzled. I asked that they persevere with walks and eventually he might try to feed her. For her part, Tequila's owner said there would be no question of anyone in her family ever intentionally or unintentionally encouraging the dog to chase black people though she admitted that it may have happened in the past.

I had a good opportunity to see the other side of the South African coin when I spent the day working with veterinarians and their staff from the Johannesburg SPCA. A group in Soweto, led by Dr Lesley Lunn, do a fantastic job caring for the many horses, cattle and other livestock which are kept by black people either as food animals or, more often, beasts of burden. Crime in Soweto between black people is particularly high, and dogs are kept to guard property, sometimes life itself. In this way they perform the same role as dogs belonging to the more fortunate whites in their spacious suburbs.

Apart from the veterinary staff at the hospital in Soweto and a few policemen, not many white South Africans ever visit Soweto. Indeed, I was told by my black SPCA guide, Enos Mofakate, that a few months earlier it would have been unsafe for me to have been driving about and watching life with him in the township. I was never aware of being in danger during my visit; all I received was friendship and hospitality.

Enos Mofakate took me to visit a man who delivered coal in Soweto, cheap coal that kept the people warm but polluted the air. At the coal yard, a black Alsatian cross bounded out and crashed into my side of the van, not into Enos Mofakate's side. There was no doubt that this was a specific act of antagonism toward me, presumably on grounds of colour, because the windows of the van were closed.

The dog was restrained so I could examine the horses, cattle and dogs, then listen and watch Enos give practical advice on animal husbandry, parasite control and nutrition. Effectively, these African paravets, who make up the core of staff at the SPCA, provide an equivalent to the Chinese barefoot doctors, working with few resources and only a modest training in the veterinary sciences. Yet they make an enormous impact because of their enthusiasm, their curiosity and their dedication to the cause of animal welfare.

In addition I was reasonably satisfied with the general quality of care which animals in Soweto received; it was mostly ignorance, lack of resources and unsuitable food that provoked the occasional instance of cruelty or neglect. I found the same in the rural areas of Southern Africa, where pet dogs are often an integral part of the household and share much the same conditions and problems as their human companions. They also serve many of the same functions as do pets to Europeans: they are used for hunting, pride is taken in their appearance, they bark at intruders, even bite when the going gets tough. In addition, they perform a vital function that dogs have traditionally served in rural Africa and other places where there is no piped sewerage system: they clear up garbage and human faeces, recycling them into harmless dog dirt.

The ultimate contrast to my experiences in Africa came recently when I visited a retired lady and her Poodle in Montreux, on the banks of Lake Geneva, Switzerland. Madame was an impressively proportioned lady in her late fifties, with a passionate interest in collecting art and bijoux ornaments. Her husband was an internationally acclaimed conductor who was on tour on the day of my visit. I was told her husband had little sympathy for dogs and did not really understand her passion for the little bitch, Minty.

The principle complaint about Minty was that she urinated indoors, or rather that she urinated in the wrong places indoors. Minty had a designated area for going to the toilet, at the base of the shower cubicle that had been installed in Madame's studio. Minty preferred to go in other places, like under the Grand Piano, in their bedroom, in the cavernous hall and in many other nooks and crannies about the house. When, I asked naively, did Minty do her business outside? We were in a third-floor apartment and I could see no evidence of easy access to a park, let alone a garden. Within a stone's throw were the inviting shores of Lake Geneva and I hoped that perhaps this was for Minty's outdoor relief.

Madame explained that they had once lived in London, where apparently all the streets were filthy and alive with diseases that were potentially dangerous to Minty. Minty had been a puppy then, and a vet had told her to keep her indoors until her vaccinations against the everyday dog diseases had had time to take effect. It struck her that as Minty took so well to doing her business on paper, there was really no need for her to go outside at all. Besides, if she did go outside, not only might she contract a doggy disease, but she might bring in the filth on her paws and spread it about the apartment. She was explaining this to me whilst lying on the floor in a loose Japanese style housecoat, and I expressed sympathy with her distaste for lying on carpets covered in dog mess. But, I asked, was the dirt from dogs outside any less desirable than Minty's, which lay scattered around her apartment even as we spoke? I was assured that Minty's dirt was most definitely OK: 'At least she didn't carry any of those unpleasant diseases that cause blindness in children.' It is also noticeable that mothers have a greater tolerance of their own babies' dirty nappies than nappies from other people's babies!

On the mantelpiece was a little finch enclosed in a glass cage. The bird was mounted on realistic-looking vegetation but was obviously stuffed. It looked weary-worn in death with missing feathers and shrivelled legs. Curious, I asked Minty's owner where it came from. She explained that this had been Mimi, who had travelled the world with her doing concerts and had even been to America, 'Where as you will know, Dr Moogiford, they are very strict about importing wild animals'. 'How did you get it past the Agriculture Department officials at the airport?' I asked innocently, knowing that the rules about importing animals into America, especially wildlife, are as strict as any in the world. She told me that at the critical moment Mimi had been popped down between her bosoms where she lay quiet, calm, and safe from discovery for the few minutes it took to pass through Customs.

I could see that I was dealing with a special sort of person here, who saw animals in a different way from me. I looked around at the paintings she had created and most of them concerned natural themes. On closer examination, though, they were man-made subjects: a flower arrangement, a cut rose, a tiger at a zoo. The theme was always the same – capture and control by man. Poor Minty was in the same boat, and I doubted my ability to change this lady's strongly held beliefs about obsessive hygiene or the rights of animals to a moderately free life. At such times I have to make concessions, and mine was that at least Minty should be driven up to the Vaudoise hills for a daily run amongst the vineyards, where not too many other dogs were walked. Minty and mistress could both wear bootees, I pointed out, if there was still a fear that they might tread in something unpleasant and contract disease.

I gave her the various golden rules about how to house-train dogs, with a straightforward emphasis upon reward for good performance witnessed by her mistress, changing diet and so on. It should have been a pleasure to be with my Swiss client, but as with some others in that country I am often depressed by their over-concern with order, cleanliness and control. Even Swiss dogs can only be expected to bend their natural behaviour a little to please over-demanding owners. To my mind it is the honesty, the innocence and the naturalness of dogs that is the sanity-saving antidote to the strange fantasies suffered by city-living people everywhere.

15
Exotica

My first visit to a zoo was when I was seven. It was quite the most exciting day of my life and I was wide-eyed with wonderment as I watched animals that I had never seen before even in books (we didn't have a television). Nowadays, when I visit a zoo, I come away profoundly depressed. The change in attitude is not just a matter of age; there has been a fundamental shift in general thinking about the rights and wrongs of keeping wild animals in captivity. I am reassured by the fact that my own children, at pre-school age, appeared to find the animals relatively less exciting than the amusement arcades, souvenir shops and other paraphernalia that are also installed in zoos.

I visit a great many zoos, both by invitation from the management to assist in the treatment of individual animals, and nowadays more often in the capacity of consultant to the charity Zoo Check, which exists to stimulate higher standards of animal welfare in zoos.

I believe passionately in the rights of wild animals to live out their lives free of human interference. I am always arguing against the trade in wild animals, whether it involves incarcerating them in zoos, 'converting' them into leather, fur, meat or horn or keeping them as pets to amuse or comfort people. It is a curious anomaly that European and North American countries provide better protection for their indigenous wildlife than they do for exotic wildlife imported from the tropics. In Britain, for example, it used to be popular to keep larks, thrushes, robins and the like in captivity. Nowadays our birds are quite properly given the full protection of the law and cannot be trapped, traded or caged. Foreign wildlife does not have these rights in either British or American law, so that parrots, finches, Mynah birds as well as rare fish, amphibians and reptiles can all be freely traded within the law.

I am in no doubt that wild animals have greater rights than do their domestic counterparts, who remain vulnerable and dependent upon the human beings who keep them. Domesticated companion animals like the dog give us an insight into the natural world which is completely lost the moment we surround a wild animal with a cage, a chain or a moat. At least our pet dogs, cats and horses are semi-free to behave almost naturally, whereas a caged wild animal is crippled by its false environment. Our priority now must be to devise some economically rewarding change of use for the many zoo buildings and cages which I hope will be largely emptied of wild animals in the coming decade.

Zoo Check was founded by Virginia McKenna and her family: husband Bill Travers and son William. They first invited me to join in 1988, because it was clear to them that the circumstances in which many wild animals were kept in zoos provoked severe behaviour disturbances which required treatment. The commonest symptom exhibited by the complex carnivores, primates and elephants was one of movement stereotypy, a compulsive jerking of the head and body, usually during repeated pacing. Such disturbed behaviour interests me greatly in dogs and horses and I take the credit for having created a moderately successful approach to therapy for these animals. If it can work for pet animals, then it may also help those poor confined bears, apes and elephants.

I was introduced to the darker side of British zoo wildlife when Virginia McKenna and William Travers took me on a tour of a municipal zoo, Dudley, near Birmingham, to inspect their polar bears and an African elephant. It was dreadful. We watched a solitary cow elephant, incongruously named Flossy, as she paced interminably amongst hay on the floor and over her own faeces, the only physical objects that were available to the poor animal to manipulate and move with her delicate trunk. Her only activity was to toss dung over herself and at the visitors. Her circumstances had dramatically deteriorated since her companion had died some six months before. Poor Flossy was now unhandleable: her facilities were decrepit and there seemed to be no keeper on hand to provide surrogate company for her. Nobody ever came to her shed. It was dark and filthy and the metal stanchions were rusty and sharp.

We moved on to the polar bears, who lived in a deep pit. A modest pool was full of filthy water, while the rest of their landscape was barren concrete. The male, Pipiluk, looked to be in physically powerful condition but paced and weaved interminably. His companion, Mosa, performed a matching two-step that fascinated me by its precision. Not even a flock of magpies stealing uneaten food from beneath their noses distracted them from this perpetual dance. Like the elephant, there was nothing for them to do except perform a mad tango. I was not in Dudley by invitation, but rather for my education about a sphere of animal abuse that I had not properly considered before.

In driving rain which suited my mood, Virgina, William and I drove on to a small private zoo. It was like entering a charnel house, with bits of dead animals lying here and there, and uneaten bones and carcases all over the place. Lions padded about on a sea of yellow mud. The cages were tiny, offering no opportunity to stretch out, let alone move about naturally. A lemur was housed in a cage part-constructed from a tea-chest, with a flimsy roof of galvanized iron flapping in the wind. Just as we were taking notes and becoming absorbed with the horror of what we had discovered, a pair of burly gentlemen approached. Virginia and William were well known to these as 'the bane' of zoo directors. We were asked to leave. This was their prerogative: it was a private zoo and although we had paid our admission money, we had no automatic right to be there.

On the journey back home, I was alternately angry and depressed at what I had seen, especially when I was told that this was only the tip of an iceberg of abuse, that extended to zoos all over the world, including the rest of Great Britain. I knew that individual exhibits from the past, such as Guy the lonely Gorilla at Regent's Park, were an imperfect inheritance from the Victorian zoo concept: to exhibit one or two of every large species of animal. But surely things had moved on a bit in this more enlightened age? Apparently not.

My first professional assignment with Zoo Check came quickly when, in collaboration with the charity, the plight of two bears at Bristol Zoo was uncovered by the *Mail on Sunday*. I read up on the natural history of polar bears and prepared to meet Nina and Misha at Bristol in the presence of the director Geoffrey Greed.

I arrived at Bristol lugging notebooks, stopwatches, cameras and the like, a naturalist on safari. I need not have bothered because the behaviour patterns I was to see could be summarized in a few simple sentences, repeated, repeated and repeated. When I arrived, it was coming up to feeding time, when I was told by the keeper they were always 'at their worst'. Misha held the high ground, stepping from left to right, right to left, his head flicking upwards at the moment his left foot touched the ground. Nina had another act running in the far corner of her den, a forwards-backwards shuffle. I got to know Nina and Misha rather well in the ensuing year-and-a-half and have noticed variations on these themes, in which they sometimes switch roles. However on any given day their performances tended to be constant.

The bear pit at Bristol forces human visitors to look down upon the animals, but they showed little interest in or awareness of me as I towered above them. Later, however, I found that when the zoo was deserted, after closing time at 5 p.m., they began to focus upon events outside their concrete and watery prison. Prison it was, except for a dark lair to which they could retreat and find privacy from one another and from the world outside.

Suddenly, from up above, rained their food for the day: dried dog chow pellets, not quite what one expects for a predator of seals. The weaving stopped and was replaced by an undignified scavenging for dog biscuits. This was the high spot of their day, but to me it represented just another lost opportunity. Everything was abnormal. Nothing in this environment moved: it was fixed and hard. The water looked dirty and was probably not used for swimming. Although these are animals which inhabit arctic iceflows where there is always a distant horizon, they had no horizontal view at Bristol Zoo except into a featureless wall. Most importantly, there was the question of food. It is not a political issue that animals should 'work' for their food: it is simply a fact that complex carnivores like polar bears spend hours hunting, waiting, and stalking in preparation for the big pounce upon a hapless prey. If they are to be kept satisfactorily in captivity, thought must be given to fulfilling these basic instincts. All wildlife literature emphasises the playfulness of polar bears, both with one another and with objects within their environment. They are intensely manipulative, just like other complex animals who sharpen and maintain their hunting skills in this way. Poor Nina and Misha had nothing to play with.

I was ushered into Mr Greed's office and found him both pleasant and interested in my preliminary analysis of the bears' behaviour. He quickly conceded a point I had wished to hear: that these were the last bears which Bristol Zoo would ever keep. I warmed to Mr Greed and accepted that here was a man who had 'inherited' a difficult situation from a previous era when it was acceptable for animals just to be exhibited, with no provision for fulfilling their natural instincts, their behavioural needs.

I began to share my ideas with him as I would with any owner of a canine patient: a mixture of changes to animal husbandry, nutrition, training, environmental manipulation, social re-groupings, drug therapy, health and so on. Even without detailed research into this remarkable species, it was obvious that substantial changes were needed. In particular, I suggested that the bears be made to work for their food, for instance by freezing fish in giant blocks of ice, so that they could play with the ice and eventually smash it to gain access to the delights inside. Then there were toys: things that floated, bounced, rattled and squidged. I donated to Nina and Misha the doggy toys which had already proved so remarkably therapeutic with disturbed Bull Terriers and Rottweilers. Would they stand up to the depredations of a powerful bear's jaws? It was worth a try. Anything was worth a try.

The question of diet is always a tricky one for zoo keepers. It is based as much upon Victorian fancies of what was thought to be good for these animals as on modern scientific and nutritional knowledge. Dog chow supplemented by the odd chunk of meat was what Nina and Misha were given, because that was what bears had always been given and after all, didn't bears live entirely on meat from seals in the wild? I retorted that seal bodies are at least thirty per cent fat, and it is a very special type of fat at that. Following the argument that we are what we eat, seals eating oily fish such as herring or mackerel contain low-boiling point fats, high in vitamins A and E and quite different from the high-melting point fats found in cattle, sheep and other herbivores. Then I pointed out that polar bears have been observed eating vegetable material when it is available during the summer. Given the chance, they would graze on arctic willow, lichen and even the seaweed that is thrown up in storms. Here was an opportunity to indulge the bears with the variety which my previous scientific research on feeding behaviour had shown was the key to pleasurable eating.

The trip to Bristol had not been wasted and I soon learned that most of my recommendations were or would soon be applied. I felt very cheered by the thought that Nina and Misha could now live out the rest of their lives in relatively interesting comfort. Such was the publicity surrounding their plight that £10,000 was raised to fund improvements in the condition of the fourteen bears at six other zoos in the UK.

In fact, the funds were spent upon an academic study of disturbed bear behaviour rather than upon practical improvements to their circumstances. To my great disappointment, a report was issued in Autumn 1990 by the University Federation of Animal Welfare (UFAW) which demonstrated that whilst all of the British polar bears were disturbed they might continue to be kept in zoos for their educational and conservational value. I profoundly disagree and meanwhile the bears continue to suffer.

On my most recent visit to Bristol Zoo in September 1990, I found Nina lying listless, covered in her own excreta. She had given up the will to live and I could see her point of view. Misha continued his table-top polka, interlaced with a frantic four-pace quickstep in the gloom of his den. The toys, mostly throwaway plastic garbage, were not being changed regularly: there was an old oak log for them to chew, the water was dirty again and they were back to eating dog chow. It was as if all the effort of the past two years had been wasted. We have not given up on them.

My affairs with polar bears deepened in intensity and frequency, and I now find myself compelled to visit any zoo which houses these poor creatures. The situation at most of them is drearily similar: stereotypic weaving is a 'normal' part of their zoo repertoire, many suffer from dental problems arising from worn, fractured or infected teeth, others have mutilated themselves and are covered in untreated sores. Treating a poorly polar bear is not like treating a poorly Poodle: each time they need a drug or dressing the animal must be confined, sedated and placed in danger of death from anaesthetic.

My worst but also my most interesting zoo visit took place in September 1990, when I was assigned to follow the trail of Mosa and Pipiluk, the pair of bears I had last watched at Dudley Zoo and previously at Regent's Park. They had been transferred to Katowice, Poland, where Pipiluk had recently died of accidental poisoning. Mosa was living in conditions which returning English tourists described as hell on earth. I telexed the director that I was on my way to offer advice and immediate financial assistance from Zoo Check to improve her lot.

Katowice is a tough and polluted mining town in the south of Poland, where not much new building work has gone on since the 1920s. Everything is worn out and grey, the people carrying the same signs of exploited weariness as the buildings. Even the weather conspired to add to the sombre mood – though it always seems to rain when I visit zoos. Imagine my surprise when I was hailed as a welcome visitor by the director and his zoo vets, Doctor Zielinski and Lander. At first the atmosphere was slightly tense, but when they understood that I was only interested in the welfare of their animals, they immediately warmed to my mission. I was to be given every possible assistance over the next two days, every door was to be opened to me. There was no doubting their sincerity.

I was driven to the polar bear cages by Dr Lander. It was still raining and I was unable to see the exquisite beauty of the Silesian Country Park which surrounds the zoo. I immediately recognized Mosa, though she could not have remembered me from our two brief encounters – at Dudley and at Regent's Park, where they had lived for two miserable decades. She had put on weight; indeed she just might have been pregnant. Her coat was in its best autumn condition, she was clean and her surroundings were spotless. But those surroundings were on a modest scale: a mere 75 metres square, divided up into two tiny pens with an interconnecting bolt-hole. Nothing in her life was soft or moved, and everything contradicted the knowledge and advice I had been disseminating about environmental enrichment for these majestic, complex creatures.

I was then taken to the adjacent pen, wherein lay another morose and depressed-looking female polar bear, Margaret. Margaret had in her twenty-four years borne twelve healthy cubs, remarkably all of them male. I doubt that the absence of daughters troubled Margaret, since the cubs had been removed from her shortly after birth. At least she had bred more than the English Mosa, who had had six pregnancies whilst at Regent's Park, all of which ended in stillbirths, infanticide or maternal neglect. These are classic signs of stress in animals. My Polish hosts were puzzled by my desire to stay in the rain and just watch, film and record the circumstances of these two bears.

A gathering of keepers formed around the polar bear cages: well-meaning gentlemen and a lady whose livelihood depended upon the survival of the zoo and who probably shared compassionate feelings towards the animals. The herbivorous animals such as tapirs, camel and bison were treated like livestock on the farms and peasant smallholdings in this part of Poland and they were in good condition, probably better than some I had visited in the UK. But carnivores are by definition dangerous animals and in public zoos they call for sophisticated security measures, concrete bunkers and metal railings.

A poor country like Poland can ill afford to hide these security measures behind scenic eye-level moats, subtle electric fences, spikes in the floor and all the other tricks of the zoo trade. What Margaret and Mosa had was flat, bare concrete, a water trough and eye-level contact with people a mere one or two metres away. For these bears, there was no hiding place, either from one another, from humans or from the camels and other herbivores a tantalisingly short distance across the fields. They had no comfortable resting spot, no pretend hunting game, no shelter from winter temperatures of down to minus 30° or summer heat of up to 40°; not even a roof to protect them from rain, snow and the like.

I was amazed that these animals had been sent to Katowice by the London Zoo, still the official owners of Mosa and of Pipiluk until his death. Surely they must have had someone inspect the proposed environment? Was there perhaps an inquiring letter or questionnaire on file to ensure that all was well? I was taken back to the office and allowed free rein on the London Zoo file for Mosa and Pipiluk. There was only a letter expressing pleasure from the London Zoo director, Dr David Jones, that Katowice would accept the bears.

I spent the next day observing the bears in the sun, recording critical dimensions of the existing cages and costing a plan for reform. There was no alternative accommodation for the bears at Katowice: every den, paddock and cage was already full. We would have to do the best possible for these bears where they were and certainly not ship them back to the UK, where London Zoo could not provide any better facilities.

I issued my report in English and Polish within a few days of returning to the UK, describing the need to create a covered den or hide for the bears, for partial shelter, for vegetable material in their diet, for trees and logs to play with, for comfortable surfaces on which to lie, for a decent swimming area, for a varied diet, for toys to play with and for veterinary attention to the bears' inevitable dental needs.

My recommendations were at first ridiculed by some of Mosa's and Pipiluk's former keepers at London Zoo, but a more positive note was struck at a meeting between the Zoo Director, Dr Jones, William Travers and myself. My report was accepted in its entirety, the necessary modification to the enclosure at Katowice Zoo being paid for jointly by the Zoological Society of London and Zoo Check. At that meeting I was heartened to obtain agreement from Dr Jones, a vet, that polar bears are not suitable animals to keep in zoos, and he will try to convert others in the British, perhaps European zoo fraternity to our point of view. For myself, I have to persuade UFAW to the same argument, by demonstrating that there are not, after all, worthwhile scientific, educational or conservational benefits to be obtained from keeping bears beyond the natural lifespan of the present inmates.

The situation facing animals in zoos is often no worse than that confronting many others on farms, in research laboratories and in collections of pet exotica. I have made it my particular *cause célèbre* only because of the human weakness which zoos reveal: hypocrisy. Zoos are managed by men (and a few women) who claim to be scientists with a serious interest in animal welfare and wildlife conservation. Yet wherever one looks, one sees short cuts, compromises and plain neglect which undermine the credibility of those concerned. This may even involve unnecessary experimental surgery or vivisection, as I recently discovered at the Institute of Zoology at Regent's Park where scientists had destroyed the sense of smell in marmosets; not for the benefit of marmosets but to satisfy human curiosity. At least I can argue that pet owners are a well-meaning if sometimes ill-informed fraternity, whose mistakes in animal welfare are usually quickly corrected once their animal's needs are explained. I regret that zookeepers are not so quickly responsive to my advice. The truth is that I just hate seing animals behind bars.

16
Pets – ambassadors to the wild

Human evolution is relatively recent: it is perhaps only 200,000 years since *homo sapiens* emerged in Neolithic times. Since then we have always been a part, latterly a highly destructive part, of the natural world. Once upon a time we were much closer to nature than we are today and exploited its plants and animals for food, protection and companionship. Some contemporary anthropologists have marvelled at the way we now adorn our houses with unproductive plants and shrubs, creating man-made habitats reminiscent of life in the jungles and plains of Africa. The favourite theory is that we are trying to hark back to our Neolithic roots. The anthropologist R. Ulrich argues that the same old-fashioned reminiscence factor is at the heart of our relationship with animals: we bring them into our homes, even into our beds, because they have been such an integral part of our own evolutionary history.

Wolves were chosen from amongst other contenders for domestication as companion animals, in part because their existing social organization was so like our own. Canine packs run along similar lines to tribes of hunter-gatherers. Domestication was probably not an especially difficult process: a few wild-caught wolf puppies quickly socialize into tractable 'dogs' without the need for selective breeding. However, a greater proportion of wolves do not make satisfactory dog-like companions, which is why I never encourage people to take them on as pets: it would be bad for wolves!

Every day, in our practice of animal behaviour therapy, I see evidence of remarkable abilities in dogs and other animals. A German Shepherd that could tell when its master was homeward-bound in his car five kilometres away; another that could distinguish between gold and other metals, and craved for the opportunity to sniff and lick the real stuff as opposed to look-alike paste. A cat that regularly commuted between present and past homes, some forty miles apart and separated by a river, motorway and other hazards. A Border Collie that had a vocabulary running to at least ninety objects, and could be commanded to 'go fetch' a squeaky banana, a bouncy ball or its mistress's slippers. Every dog in the land learns to recognize his owner's car, to 'read' the signals before people go out to work or pack up before a holiday. By any standards these are remarkable achievements and I don't pretend always to know how they come about.

The pleasure and interest which the company of animals gives to their owners can never be over-emphasized. Even the most horrendous characters described in this book were at other times a source of pride to their owner. On strictly psychological grounds, we know that the simple process of caretaking or nurturing animals fulfills important needs in people. It is an exercise in generosity of spirit, in altruism, in the collective glue that keeps society functioning. In return for affection, social animals like the dog shower us with uninhibited, unconditional love. This has an important impact upon our self-esteem, to the extent that people who own dogs report a larger circle of friends, have higher estimations of their own happiness and believe that their lives are more worthwhile than those who do not. Much of the secret of this lies in the dog's availability for shared experiences. Human social behaviour is dominated by a tendency to form coalitions, to co-operate with others and those same tendencies are exercised in relationships with dogs.

The importance of dogs goes beyond the immediate personal gratification that I have outlined above. Dogs, indeed all companion animals, provide a privileged seat from which to observe the natural world. By just watching dogs in the park we can learn all kinds of things about genetics, temperature regulation, food preferences, chemical signalling, predator-prey relationships, the impact of animals upon vegetation and most importantly of all, about the adaptability of individual animals in changing circumstances. These are all crucial lessons because they may stimulate the shift of attitudes which is required if we are to make mankind a more sensitive and informed guardian of Planet Earth. Some people may be surprised to hear me claiming a green element in dog ownership, if they are accustomed to thinking of dogs as creatures that despoil pavements and parks with faeces, chase children or knock over old ladies. These negatives do have to be addressed, but they are easily corrected and should not be permitted to detract from the larger benefits of dog ownership.

A couple of Icelandic dog owners recently visited the farm and described to me the attitudes of Icelanders to dogs now that they are at last able to keep dogs. Before a recent law was passed which liberalized dog ownership, having pets was like having contraband: people hid them indoors, in attics even, like frightened fugitives from the secret police. When they were 'liberated', dog owners were to be seen out on the fells enjoying the wildlife and scenery which Iceland has in such abundance. By contrast, the traditionally dogless Icelander would stay indoors through the long harsh winter, unaware of the natural world outside. There are precious few mammals native to Iceland and farm animals are usually intensively reared indoors, invisible to the substantial urban population of Reykjavik and elsewhere. Abundant bird and fish life is all very well, but Icelanders need to touch warm furry creatures as much as any other nationality and dogs can now fulfill that need.

The dog deserves the high status which it has acquired in Britain and I fight to support those who wish to keep it that way. If we are lucky to have dogs, they in return are fortunate to have us. Most of the dogs I see lead fairly pampered existences in the countries of Europe, Asia and America around which I travel. I value one animal's life as much as another and indeed have a slight prejudice toward the wild animal, honed as it is by nature's evolutionary forces. Accordingly, I am content to regard pets as ambassadors to the natural world, raising our sensitivity about conservation issues and about the species that need our help: animals on whom we have too often turned our backs in the past. I am an enthusiastic supporter of the increasingly effective and intellectually well-founded animal rights groups, who take exception to unnecessary and exploitative industries like fur farming, blood sports, vivisection in bio-medical research and the use of animals for entertainment in circuses and zoos. Hyprocrisy, conflicts, double standards and real dilemmas are everywhere in the world of animals, and individuals like you and me can only do our best to right the wrongs over which we have the power. Even with the progress that is all around I do not expect my casebook to slacken in the years ahead.

INDEX

Afghan Hounds, 50–1
Airedales, 175
American Pit Bull Terriers, 149–55
amphetamines, 164–5
Animal Behaviour Centre, 16–19
Anne, Princess Royal, 127, 131
'Assistance Dogs', 115–16

Baskerville muzzles, 38, 52
Beagles, 113, 114
Bearded Collies, 74, 134, 137–8
beta-blockers, 30, 38, 42, 75–6
Bip, 178–9
Border Collies, 96–101, 106, 222
Border Terriers, 175
Bowden, Andrew and Benita, 136–7
Boxers, 47–50
Boyde, Carl, 16, 66, 136, 188
breeding, 32, 83, 159–60, 167–8, 173–5
Bristol Zoo, 214–16, 217
Bull Terriers, 31, 32, 68–71, 155–7, 174–5
Bulldogs, 53–5, 161

Cairn Terriers, 161
Cape Hunting Dogs, 45–7
cars: car craziness, 101–6, 194–5
  chasing, 96–101
  fear of, 109–10, 203–4
castration, 28–9, 30, 65–6
cats, 131–2, 197–9, 200–1, 222
Cavalier King Charles Spaniels, 90–2
chewing, 41–2, 44
choke-chains, 13–14, 20–1, 25, 179, 181, 183, 196
clubs, breed, 160
Cocker Spaniels, 7–8, 32, 116, 163–8, 166–9
collars, 25–6, 179
Collies, 74–80, 96–106, 134, 222
conditioned-aversion learning, 114
coprophagia, 113–15
Corgis, 28, 127–31
Corson, Professor Samuel, 164–5
coyotes, 45, 114
Cross, Celia, 122–3
Crufts Dog Show, 156, 160–2

Dachshunds, 92–5, 161–2, 201–2
Dangerous Dogs Act (1989), 156
Deerhounds, 23–4, 175
defecation, 85, 87–8, 89–90, 92–5
Delta Group, 12–14
desensitization, 78–9
diet, 170–2, 193
Dobermanns, 194–5, 203–4
dog shows, 160–1
Dog Stop alarm, 28, 53, 102, 130
Dorgis, 127
Dudley Zoo, 213–14

Elizabeth II, Queen, 28, 127–31
'errorless learning', 22–3

faeces, 85, 87–8, 89–92, 113–15
fear, 73–84
feral dogs, 177–8
fighting, 28, 29
Flat-coated Retrievers, 175
flooding, 81–2, 138
Fogle, Dr Bruce, 13
forensic work, 141–58
Fox, Michael, 59
France, 191–203

genetics, 31–2, 174
German Shepherds, 32, 51, 52, 54, 56–7, 62, 106, 116, 117–20, 134–6, 144, 162–3, 168, 221–2
Golden Retrievers, 161, 168–72, 173, 175
Great Danes, 26, 86–9, 109, 134–6
Greed, Geoffrey, 214, 215–16
Greyhounds, 120–3, 175
Guide Dogs, 89, 111–15
Guide Dogs for the Blind Association, 112, 115
Gyp, 9, 22, 111

Hallgren, Anders, 14
Halti headcollars, 27–8, 115, 127
Hardwick Court Farm, 16, 18
headcollars, 26–8, 52, 115
Hearing Dogs for the Deaf Organization, 115
hepatic encephalopathy, 170–1
homoeopathy, 30, 192
hormones, 28–30, 70–1, 83, 91, 92
hyperventilation, 73, 75

inbreeding, 173–4
instrumental conditioning, 24, 27, 120
Irish Setters, 17, 161, 175, 178
Irish Wolfhounds, 26–7, 132–3

Jack Russell Terriers, 26–7, 106–9, 130, 139–40, 205–7

Katowice Zoo, 217–19
Kennel Club, 159, 160, 168, 173, 174
Kerry Blue Terriers, 207–8
Koehler William, 20, 179, 181, 189

Labradors, 25, 39–44, 80–3, 111–15, 161, 168
Lane, Carla, 132–3
leads, extending, 25, 184
Lenska, Rula, 133–4
Lester, Jim and Merry Lyn, 137
liver function, 170–2
London Zoo, 214, 219, 220
Long-haired Dachshunds, 161
Lurchers, 133

McKenna, Virginia, 213–14
Miniature Schnauzers, 192–4
Mofakate, Enos, 209
Mongrels, 39, 74, 133–4, 175, 184–9
Most, Konrad, 20, 179–80, 182, 189
Mugford, Ruth, 26
Mugford, Vivienne, 27, 51, 52, 114, 127, 154, 203
muzzles, 38, 51–2
Myth, 128

narcolepsy, 48
National Canine Defence League, 137, 154
noise, fear of, 74–8
Norfolk Terriers, 175
Norwich Terriers, 175

oestrogen, 70, 71, 85
Old English Sheepdogs, 124–5, 141–5, 161
Oppenheim, Sally, 139–40

pack structure, 21–2, 60, 71–2
Payancé, Dr Patrick and Katherine, 191–203
Pearsall, 20
Pembroke Corgis, 130
phobias, 73–4
pinch collars, 179
Pit Bull Terriers, 55–8, 149–55
play, 30–1
polar bears, 213–19
police dogs, 117–20, 141
Poodles, 175, 199–200, 209–11
pregnancy, 83
preputial gland, 85
Pro Dogs, 116, 137
progestagens, 29
puppy crates, 44
Puppy Playgroup, 83–4, 86, 189–90

response substitution training, 24
Retrievers, 161, 168–72, 173, 175
Rottweilers, 11, 30, 56–7, 58, 70, 144, 172–3
Rough Collies, 74, 77–80, 101–6, 134
Royal College of Veterinary Surgeons, 14
RSPCA, 57

Sam, 17–18, 26, 28, 52, 57, 75, 81, 83, 97–8, 110, 123, 134, 138, 144
Senn-Gupta, Amita, 161–2
Setters, 17, 30, 161, 175, 178
sexuality, 68–71
Shelties, 74
Shih Tzus, 204–5
Skerritt, Geoffrey, 166, 168
Skinner, Barry, 25, 120
Smooth-haired Dachshunds, 161–2
sniffer dogs, 116–17
Society for Companion Animal Studies, 14
South Africa, 207–9
Spaniels, 7–8, 30, 32, 116, 163–8, 169
Staffordshire Bull Terriers, 146–9
Stewart, Ed and Ciara, 134–6
Stewart, Rod, 205, 207
stud books, 174
Sundgren, Dr P. E., 173–4

tail-docking, 57
teething, 41–2
Terriers, 39
testosterone, 28–30, 66, 91, 92
Thatcher, Margaret, 14, 138–9
training, 178–90
Travers, Bill, 213
Travers, William, 213–14, 219

USA, 203–7
University Federation of Animal Welfare (UFAW), 216–17, 219
urine, 85–9, 90–2

Van Heeren, Joseph, 45–6
vomiting, 177, 192–4

Weimaraners, 30, 60–7, 70, 139
West Highland White Terriers, 70, 136–7
wild animals, 212–20
Wild Dogs, 45–7, 176
Willis, Dr Malcolm, 162
wolves, 22, 45, 59–60, 68, 71–2, 73, 176, 221
Woodhouse, Barbara, 13–14, 20–1, 26, 179, 180–1
working dogs, 111–23

Yorkshire Terriers, 90–2, 155–7, 181

Zoo Check, 212, 213–14, 217, 219